Faculty Guide for
Moving Teaching and Learning to the Web

Second Edition

Judith V. Boettcher

Rita-Marie Conrad

League for Innovation in the Community College

The League for Innovation in the Community College is an international organization dedicated to catalyzing the community college movement. The League hosts conferences and institutes, develops web resources, conducts research, produces publications, provides services, and leads projects and initiatives with more than 750 member colleges, 100 corporate partners, and a host of other government and nonprofit agencies in a continuing effort to make a positive difference for students and communities. Information about the League and its activities is available at www.league.org.

The opinions expressed in this book are those of the authors and do not necessarily reflect the views of the League for Innovation in the Community College.

Requests for permission should be sent to
League for Innovation in the Community College
4505 E. Chandler Boulevard, Suite 250
Phoenix, AZ 85048
email: publications@league.org
Fax: (480) 705-8201

Copies of this publication are available through the League's website at www.league.org, or by calling (480) 705-8200.

Please cite this publication as follows:
Boettcher, J., & Conrad, R-M. (2004). *Faculty Guide for Moving Teaching and Learning to the Web, Second Edition*. Phoenix: League for Innovation in the Community College.

Printed in the United States of America

ISBN 1-931300-41-0

Contents

Foreword

How do you update a book about technology when technology is changing so rapidly? How do you update a book about education when new ideas of teaching and learning are emerging yearly? And how do you update a book that combines the latest in learning and teaching with the latest in technology and keep both timeless?

Boettcher and Conrad have again accomplished these feats by holding strong to the same principles they developed in the first edition of *Faculty Guide for Moving Teaching and Learning to the Web*. These are principles of learning and technology that are not time bound, even though the applications of technology in teaching and learning have changed.

But Boettcher and Conrad have done more. Not only did such change in learning and technology take place, but something else has changed profoundly: the penetration of the technology that pervades our lives and, even more important, the lives of the young, who as students are moving in an environment that is far more integrated in technology than many of us are. Thus, this text could not be written about even the most current or most imagined technology and teaching alone. It must reflect the differences in the role of the learner, the instructor, and those who support and assist all the efforts to use technology appropriately. This text adds to the basic principles of teaching and learning and technology and incorporates powerful notions of the basic principles of change.

What we now have, and what Boettcher and Conrad add to this work, is the interplay of technological concepts of teaching and learning with change. The authors continue to use strong, cogent ideas such as the Zone of Proximal Development and the understanding that learning progresses in broad stages with overlaps and regressions. They continue using the web as a true breakthrough in interactive presentation, response, collaboration, and involvement. But more, the authors have expanded on the "Star Trek" metaphor of the holodeck, through which new teaching and new technology will easily highlight the fabric of change across time. The holodeck continues to provide timeless ideas to be tested in new and unusual surroundings. Just as the versions of "Star Trek" have evolved, as has the holodeck, the authors allow us to delve into the change brought about by the transformation in our culture that is just starting. The authors use and contrast ideas that may succeed in one venue and fail in another. Succeed with a set of students versed in instant phone messaging, compact abbreviations, and other code. Fail with other sets of students and teachers who do not see that the change is deeper than the winds of fashion. The holodeck remains the stage where such fashions can be tried and tested to find which fade and which endure with opportunities for graceful failures as well as successes.

In a real way, you are about to use this text as your holodeck on a teaching and learning journey. But as with the new versions of "Star Trek," you have a new holodeck with expanded capabilities: enhanced roles for each user, and even more intriguing relationships. You are about to continue on such a journey in your teaching and learning, where you will be faced not only with a constantly changing environment, but also a metamorphosis in the very pervasiveness of technology in our daily lives, with the demand for educators to understand this profound pervasiveness. This text continues to provide the navigational tools for you to expand your understanding of your own teaching and learning environment; it continues to provide that adventuresome spirit that moving into the unknown brings. In addition to all the continuing features, an expanded section on stories is worth the price of admission on its own. Chapter 9 contains a series of case studies with foreshadowing and summaries. The breadth and complexity of the stories makes real the difficulties and joys of developing new distance learning materials, courses, and programs.

Best yet, the authors continue with the grounding of the great ideas of technology and the great ideas of teaching and learning, and add the great ideas that this depth of involvement by our students brings. You will discover multiple interactive pathways though constantly expanding education worlds. I wish you an exciting and challenging journey.

Carl Berger
Professor and Dean Emeritus of Science and Technology Education and
Director of Advanced Academic Technologies
University of Michigan

Acknowledgments

This book is the coming together of a serendipitous set of people, ideas, and events over a period of over 10 years. However, the particular catalyst behind this book was a three-day tour across northern Wisconsin in May 1998. On that road tour, Terry O'Banion and Judith Boettcher had time to brainstorm about a book that might be a guide to faculty about the use of the emerging online environment in teaching and learning. We knew that some faculty approached using the web in teaching and learning with bravado, genius, and enthusiasm. We knew that other faculty were curious about the web, but much too busy in their work and comfortable and engrained in old habits. Still other faculty preferred not to think about the web at all, but to leave it for others, please! So an important acknowledgment goes to O'Banion for his encouragement to prepare a guide that would explain, encourage, and suggest ways for faculty to embrace the web joyfully for teaching and learning.

There are a host of others we also acknowledge. We thank the staff at the League, including Cynthia Wilson, Cindy Miles, and Ann Doty, who guided us through the first edition, and Boo Browning, who was very patient in waiting for the second edition. The world of the web and online teaching and learning had changed even more than we had thought about during the interim.

The guide is longer than we expected and, with its very expanded faculty story section, we believe it is much better. We also acknowledge our colleagues and students at our current and former institutions. These associations have contributed greatly to our learning and experimenting with effective online teaching and learning. We thank our colleagues at Penn State University and Florida State University, our newer colleagues and students at Capella University and the University of Florida, the staff and volunteers associated with CREN, a nonprofit higher education association, as well as all our friends and colleagues in the instructional technology profession. The interactions, discussions, and brainstorming sessions helped to inform and shape the ideas in this book.

We also recognize the contributions of all who participated in various versions of the online and distance learning workshops offered through *Syllabus*, the readers of the *Syllabus* distance learning columns, and especially the faculty who contributed their accounts to our online-stories chapter. The interactions with this community helped crystallize the real-life campus questions and strategies faced by faculty, staff, and students.

Finally, we acknowledge our husbands, Gil and Larry, for their patience and support while this book was being written – again. Writing and rewriting and reading stories took precedence over cooking, sailing, traveling, and deck time. To all, thanks! We hope this guide will contribute in some small way to a new joy and enthusiasm as you see the knowledge networks being formed in your students' minds.

Judith V. Boettcher, Designing for Learning, University of Florida
Rita-Marie Conrad, Capella University

Preface

Since the writing of the first edition of this book, the world of teaching and learning has shifted and reshaped itself. Higher education institutions of all types and sizes have made significant strides in integrating the online environment and tools into fulfilling their missions of teaching, learning, and research. The online and mobile technologies now available enable us to create teaching and learning environments that are more interactive and collaborative than any that have been possible before. Our higher education institutions are in the knowledge business. We create knowledge, we analyze knowledge, and we organize knowledge. We archive knowledge; we share it and we help others acquire and use it. As educators, we use the core processes of communication and interaction with each other in teaching and learning. The new communication and knowledge tools support these core processes with faster, more personal, more flexible communication than we have ever had. We offer the 11 chapters of this text as a guide for applying these new tools and as evidence that we are living in a tremendously exciting time in education.

1. The Online World of Higher Education: Where Are We?

This chapter begins with a brief history of the internet, from its beginnings in 1966 as a tool to support the sharing of scarce computer resources among scientists across the country. The power of the internet to support communications came later. It is these communications applications that support the core processes of teaching and learning. In this chapter, we also describe the basics of how the internet works, how the web developed, and how fast the use of these technologies has developed in what is now commonly called net time. This chapter helps to build a conceptual understanding of the web infrastructure to clarify its usefulness for teaching and learning. These concepts are fundamental to knowing how to design and plan for online teaching and learning.

2. Principles of Technology and Change to Guide Our Journey to the Web

This chapter describes the principles behind the technology innovation adoption curve and the change processes that accompany the adoption of technology innovations generally. These principles highlight the need for campus policies and a campus infrastructure that support successful adoption and transformative reshaping of new technology-enriched learning environments by faculty, staff, and students. This chapter also provides some telling statistics and trend lines about the adoption of technology innovations. Some of these statistics include factors important to teaching and learning programs, such as personal computer ownership by faculty and students and campus strategies for addressing technology needs and support.

3. What We Know About Teaching and Learning

Here we introduce the online environment, the first truly major shift in instruction that has occurred in the last 500 years. It is the shift from the classroom as the primary center of organized instruction to the online environment as the primary center of instruction. The net is now the gathering place.

This chapter provides background in the pedagogy, including an examination of how the basics of the teaching and learning processes are really communications and dialogue processes. The fundamental ideas of five educational theorists – Skinner, Bruner, Vygotsky, Dewey, and Knowles – provide support for rethinking the core processes of teaching and learning. When an environment is changed, it is wise to reexamine the core assumptions of the earlier model. New environments often enable us to address longstanding problems easily and affordably. At the same time, new environments bring their own new problems.

4. Envisioning, Planning, and Identifying Resources for Teaching Online

With this chapter, we begin the how-to section of the book. The first part of this chapter addresses questions of focus by providing two layers of decision-making and planning tools. How does one choose what courses should be offered in the online environment? How does a faculty member prepare for and actually begin teaching online? What types of tools, resources, and infrastructure are needed? What sort of design and development time is needed? Three different types of courses – online, webcentric or hybrid, and web-enhanced – are described in this chapter. Worksheets on the two design decision layers help to determine the focus of an online course project and the types of resources, support, and infrastructure that may be needed.

5. Instructional Design Guidelines for Moving Teaching and Learning Online

This chapter is the primary design chapter of the book. If a faculty member is going to design a course for the web, what will it look like? How will it be similar to and how will it differ from a traditional on-campus course? What will it have in common with traditional distance learning courses? In this chapter, we analyze the structure of traditional courses, focusing on the three-credit course model. We describe the expectations for time and workload on the part of faculty and students, and consider what the expected instructional and learning outcomes will look like, given these expectations. Finally, a major section of the chapter is devoted to the process of instructional design. This section contains a list of 10 simple guidelines for designing and developing courses.

6. Steps in Developing Web Courses

Here we present a step-by-step process for developing web courses. For all practical purposes, the design and development of courses today is still a cottage industry. Faculty members design, redesign, update, and change their courses every semester, using the *bundled* model of being responsible for the three Ds: design, development, and delivery. No course is quite like any other. This is both the challenge and the drawback of our current models. In this chapter, we look at the kinds of expertise needed to design and develop the course materials that make up the digital content for teaching and learning in an online classroom. This chapter also features an eight-step process for systematically designing and developing an online course. We also describe different designs for courses according to the amount of prepackaged or dynamic content and time used for different types of dialogues, such as large group synchronous activities, small group activities, and individual dialogue with resources.

7. Creating and Sustaining Online Communities

In earlier generations of distance learning, students were often isolated, not only from the instructor, but from other learners as well. Today's technology tools support many types and degrees of interactivity, enabling students to engage more actively in the teaching and learning processes, including interactions with fellow students and experts. The strategies for promoting online interaction have grown exponentially over the past few years. This chapter discusses the nature of online collaboration and community and strategies for nurturing community-centered learning online.

8. Tools and Resources for Creating Online Courses

Tools and resources to support faculty and students with the tasks of teaching and learning in the online environment have grown dramatically, keeping pace with the growth of internet and web technologies. This chapter provides an overview of the evolution of course management systems (CMSs) to their current role as an integrated part of the teaching and learning environment and a fundamental component of a modern campuswide digital infrastructure. The design and functions of these systems are provided along with a process for deciding which CMS might be right for your campus. This chapter also presents an overview of some of the newer categories of tools and applications that faculty and students are using, including content resources and learning objects, and some of the newer audio and video tools, addressing the question, "Can I really lecture online?" These newer categories also provide a glimpse of how the teaching and learning online environment is changing the roles of teachers and students.

9. Stories About Online Teaching and Learning

The stories written by faculty and faculty support personnel in this chapter are special treasures, providing insights into the life and times of faculty as they have been designing, developing, and delivering courses online. While much of what faculty are doing might be anticipated, the creativity and adaptivity of faculty and students within the online environment continue to be sources of amazing revelation. The first edition of this book featured eight stories; this edition features updates from some of the original stories that started back in the earliest days of web technology in 1994 to 1996, plus many new stories. Each story is a separate and joyful testimony to the teaching and learning experience. This chapter provides accounts illustrating the three basic types of courses: web-enhanced, webcentric (hybrid, blended), and fully online courses. Common to all these narratives are the changes the online environment is making in three aspects of higher education:

- Changes in the amount of *time* faculty and students spend collaborating with each other and in the *types* of interactions between faculty and students and between students

- Changes in the faculty and student *roles*, with students stepping forward and into the role of active learners, and the faculty member becoming more of a mentor, director, and coach

- Changes in the types of *resources* that are being used in teaching and learning environments

10. Issues in the Online Environment

This chapter addresses filling in some of the cracks. We focus on issues educators never seem to have enough time to explore in depth. Our discussion serves as a starting point for discussion and a snapshot of five issues:

- Class sizes in online courses
- Remote management of interactions with students and between students
- Copyright issues and intellectual property policies

- Assessment and evaluation
- Balance of life and learning

11. Perspectives on the Future

Where will we be in teaching and learning in higher education in the year 2010? This chapter provides a glimpse into what the higher education enterprise might feature just a few short years from now. The predictions are organized around six components of higher education: (1) the higher education enterprise as a whole, (2) degree programs and continuing education programs, (3) the institutional infrastructure, (4) faculty and student tools and roles, (5) content resources, and (6) research into the science of learning. The second part of the chapter is a science fiction fantasy about what learning might be beyond the year 2010. "Student-Centered Learning in the Lasting Experiences Ltd. Holodeck: As Good as It Gets!" was first published as a column in *Syllabus* in June 1998. Amazingly, it still seems to work as a vision of where we might arrive in the year 2025.

Chapter 1

The Online World of Higher Education: Where Are We?

Five years ago, the primary purpose of this chapter was to provide an introduction to the history and development of the internet. Five years ago, the use of the internet for online learning was only on the edges of awareness for most faculty. Many faculty and administrators quietly suspected that the internet was only a fad. Some secretly hoped that if they ignored it, it would go away. What a different place we find ourselves in today!

At the other end of the spectrum back then were many innovative faculty who were energized by the promise of the internet and its related technologies, such as dynamic modeling, mobile computing and real-time access to information. These faculty delighted in pursuing the internet applications, believing that these communication-focused technologies could help solve persistent problems of teaching difficult concepts, managing large classes, and reaching disengaged students. Some administrators saw the internet and a new online learning environment as the solution to many of the cost problems in higher education. Surely, the thinking went, a digital infrastructure would be less expensive than a physical campus infrastructure, and surely class sizes would be increased significantly! And of course, the online courses would bring in many more tuition monies. Well, optimism combined with technology innovation is a very good thing.

Where are faculty and administrators with the online paradigm now? According to recent surveys by Green (2002, p. 9), about one-third of all courses offered in higher education have websites associated with courses, whether these courses are offered online or on campus. Currently, there is a large variance across types of institution. For example, the data indicate that approximately 25 percent of all courses at community colleges have websites, while approximately 50 percent of courses at private institutions have websites. What would you estimate the percentage to be of courses at your institution or in your department that have websites?

> **What would you estimate the percentage to be of courses at your institution or in your department that have websites?**

Whatever the number of courses with websites at your institution, and whether or not that is a good metric to be using, we can safely say that the internet and the web have not only arrived on higher education campuses, but that they have caused a shift from the physical classroom to the online environment for many teaching and learning activities. This shift is changing relationships between teachers and learners, changing communication patterns and expectations, and engaging students in active and collaborative learning.

What are the technologies driving this changing landscape? And what are the characteristics of these technologies that make them so powerful for teaching and learning? This chapter provides insight into the technologies supporting the paradigm of online learning that is now with us. It also supports future thinking, as the current paradigm is only temporary. The communications and internet technologies are projected to continue to evolve at the pace of Moore's Law for a minimum of another 20 years (Kurzweil, 1999), and the Law of Accelerating Returns means that the pace of change will continue to increase.

This means that our higher education community and partner communities, such as business and government, will be designing, shaping, and creating new teaching and learning paradigms for at least the next 15 to 20 years. We used to think that if we all made it to the year 2015 – a totally gut estimate of the completion of the analog-to-digital revolution – we might achieve a measure of stability in teaching and learning paradigms and related industries. Our thinking now is that the technologies and online environments will become ever more responsive to who and where we are, for everything we need to know or do. Finding a point of relative stability will probably elude us. The last chapter in the book examines future possibilities and trends.

For now, the accelerating pace of technological change means that a focus on the core principles of teaching and learning is highly recommended. The core principles of teaching and learning and the core principles about how our brains process and store information remain fairly stable. These core principles can serve as touchstones to inform the design of our teaching and learning programs, institutions, and services.

This chapter also provides a bird's-eye view of the basic evolution of the internet and the fundamental web applications. The power of the internet and its associated web applications support the myriad types of interactions, relationships, and events that are the core of the teaching and learning experience. We start by stepping back and taking a long-view look at the technologies that are serving our teaching and learning communities. Technologies surprise and delight and challenge us; we can certainly enjoy the process as well as the results.

Where You Were When the Web Happened?

It is probably safe to say that the global village that Marshall McLuhan envisioned has arrived. In the more than 35 years since he said, "We now live in a global village . . . a simultaneous happening," we have seen the accumulation of invention upon invention, most of which seemed to be supportive of current structures. Then, a set of critical technological developments caused the world to truly shift to another level, a different place. This invention made possible the global village and the "allatonceness" described by McLuhan (1967, p. 63.) The critical technologies behind this shift are, of course, the internet, the web, mobile and wireless computing, and their related applications.

In a 1998 interview, Robert W. Lucky, a telecommunications researcher at Bellcore, said, "It is easy to predict the future; what is hard is predicting what people will do with the technology" (1998, p. 72). Lucky also observed, "The web is an astounding example of the lack of foresight. Nobody saw this – in industry or anywhere else. In retrospect, the web is the most obvious thing you ever heard of, and it is such a world-class idea" (1998, p. 74).

Those of us who are old enough can remember where we were when we first heard the news that J.F.K. had been shot. Almost all of us remember where we were on the morning of September 11, 2001. However, most of us do *not* remember where we were when the web came to be. The web did not happen as a single stunning event in time, but it did happen quickly.

In less than 10 years, this set of technologies has transformed how people interact with other people, with other resources and services, and with organizations. Technology is fundamentally a democratizing function, changing relationships among people and organizations. Many of us now find ourselves talking in terms of "before the web" and "now that the web is here," of before and after the emergence of Wi-Fi wireless.

By 2004, we completed the first phase of the web as a disruptive technology, a phase of using the web to do things we have always done. We are in the middle of Phase Two, one of innovation in how we do things, and we are well on our way to the third phase of exploiting transformational possibilities (Rosenbloom, 1999.) Then, of course, we start over with another set of disruptive technologies, overlapping these phases. Some of the technology developments that will be re-inventing the internet are already under way. These technologies include grid computing, ubiquitous computing, and the PlanetLab initiative (www.planet-lab.org), which has as its goal a much smarter internet, with more of the computing being done by smart network nodes.

In early 1998, it was estimated that over 120 million people worldwide were using the internet, mostly for communication. The number of online users worldwide in September 2002 was estimated at over 605 million, of which almost 183 million were in the U.S. and Canada (www.cyberatlas.internet.com). Data from The Pew Internet and American Life Project suggests that over 5 million adults had taken a course for credit online by the last quarter of 2001 (Lenhart, Simon, & Graziano, 2001). The results from Year Three of the UCLA Internet Project – reporting data from 2002 – suggest that 71 percent of Americans are now online, with the average number of hours per week at 11.1 hours.

Another brief study in 2003-2004 of elementary school children in "the top 15 wired cities" estimates that half of the children in these cities go "online at least four times a week, and 20 percent are online every day." Other studies suggest that the online activities are gaining time among young adults away from television and other media. A trend among college students is that one technology, the laptop computer, is becoming their one and only technology, through which they listen to music, watch movies and television, take courses, and surf the web (Carnevale, 2003).

The Internet Environment and Higher Education

Many questions persist about teaching and learning online. How is higher education responding to this new paradigm? A new set of reports is turning these analyses to the outcome question. What are the skills, attributes, and knowledge that college graduates should be expected to acquire? The *Building of a Nation of Learners* report from the American Council on Education (www.bhef.com) lists the 12 desired characteristics, skills, and attributes that are expected goals for students in higher education. These goals include cross-functional skills such as leadership, teamwork, and time management. It is serendipitous, perhaps, that these are the very skills that the new environments and tools make it easier to teach. As we are designing new models and new paradigms, we will want to design and build in the processes and systems to support the acquisition of these skills in addition to knowledge acquisition.

As many pundits have said, the web changes everything. The higher education landscape now includes wholly online for-profit institutions offering online degrees in almost any subject or content area and at any degree level. Most public and private higher education institutions are also now involved in online learning, offering complete graduate degrees and an abundance of certificate programs aimed at working professionals. According to two research studies quoted in a recent report, 84 percent of four-year institutions offered at least one distance education course in 2002, and an estimated 1.5 million of the 19 million students in higher education took at least one online distance education course in the 1999–2000 school year (ACE-BHEF, 2003, p. 17).

The body of knowledge available about online learning is already rich and rapidly expanding. One of the many excellent resources on the progress of effective use for technology in higher education is the Center for Academic Transformation at Rochester Polytechnic Institute. An important series of monographs from 1996 through 2003 about the design and effectiveness of online learning is available on the internet (www.center.rpi.edu). More resources are listed in the references list.

Ongoing research and experimental use of technologies and tools are essential to identifying which capabilities of the web can best support the goals of high-quality teaching and learning. The pressures for higher education to become more efficient and to reduce costs of educating the new generations of college students are rapidly growing. At the same time, our information-based world economy is demanding services for the ongoing updating and education of its workers.

An analysis by Dolence and Norris (1995, p. 7) suggests that all workers should be spending up to 11 percent of their time learning. This means that we all need to be incorporating learning into our lives. We already see ourselves learning at work, at home, at the steering wheel, and at meals. We are also learning in short bursts and over extended periods of time. We are learning anywhere, anytime – just like our students.

> **We already see ourselves learning at work, at home, at the steering wheel, and at meals.**

What Is the Internet?

Although internet and web are now household words, for some people these technologies remain a mystery. Simply stated, the internet is a network of networks. Before the development of a common language or internet protocol (IP) for all computers, communication between or among computers was difficult and at times impossible. In 1982, the development of a common network language, TCP/IP, enabled the loose collections of computers on local networks to be linked together to form a hierarchy of local, national, regional, and global networks. The formal definition of the internet is "a global network of networks enabling computers of all kinds to directly and transparently communicate and share services throughout much of the world" (Internet Society, www.isoc.org). For those curious about the development of the internet, a rich set of resources about its history is provided at www.isoc.org/internet/history. The Internet Society (ISOC) is an international organization formed in 1992 to coordinate a spectrum of activities focused on the internet's development, availability, and associated technologies.

A network's design, operation, and traffic volume determine the number and variety of network paths along which data messages travel. In fact, a data message might be divided into many smaller packets that travel on different paths across the network and then are reassembled before arriving at a mail server or at a personal computer or cell phone. Thus, even though the network is very fast, it is neither instantaneous nor 100 percent reliable. Data can get lost, which means that messages can get lost. The longstanding student excuse, "My dog ate my homework," has evolved to, "I sent it in. I don't know why it isn't there." And the student might be right! Technologies such as time stamping and the confirmation of receipt of messages and secure interchange protocols are starting to address these problems. Soon, the excuses will change again. For information about the internet infrastructure, IP addresses, web pages, instant messaging, the site www.howstuffworks.com/index.htm is very useful.

The Origins of the Internet

The beginnings of the internet can be traced to a small government agency, the Advanced Research Project Agency (ARPA), that supervised and directed funding of computer research in the early 1960s. This agency supported a cadre of computer scientists located at research universities across the United States. These scientists quickly developed a number of different computers, each with its own operating system, command language, and way to send data from point to point. The computers were expensive to design and build, and difficult and costly to use. In an effort to be more productive, the scientists began searching for ways to communicate with each other via these systems and to share the resources of these scarce and expensive computers.

In 1962, as the programs funded by ARPA were beginning to expand their focus beyond the calculating abilities of computers, J.C.R. Licklider joined ARPA as a division manager. Unlike many of the agency's computer scientists, Licklider was a psychologist who had migrated to the field of computing. Bringing a new perspective to the agency, he was particularly interested in interactive computing. He envisioned the computer as a tool that would be able to "act as an extension of the whole human being" and to "amplify the range of human intelligence" (Hafner & Lyon, 1998, p. 27).

Licklider's vision encouraged the concurrent development of interactive computing, number-crunching computing, and network computing. Our use of the internet and the web in teaching and learning is, in many ways, a realization of his early vision.

The Growth of the Internet

Once scientists developed the ability for computers to talk to one another, email quickly became the most popular application; however, the cost and complexity of computers hampered early growth. Increased use of the internet came with the introduction of personal computers in the mid-1980s. By 1987, the number of host computers linked to the net had grown to more than 28,000; and by 1990, the number had reached more than 300,000. Data from January 2003 suggest that number is now over 171 million. What does all this mean to teaching and learning? The bottom line is that learning is accessible 24 hours a day, seven days a week, and that educational opportunities are global and ubiquitous. For more data on the growth of the internet, Hobbes' Internet Timeline v6.1 at www.zakon.org/robert/internet/timeline is an excellent resource. This timeline continues to grow and welcomes contributions (Zion, 1993-2003).

The driving force behind this extraordinary growth was email, one of the most famous killer applications. A killer application is one whose benefits are so powerful that people will purchase computers, software, and network access just for the ability to use it. Email and communication services are major contributors to the explosive growth of the network, while electronic commerce has an increasingly prominent presence as well.

In the late 1980s and early 1990s, the internet was only user friendly for professionals in computer science, engineering, and other technical fields. It was less hospitable for nontechnical users such as faculty members, staff, and students. We didn't know it at the time, but we needed the web.

The Origins of the Web

At the European Laboratory for Particle Physics in Switzerland, a young physicist, Tim Berners-Lee, helped launch the phenomenon of the World Wide Web as a "shared information space through which people (and machines) could communicate." In 1990, Berners-Lee created the first version of this "shared information space" by developing an enhanced protocol, HyperText Transfer Protocol (http), for sending information over the internet. This protocol made point-and-click navigation available on the internet, moving to the net what had only been available on the personal desktop computer. This navigation system evolved into the first graphical browser, Mosaic, developed by Marc Andreessen and other students at the University of Illinois and announced on a number of lists in March of 1993. Andreessen is a cofounder of Netscape Communications, a company that at one time commanded almost 80 percent of the internet browser market. It seems safe to say that 1993, the year the first graphical browser was developed, was the birth event of the World Wide Web. Do you remember where you were and what you were doing in March of 1993?

Email and the Growth of the Internet and Its Uses

For many people, email continues to be one of the primary reasons to go online and stay online. Email is still being reported by both experienced and new internet users as their top online activity, followed by web surfing or browsing for information (UCLA, 2003). A UCLA report indicates that internet usage is a whopping 97 percent in the two age ranges of 12 to 15 years and 16 to 18 years. The widespread use of the internet for email, instant messaging, information access, and entertainment means that concern about students being comfortable in the online environment is no longer the issue it was even five years ago. However, this does mean that faculty may be less experienced and less comfortable on the internet than students.

The list of internet activities and the percentage of users as reported in the UCLA Year Three study is interesting. Email and instant-messaging activities are reported by almost 90 percent of users overall. Also, users are relying on the internet for accessing information of all types, from medical to travel to entertainment information. While they overwhelmingly use the web for information purposes, however, many users question the accuracy and validity of the information on the web. A question in the UCLA study asked if users believed most or all of the information on the internet to be reliable and accurate. Over the three years of the study, the number of users believing "most or all of the information online to be reliable and accurate" declined to 52.8 percent in 2002, from 58 percent in 2001 and 55 percent in 2000 (p. 38).

Table 1 from the UCLA study shows the top 10 most popular internet activities. This data suggests that the use of the internet for accessing information is a comfortable, already well-ingrained habit among internet users, but that its use for teaching and learning is not as automatic. As we move more teaching and learning transactions to the online environment, we need to plan more explicitly for what skills teachers and learners need to develop to ensure effective and accurate learning on the internet.

Table 1.1   The Top Ten Most Popular Internet Activities by Percentage of Users

Email and instant messaging	87.9%
Web surfing or browsing	76.0%
Reading news	51.9%
Accessing entertainment information	46.4%
Shopping and buying online	44.5%
Hobbies	43.7%
Travel information	36.2%
Medical information	35.5%
Playing games	26.5%
Tracking credit cards	24.2%

(Source: *The UCLA Internet Report, Year Three*. 2003, p. 21.)

Current Campus Network Infrastructures

The basic infrastructure of the network consists of hardware in the form of network servers, wires and cables, routers, and computers of all sizes and types. The network also relies on software and applications that, fortunately, are now fairly standard. A very simple model of a hardware portion of the network is illustrated in Figure 1.1.

Faculty and students may connect to the internet through personal computers, modems, and local phone lines or cable networks linking them to a local internet service provider (ISP). The process is relatively simple. When a modem – either a telephone or cable modem, attached to the computer, possibly wirelessly – links into the ISP, a modem-to-modem link is established over a regular phone or cable line. Once the link is established, the router and server check for the account and password of the user before approving access to the internet. If approved, the user can access any content, web service, information, or server.

Accessing the internet from an office works in much the same way. For example, faculty and staff offices and student computer labs on a campus may be linked to a local area network (LAN). Generally, the LAN hooks the entire faculty and support staff to a special computer called a router that serves as a gateway to the larger regional and global networks.

Figure 1.1 Simple Network Model

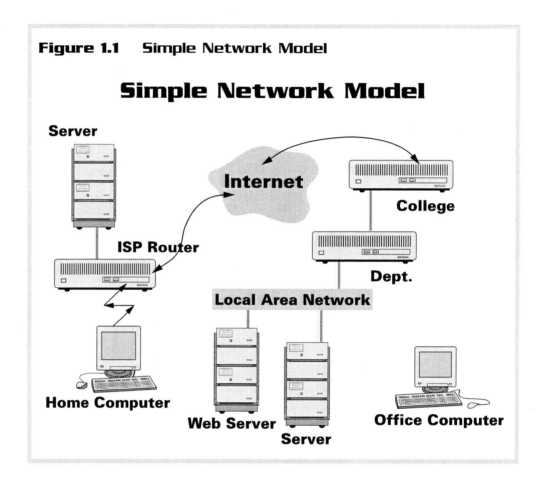

Simple Network Model

The global internet is built from multiples of these simple components. As a consequence, the internet is both very robust and very fragile. Its power comes from the redundancy that is provided by a network of computers offering multiple paths. If one router, server, or computer is broken, slow, or problematic, the data are still transmitted successfully and quickly across the network, because the routers and gateways use alternate pathways. The system is strong, but the ability to use the network is very dependent on immediate access points. If the college router is down or overburdened, we experience the frustration and anxiety that come from a slow or unavailable network. On the occasional morning or afternoon that network problems occur, the pace of work changes dramatically. If the department router is down, we may be unable to access data, applications, or email. Reaction may be similar to the discord experienced when the electrical power is interrupted. We change how we work. We change our expectations. We have another cup of coffee. We gather in groups to talk about what we can't get done. Or perhaps we walk over to the local coffee shop or the next wireless access point with our laptop computers.

Given the design of the network, the potential exists for multiple points of failure, including performance problems with network hardware or software. As a result, one of the core principles of planning for teaching and learning on the web is to plan for multiple servers, backup servers, and network redundancies. Also, given the need to be available for learning anywhere, anytime, we need to plan for 24/7 access.

Network Software and Web Applications

In addition to the hardware, layers of software support the network and other applications. Sometimes called middleware, these layers include the software on the network for routing, management, and data flow; the software on web servers to control access; and the software in the browsers used to access the servers. Middleware can also refer to the components of the software on the server that manage course websites.

Current Campus Network Infrastructures

The infrastructure currently available on most campuses effectively supports the popular and basic uses of the internet for communication, collaboration, and research. More advanced network technology projects, such as Internet2, are bringing high-bandwidth performance networks to many campuses, making videoconferencing and other high-bandwidth applications readily available. Many campuses are installing wireless capabilities in conjunction with their high-speed wired networking core.

Some of these advances are making significant differences in the types of events that can be easily offered as part of the teaching and learning experiences. But it is good to remember that the primary benefit of many of these advances in networking technologies is in making the basic communication and research capabilities more readily available whenever and wherever students and faculty are.

The core design features of the various communication applications – email, instant messaging, videoconferencing, chat rooms, bulletin boards, threaded discussions, and simulated environments – remain constant. These features provide a convenient way for faculty to communicate with students quickly, easily, and from almost any location, and for students to communicate with other students and resources. Email is also helpful in communicating with groups, from large classes to small project teams.

Email Software on the Internet

Internet access and email are in some ways similar to the postal service, but the digital systems are still relatively fragile. The language of email has its corollaries with the postal service and with telephone systems. We have email mailboxes, email addresses, online directories, yellow pages, and computers dedicated as mail servers. Our computing appliances, including computers, hand-helds, and cell phones all have, or soon will have, internet protocol (IP) addresses. Online directories enable us to track down friends and family, and the amount of junk email rivals that of traditional or snail mail.

The setup and installation of software for communicating over the internet is now much easier than it has been. Several items are necessary for email and online access:

- **Hardware** to access the net, usually a computer and modem, but increasingly a hand-held or cell phone.
- **Software** to help manage email. Mail software can be a simple application provided by an internet browser, such as Internet Explorer, Safari, Netscape, or more specialized mail programs such as Eudora, Microsoft Outlook, or many others.
- An **internet account** that provides access to the internet. This account can be arranged with a local ISP, or a college may offer options for faculty, staff, and students. Free internet accounts are also available, but these often come with many pop-up ads and other distractions.
- An **email account** for sending and receiving messages
- A **mailbox** on a mail server, where messages are stored until they are retrieved. The mailbox is often set up at the same time as the internet access account; however, other options are available. For example, a user may arrange for internet access with an ISP, but use an email account at school or work. Storing email is also a consideration, as users may elect to keep messages on the personal computer, on the mail server, or on a disk.

Basic Principles

For many who entered the teaching profession before the advent of personal computers, the internet and its associated communication technologies now provide an entirely new teaching and learning environment. We might be rethinking what a course is, what a class is, what a book is. We might re-examine our roles as teachers and rethinking students' roles and responsibilities. The web and internet world is a new place, and new rules, challenges, and opportunities apply.

Designing teaching and learning for the internet, whether as a fully online course or as part of a regular campus course, is hard work, but it is an energizing and satisfactory challenge. The good news is that we don't have to do it alone. The many faculty-experience stories in this guide are enjoyable community testimonials to teaching and learning in this new environment.

As we explore the processes and implications of using the web for teaching and learning, we want to emphasize certain principles:

- The internet, the web, and associated communication technologies will continue to change and grow, according to the Law of Accelerating Returns.
- The design, development, and delivery of teaching and learning experiences will need to be flexible and future-oriented, as well as effective.
- Institutions must plan for the growing sophistication of the digital infrastructure to support the new internet space for teaching and learning. Technology plans need to include upgrading of networks and redundancy of services to ensure that they are always on, always available.

Moving teaching and learning experiences to the web requires knowledge, skills, and tools. The next chapters describe core learning principles and processes to help make this an effective and joyful experience.

Chapter 2

Principles of Technology and Change to Guide the Journey to the Web

This chapter provides an overview of changes in communication technologies over the last century, a description of the technology dissemination process, and a set of principles for the wise and manageable use of technology. These principles reinforce campus policies that advance faculty, staff, and student change to the technology-enriched learning environment.

In addition, this chapter illustrates how the design of new teaching and learning environments can sustain cherished professional beliefs and principles while supporting the need for efficiency and effectiveness. Significant statistics and trend lines about the adoption of technology are presented, including data on personal computer ownership by faculty and students, ease and affordability of web access, and campus strategies for supporting the technology needs of faculty and students.

Introduction to Technology and Education

Just what is educational technology? The root of technology, *tekhne*, means art or skill. The *American Heritage Dictionary* definition states that technology is the "application of science, especially to industrial or commercial objectives." To fit our idea of educational technologies into this definition is a bit of a stretch; our purpose would be better served if the definition also included "for educational objectives." We propose the following definition of technology in education:

The technology of education is the set of tools and techniques used to extend or enhance the ability to learn, collect, and organize data and information, solve problems, and support communication exchanges between and among faculty and students.

Thus, paper, pens, pencils, books, television, radio, and audio-video recording and playback devices are all educational technologies that enhance learning and communication. The difference in today's technologies from those of an earlier age is in the kinds of technology we have available, when and where we are using them, and the speed at which technology is changing.

In the early part of the 20th century, before paper and pencils were broadly affordable, students had miniature chalkboards called slates, which provided very little space for storing and analyzing thoughts and information. At that time, they were used primarily for drill and practice of basic knowledge. By contrast, we see today examples of complete classes of students in Grades 5 and 6 with laptops to call their own. And many of today's college students also have their own computers. What a difference tools can make!

In fact, laptops are gaining momentum over desktop computers. The cost of laptops has decreased markedly since 2000, and now they make up almost 30 percent of all computers sold. Laptops are lightweight – many are under five or six pounds – and include wireless capabilities to take advantage of the new mobile computing with wireless hotspots. This makes accessing the online learning environment whenever and wherever you are as easy as ordering coffee. The broad definition of technology as any tool or technique to enhance or extend the brain means that we want to keep monitoring the developments of technology to see how they can make a difference in teaching and learning. How quickly do we adopt new technology?

Principle One: Good Use of Technology Takes Time

In the late 19th century, the best way to communicate across long distances was by telegraph, and in the United States, Western Union dominated the use of the technology. When the telephone came along in about 1876, research and market analysts at Western Union judged that "this (new) telephone has too many shortcomings to be seriously considered as a means of communication. This device is inherently of no value to us." Now, a derivative of that early telephone technology is with us everywhere, hanging from our belts, in our purses, our cars, our pockets. Today, one phone number can find us anywhere.

> **One fundamental principle of technology dissemination is that good uses of technology take time to develop.**

Typical of fledgling technology, the 1876 telephone was awkward, expensive, and didn't seem to fill any particular need. One fundamental principle of technology dissemination is that good uses of technology take time to develop. Therefore, we need to be patient with each other and ourselves as we innovate and learn.

Another major 20th century technology, the radio, was also initially received with derision. An associate of David Sarnoff, later the head of RCA, looked at this technology and remarked, "The wireless music box has no imaginable commercial value. Who would pay for a message sent to nobody in particular?" Now, of course, we have radios and smart phones, and entire industries depend on broadcasting messages, movies, sitcoms, and educational programs to no one in particular. We also now see a future with narrowcasting emerging as a powerful force, reaching out to specific interests of folks all over the world. If you are a former Minnesotan and still love listening to WCCO, you can do that with the web. And with satellite radio technology, it is possible to access National Public Radio wherever you might be.

Principle Two: Not All Technology Thrives or Survives

The telephone and radio, two examples of successful innovation, lead us to the second principle of technology change: Not all technology evolves to be a practical or dominant force in our daily lives. We know that high cost and difficulty of use are major deterrents to the adoption of new technology. Technology does not become cost effective until it is commercialized and widely available. For example, videotapes were not widely used in distance education until VCRs were in the majority of households. And VCRs are rapidly being replaced or superseded by recordable DVDs. This principle, that not all technology survives or thrives in its original form, reinforces our natural abhorrence of change and also reinforces the philosophy that educators are wise to wait and watch how technology develops before deploying new technologies broadly.

In a study of the diffusion of innovations, Everett Rogers (1995) noted that the critical time for a new innovation is when the technology has been adopted by 10 to 20 percent of a population. The theory of innovation suggests that after technology reaches this percentage range of a group, "it is often impossible to stop the further diffusion of a new idea, even if one wished to do so" (Rogers, 1995, p. 259). This important attribute of the theory of innovation enables us to identify when a technology has reached the no-turning-back point, and allows us to plan for widespread use and integration.

For example, when the ownership of personal computers reached the 25 percent diffusion point in 1992, it became relatively safe to predict that at some point in the not-too-distant future, close to 85 percent of the population would have personal computers of some type. So, even if one chose to wait and watch, serious planning for computing should have started about 1990. By this time, the education community could have recognized its need to accommodate and embrace personal computer technology.

A compelling reason for this adoption was the personal computer's ability to manipulate data. Information, dialogue, and communication are the fundamental processes in our daily work of research, teaching, and learning. A second compelling reason was that it had become clear that this technology and many related technology innovations would soon be available and in the process of diffusion.

Think about which technologies are just now being tested and adopted by innovators. Where are smart phones, the tablet personal computers, the ipods, and other handheld devices today? What are the location-based services providing and what is being downloaded and accessed from the web? Some of these technologies may be too costly, too bulky, or not sufficiently useful or convenient now, but what might they be like or do in 5 or 10 years? What difference can they make for teaching and learning?

Principle Three: Continued Technology Growth Can Be Assumed

Knowing the approximate rate at which the technology is going to be improved in power and reduced in cost is useful. Gordon Moore, former President and CEO of Intel Corporation, observed in a 1965 paper that "the number of components on computer chips was growing exponentially. This observation gradually evolved into an industry rule of thumb that the power and price of technology would be doubling every 18 months." This rule of thumb is now known as Moore's Law, and it has held true for over 30 years. In recent years, experts have thought that the fundamental laws of physics would put a stop to this rate of development. The current belief, based on an International Technology Roadmap for Semiconductors (ITRS), is that this type of growth rate will continue at least until about 2016 (Tuomi, 2003). And then we might see continued acceleration, based on the technologies envisioned by Kurzweil, of genetic engineering, nanotechnology, robotics, and artificial intelligences (Kurzweil, 2003). So, despite the already impressive base of technology tools, the best planning assumption is that change will be continuing at an exponential rate.

We have already discussed the web and its exponential rate of growth. While the personal computer, when not networked, is a powerful teaching, learning, and knowledge tool, it becomes formidable when it is networked to other computers and to the internet. When the computer is networked, it becomes a communication and research tool that is unlimited in possibilities. The networked computer supports all the dialogue, communications, and study processes that are at the very essence of the teaching and learning transaction processes.

A 1998 campus computing study reported that the use of email as an instructional resource in community college courses exploded between 1994 and 1998, rising from 3 percent to 26 percent (Green, 1999, p. 4). (Note that the magic point of innovation adoption was reached.) In public universities during the same period, use of email in courses increased from 10 to 56 percent. A follow-up study in 2003 reported that "more than two-thirds (69.5 percent) of all college courses now utilize electronic mail in college classes" (Green, 2003, p. 9).

Another useful metric is the number of college courses with course websites. Between 1995 and 1998, the percentage of courses with web pages rose by 300 percent in public research universities and grew 500 percent in private research universities. Increases at community colleges were less dramatic but still significant, growing from about 6 percent to 14 percent (Green, 1999, pp. 3-4). A 2002 survey reports that 34.8 percent of all college courses have web pages. Another category tracked by the survey is the number of courses reporting the use of internet-based resources. The survey results indicate that fully 50.3 percent of all courses now use internet-based resources. With these survey results, we can assert with confidence that the web and its related communication technologies are significant change forces.

Certainly, the point of successful diffusion has been reached, and there is no turning back, even if we desired it. These integrated technologies – personal computers, handheld devices, cell phones, wireless, networking, and the web – are here to stay and can support some much-needed changes in education.

> **Certainly, the point of successful diffusion has been reached, and there is no turning back...**

Principle Four: People Adopt Innovation at Different Rates

The rate of adoption of new technology by individuals generally follows a bell curve, with limited numbers of creative adventurers and timid souls, and most others somewhere in the middle. Rogers (1995) found that individuals fell into a distribution of five categories of their adoption of innovation: (1) the innovators (2.5 percent); (2) the early adopters (13.5 percent); (3) the early majority (34 percent); (4) the late majority (34 percent); (5) and the laggards (16 percent). A description of each of these categories is provided in the following paragraphs.

Innovators. Another way of describing the innovators (2.5 percent) is that they are adventurers and thrill seekers. Innovators are also easy to spot. They always have some of the latest technogadgets, and they spend much of their time and resources testing, exploring, and trying new technotools. Innovators boast to others about the capacity of their hard drives, the speed of their processors, the extent of their computer memory, and the software innovations they are using. In the last two or three years, they have probably been boasting about the wireless networks in their home, their smart phones, and their new advanced PDAs with keyboards. Innovators often form information-sharing relationships with other innovators, receiving mutual support and feedback in their exploration of these tools. In higher education, innovators serve as gadflies to encourage and push administrators to plan for technology integration into teaching and learning. They are the cadre of faculty who regularly submit project proposals for testing and developing the use of technology for teaching, learning, and research. Many innovators are also effective visionaries and champions of new ideas, and often volunteer to help with strategic planning and technology committees.

Early Adopters. Early adopters (13.5 percent) have many of the characteristics of innovators, but they are generally more cautious in their enthusiasm. Early adopters like to test new technogadgets and tools to see how they might work in various situations. They often have smaller technology budgets as well. Early adopters generally carefully assess an innovation and consult with innovators before making purchases. They also commonly serve as consultants to others who are seeking information about the effective use of technology. While the innovator is often considered far out from the majority in their use of technology, early adopters are closer in peer relationships and serve as important bridges between innovators and members of the early majority.

In higher education, early adopters also serve on committees as resources to decision makers about strategic technology decisions. They might brag about their new technotools and gadgets, but they generally do so after careful assessment of how various tools work within specific contexts and for specific teaching and learning purposes. Early adopters and innovators are the members of the campus community who have consumed many of the resources of the computing help desks. Innovations in technology tend to be more difficult to use when they are new and may be unreliable or unpredictable because appropriate infrastructures are not in place to support them. Thus, both innovators and early adopters tend to have a high tolerance for ambiguity and uncertainty and are good independent problem solvers. They are also very important resources for campuses in their roles as visionaries, champions, and implementers.

Early Majority. By the time the early majority (34 percent) embraces some of the newer technologies, the often ad-hoc services and strategies for supporting the use of tools become quite strained. It is at this point that strategic infrastructure decisions and support structures need to be in place. Before the early majority comes on board with the use of technologies, the number of faculty and staff to be supported is only in the range of 10 to 15 percent. By the time the early majority is interested and ready to implement, the number of students, faculty, and staff who need support at this stage approaches the total of innovators, early adopters, and early majority – a number nearing 50 percent of the campus community. By this time, the technologies need to be easier to use and less expensive, and more documentation and people resources need to be in place. For example, once the use of the internet in the classroom became a desired feature, outfitting classrooms with network connections, projectors, and support personnel was a real challenge for campuses.

The characteristics of the early majority – deliberate, cautious, precise, and questioning – result in much higher expectations of technology and the support infrastructure. The best approach for encouraging faculty to use new technology is to have members of the innovator and early-adopter groups share their successes. Occasionally, there can be drawbacks to innovators meeting with faculty, but such meetings are usually worth the risk.

Late Majority. Members of the late majority (34 percent) adopt new technology at the point when hanging on to the old technology becomes more problematic than moving to the new. Late majority members are skeptics and generally have fewer resources to support their transition to new technologies. By the time members of the late majority begin using the new technology, the number of bugs are much reduced and, generally, the technology is much easier to use. By this time, more support infrastructures are in place, and more colleagues are knowledgeable about the technology. The late majority generally want to use the tools to do their work and aren't interested in how the technology works; they care only that it does work, and that it works reliably. The late majority can be predictably impatient and difficult, and they are likely to complain if the new technology is unreliable. They have very high expectations, assuming the new technology has to be better and more reliable than the old technology, or all these other folks wouldn't be using it.

In higher education, members of the late majority often are found on tenure-review and curriculum-review committees, and they often are members of the faculty union and faculty senate who are comfortable with predictable results and consequences. Applying known principles of change can help communicate, persuade, and engage the late majority in adopting useful teaching and learning technologies.

Laggards. Laggards (16 percent) adopt new technology only when they have no other choice, such as when meetings are only held with technology, or when familiar tools are no longer supported. (*Where have all the slide projectors gone?*) Intensive initial training and support – including handholding – can help laggards adopt new technology. If little additional support is provided, however, laggards use the technology inefficiently, if at all. Stories flourished in the late 1990s of new computers, still in boxes, sitting in corners of offices. Many stories also circulated describing the ways laggards were only brought on board for the use of email when managers or administrators chose to only send important information and invitations to important events only through email. Faculty, strongly encouraged to use websites for their courses, might instead leave the website in the hands of students or student assistants.

Laggards can be quite inventive in avoiding the use of new technology. A laggard knows that few administrators have the time or the need to force the use of new technology, and many laggards plan on retiring before they need to learn anything new.

> **A person's state of readiness for the use of technology for teaching and learning also predicts the speed at which that person will want to include technology design in teaching environments and courses.**

Where Do You Fit? When reflecting on which innovation group fits you, remember that you can be an innovator in one category of technology and a laggard in another. Keep in mind that readiness to accept new technology is neither good nor bad. Instead, it clarifies why a person responds to technology in a certain way. A person's state of readiness for the use of technology for teaching and learning also predicts the speed at which that person will want to include technology design in teaching environments and courses. The principles behind technology adoption and the change processes that accompany technology adoption lead to changes in the ways we perceive and function in faculty and staff roles. However, many new technology innovations are needed before the stage is set for a full paradigm shift.

With all the new technologies now at our fingertips wherever we happen to be, we in the higher education community are in the middle of the largest paradigm shift in education in hundreds of years. We need to look at the process of paradigm shifting so we can fully participate in it.

Stages of a Paradigm Shift

As new technology is introduced into an environment, we can predict the way it will first be used. One of the difficulties of new, unrefined technology is the lack of practical and convenient uses for it. Another difficulty is that there is usually little or no infrastructure for its use. Cell phones didn't really didn't take off until a network of cell towers blanketed the earth and convenient one-price monthly plans were available. Innovative technologies are often used in safe, undemanding environments that enable a lot of experimentation. This is one reason many new technologies are tested in games. As a technology evolves and matures, four general stages of technology adoption occur.

Stage 1. In the first stage of technology adoption, people use new tools to do the same thing in a new way. The first educational use of the computer, for example, was for drill-and-practice applications or tutorials. At that time, we thought that the primary function of teaching was to dispense information. A well-known early CEO of computer tutorials and programs used to say, "If a computer can replace a teacher, then it should!" He tended to keep his publicists busy.

Early computer teaching programs presented the contents and the exercises from popular workbooks in reading, math, and language. Computers were sometimes called expensive technological workbooks, and with good reason. As another example, the initial use of a video camera was to take moving pictures of a stage play. In this first stage of adoption, difficulties lie in justifying the benefits of new technology and determining whether it is as good as the old technology.

Stage 2. The second stage of technology adoption is using the technology to improve the efficiency of existing processes. Word processing evolved to speed the process of writing letters; spreadsheets evolved to speed the process of budgeting. Little or no thought was given to how word processing and spreadsheets would shift and redefine the work and roles of secretaries and managers.

In higher education, one of the first uses of computers by faculty in teaching was to deliver more visually effective lectures. Efficient simulations of difficult concepts save faculty time and students frustration in learning complex processes, relationships, and interdependencies. Early efforts with improving lectures involved faculty spending many hours moving yellow-pad lectures to HyperCard. Later, many of these same faculty moved their animations to Macromedia Director, and later to the web. Over time, classrooms have become equipped with computer projection equipment so that the improved lectures and animations can be displayed to students. In this second stage, justifying the cost and time investments of new technology is still difficult, largely because all the costs and time are generally added to existing processes. Few efficiencies are yet apparent; technology is viewed as an expensive add-on.

Stage 3. In this stage, costs generally decrease as tools become better, less expensive, and more available. In higher education, faculty have discovered that faculty-to-student communication can be enhanced by the use of email and synchronous and asynchronous group meetings. Faculty have also discovered that holding office hours on the web is a real benefit. At this stage, we generally see some economies of time.

As any technology achieves greater dissemination, the functions supported by the technologies need to be re-examined. At this stage in our higher education environment, we have been asking ourselves fundamental questions about the teaching and learning processes around which our campuses have been structured for so long. Some of the questions asked at this stage are, What exactly is a course? What is the origin of the now accepted three-credit Carnegie unit? How many times do students and faculty really need to get together physically? We have been in the classroom-and-books paradigm for hundreds of years. We are loath to change anything that has worked for so long, but computer technologies have transformed the environment in which we operate so greatly that we are now at Stage 3 of the paradigm shift: using the new technologies to create and invent new processes.

Stage 4. This stage is the transformational stage. Here, new tools are used to solve old problems. For example, one of the most significant problems with many distance education models of the past was the lack of interaction, within a reasonable time frame, among the participants. New communication technology overcomes that problem.

In solving the problem, however, we have discovered another challenge of distance learning: increased expectations from students. If faculty can communicate regularly and consistently, student expectations rise, creating greater demands on faculty time. A comprehensive paradigm shift requires a whole new set of tools, applications, and services. We are not there yet.

While new communication technologies have arrived, the software and services are in a relatively immature stage of development for teaching and learning purposes. In many ways, we are using new technology to do our teaching and learning in the same old ways. The need for patience is clear, as is the need for planning. Improved tools are emerging that are less costly, easier to use, and integrated into the fabric of a campus environment.

In *Paradigms*: *The Business of Discovering the Future*, Joel Arthur Barker (1993) asserts the most important lesson of paradigm shifts: "When a paradigm shifts, everyone goes back to zero" (p. 140). This means that in using new technology for teaching and learning, all faculty become novices again. For administrators, this means that faculty require support in becoming proficient in the use of tools for teaching and learning. It means new infrastructure and new services. It also means recognizing the need for time and energy for the change.

What Will the New Environment for Teaching and Learning Look Like?

One more principle guides the theory of innovation. We often think that creating a new environment simply may not be possible. We may think we are too stuck in our ways to change the current paradigm. Change is difficult; it takes time, energy, resources, and changed minds and attitudes. So how do we make this happen? How might it be possible?

Tracy Goss (1996), in *The Last Word on Power*, states, "When you declare a new context, you create a new realm of possibility, one that did not previously exist" (p. 19). Goss provides an example of this process by reminding readers of the power of the statement made by John F. Kennedy when he declared that we would be on the moon by the end of the 1960s. He created a context in which getting to the moon was believed to be possible. He, and the American public by agreeing to it, created a belief system that this was possible. Resources and talent were allocated on the basis of this belief system.

In a similar fashion, the higher education institutions that mandated 24-hour student access to computing and networking in the late 1990s created a new context for teaching and learning. This new context supports the fundamental processes that occur in teaching and learning: communication, dialogue, creating knowledge, researching and analyzing information, and sharing knowledge and ideas.

For many decades, some might even say centuries, we used the classroom as the beginning and ending point of the course or higher education learning experience. The classrooms of today and the future are assuming new and, in some cases, unfamiliar shapes. We are experiencing a shift from the classroom as the primary place of organized instruction to the web as the center for instruction. The course website is now the communications hub and the teaching and learning space for many of the experiences of the course.

Figure 2.1 shows a possible midstate of the new teaching and learning environment to which we may be moving. This graphic shows the center of organized instruction as the web. This does not mean that the classroom disappears; it means that the primacy of the classroom is past.

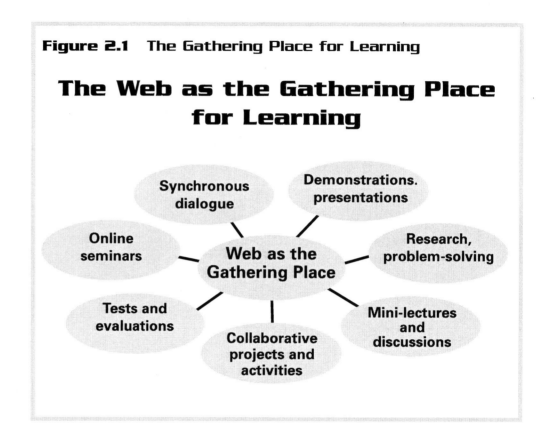

Figure 2.1 The Gathering Place for Learning

The Web as the Gathering Place for Learning

Consider the traditional elements of higher education course experiences: class meetings, independent and group study time, individual and group projects, tests and evaluations, demonstrations, and discussion. Which of these communication experiences must occur in a shared physical space at the same time? Which of them benefit from being in a traditional space? Which of these experiences might benefit from being in a networked gathering space? Many studies in the late 1990s and in 2000 to 2003 examined the impact of a new balance of class meetings, individual and group study, and research. The new paradigm may seem to be only a shift in the emphasis of meeting places, but it will change almost everything.

Chapter 3
What We Know About Teaching and Learning

After more than 150 years of educational research, we have a significant body of knowledge about what increases the probabilities of effective teaching and learning. But little is known for certain. Why don't we have more certainty about what works in teaching and learning? Berliner (2003, p. 18) suggests two primary reasons: (1) because the context in teaching and learning cannot be controlled, and (2) because context includes an abundance of interactions. Context and interactions: a concise summary for thinking about teaching and learning. These two characteristics capture many of the challenges in designing and doing teaching and learning. Finding ways to deal with the dual challenge of specific contexts and the distinctive interactions of teaching and learning experiences may help us make more progress in educational research.

Despite the challenges inherent in educational research, we have seen great progress in the last 20 years from research about how people learn and think (Bransford, Brown, & Cocking, 1999; Fauconnier & Turner, 2003; Howard, 2000; Pinker, 1997, 2003). The decade of the 1990s was proclaimed the Decade of the Brain to focus attention on the structures of the brain and how these structures result in mind, consciousness, and emotion. Demasio (2000) states that emotion is "an adaptive response, part of the vital process of normal reasoning and decision making," and that emotion is "critical to learning and memory." The research from this decade will be enriching and affecting our views and decisions about teaching and learning for years to come.

Most faculty find it difficult to make effective use of research knowledge. We have come to rely on instincts, habits, and traditions that are readily available to us rather than pursue the principles identified by researchers. And it takes time for information to be learned and integrated into our thinking. The novelty and ubiquity of the online environment brings the need for everyone involved in teaching and learning to develop explicit knowledge about the best practices in designing effective educational experiences. Our personal experiences might not have prepared us for the possibilities of the online environment.

In one respect, we are very fortunate. The new context encourages us to re-examine the fundamental processes involved in teaching and learning. A fresh

> **A fresh look at how we teach and how students learn can help us identify core principles for designing and creating effective models of teaching and learning for online learning.**

look at how we teach and how students learn can help us identify core principles for designing and creating effective models of teaching and learning for online learning. These principles can serve as solid reference points so we do not get lost as we adopt and embrace the new technologies.

This chapter provides perspectives about designing for learning. They include the change processes for moving to online learning, codes for designing learning, and a summary of learning principles derived from major theoretical schools. Those perspectives and theories can guide the design of effective teaching and learning, whether in the classroom or online. We hope that by using this chapter as a resource, you will feel more confident about your choice of learning strategies and your design of learning experiences.

The Web as Gathering Place

As the online environment takes its place as the new gathering place for teaching and learning, it may for some courses replace the classroom as the primary site of organized instruction. Shifting from the physical space of the classroom to the virtual space of the online classroom encourages us to ask questions about the functions, rules, and freedoms we have in this new environment.

Moving from the traditional classroom to the online environment does not mean that the physical classroom disappears. Rather, the web likely becomes the primary place of interaction, and the classroom assumes a secondary role. Students will register for classes and purchase and subscribe to class materials and resources online. If it is a campus-based course, students will go to the course website for the syllabus, course goals, objectives, and requirements and to meet the faculty member via a video clip introduction. They will introduce themselves to their fellow students online. The classroom will continue to be used for instructional events for which it is best suited and for gatherings and meetings. However, the number of times we use a classroom may be reduced, while the number of hours we spend in a classroom for a particular meeting may increase.

Why Do We Teach the Way We Do?

Many faculty in higher education have a great deal of experience in designing and delivering instruction, but they might not have had the time or opportunity to learn about teaching and learning research in any formal way. Rather, postsecondary faculty generally come to the teaching experience with a high level of competence in a content area. They then learn about teaching and learning through peer observation, collegial discussion, trial and error, and their own educational experiences. Many faculty are unconscious competents in the discipline of instructional design. We know how to teach and have good intuition about what works, but we don't necessarily know why. Given the need to adapt to a new environment, it is important to learn the *why* of what we know.

The current classroom paradigm for teaching and learning has many constraints. Many have adapted to these constraints and accepted them. Yet the principles of effective learning suggest that new environments that supplement the classroom are needed. Consider the difficulty of holding small group discussions in a large lecture hall with immovable seats. How effective is collaborative work in a computer lab where students cannot see their classmates over the monitors? How interactive can a class of 400 students be in the hour allotted for class? What interactive strategies for learning large amounts of content are useful to students?

These are only a few examples of the many challenges associated with implementing interactive learning, the engaged learning now so strongly recommended by researchers. The wonder and power of the online environment is that it provides an entirely new context for teaching and learning. It removes the physical and time constraints for instructors as well as learners. Moving a course to the web presents the perfect opportunity to re-examine the core principles of teaching and learning and to create a new pedagogical framework for practices.

> The wonder and power of the online environment is that it provides an entirely new context for teaching and learning.

Perspectives and Principles for Designing Learning

Building a Foundation of Learning

Pedagogy is the art or science of teaching. It can guide us in rethinking the teaching and learning process for new environments. The fundamental unit of pedagogy is the educational experience, which contains these four elements:

- The learner
- The teacher
- A task to be completed with the help of a teacher
- The knowledge needed to complete the task

This description of the four core components of the teaching and learning process is from Vygotsky (1962) and his theory of the Zone of Proximal Development (ZPD).

Viewing all teaching and learning as a series of educational experiences sounds elegant and, in fact, it is. Every learning experience engaged in by a learner has these four elements. The learner is a given. The teacher element is either (1) explicitly present synchronously or asynchronously, at a distance or face to face, or (2) implicitly present by virtue of directed instruction or by virtue of being accessible if needed. The task to be completed is in a student's zone of proximal development, and the knowledge to complete the task is present in the form of resources and tools available to the student. This description of any learning experience combines the basic principle of readiness with the principle of manageable steps in learning supported by a teacher.

One might observe that teaching and learning with these four critical elements can happen anywhere, anytime. Learning happens when a young child helps a toddler build a tower of blocks; when parents show teenagers how to barbecue chicken or drive a car; and when adults learn how to use new software, repair marine engines, or integrate new tools into teaching and learning processes. Teaching and learning experiences occur every day in many scenarios. Some of these experiences are structured and formal, while others are unstructured, informal, and casual. All fit the definition of a learning experience.

Vygotsky's four-element learning model provides a good place to start a quest for the fundamentals of learning. The most significant aspect of this learning model is the focus on the task to be performed by the learner. As Samuel Johnson has been quoted as saying, Nothing so focuses a designer of instructional events as knowing the particular task or problem that a student must learn to solve. This task focuses and engages the learner and specifies an assessment of the learning. The learner who solves the problem or completes the task can move on to another problem or task.

Thus, our design task centers on the learning and the learner wherever the learner may be, and reduces the importance of the physical *where* of teaching.

Strategies for Instructional Design

The field of pedagogy includes the principles of instructional design that specify instructional strategies for teaching and learning. An instructional strategy is a simple concept: It is a communication activity that engages the learner in a task and assists the learner in acquiring the knowledge, skill, or attitude necessary to complete the task. Instructional strategies include, for example, lectures, discussions, problem solving, interviews, panel presentations, study projects, and assessments.

The instructional strategies that assist learning are generally based on one or more of these three modes of dialogue and communication in teaching and learning:

- The dialogue between the instructor and the student
- The dialogue between the student and instructional resources
- The dialogue between and among students

Scholars have suggested that a useful design goal for undergraduate education be an approximate balance of these three dialogues (Pelikan, 1992, p. 61). It can also be a useful design goal for courses, especially online courses (Boettcher, 1995). Designing learning experiences with a balance of these three modes of communication can be just as easy or even easier in an online environment than for campus courses. In the online environment, the spatial and physical limitations of the classroom vanish. Communication in the online environment can be synchronous or asynchronous, can be one-to-one dialogue, or one-to-small group, or one-to-many dialogue, as in broadcast email or website communication.

Instructional Design for Faculty

A principal characteristic of instructional design is its iterative and multileveled nature. In other words, instructional design is seldom truly complete, and effective instructional design usually requires design at institutional and infrastructure levels as well as at program, course, activity, and assessment levels (Boettcher, 2003). The process that follows applies primarily to the design at the course, activity, and assessment levels. A more complete discussion of instructional design is in Chapter 5. This overview is provided here as grounding for thinking about learning theory.

Instructional design can be described as a four-step process.

1. Analyze the Course. Course analysis is usually done by the faculty member. For many online programs, a more extensive marketing and mission analysis is completed at the program level. This analysis questions whether the program is a match with the students and their needs and expectations, whether it will attract sufficient students, and whether there are sufficient experienced faculty to support the program.

The initial course analysis examines the following:

- Learner characteristics
- The learning contexts of the expected learner – where and when students will be learning
- The knowledge, skill goals, and expectations of the learners
- The knowledge and skill requirements of the instructor
- The relationship of the course to the context of the larger certificate or degree program

2. Determine Goals and Objectives. The second step asks the following Instructional Design 101 questions. If you ask no other questions while planning a course, these are the most useful and fundamental. At the end of the course,

- What do my students need to know?
- What do my students need to be able to do?
- What do my students need to think as a result of the instruction?

3. Design the Learning Experiences. The third step focuses on the design of the unit or modules and the learning experiences within those units. During this design step, faculty generally do the following:

- Frame the body of knowledge and select the core and recommended content.
- Identify and select a set of teaching strategies and resources.
- Determine the procedures and processes for assessing student learning.

4. Plan Evaluation of Course. The fourth step focuses on evaluating the design and effectiveness of the course and the program. The plan includes evaluating three dimensions of the program:

- Program design
- Instructor evaluation
- Delivery of the program

In the process of instructional design, we all make decisions based on our own theories and practices of learning. Here is an overview of some of the principal schools of learning theory. Immersing yourself in a learning theory or embracing principles from a set of theories can be the basis of your own theory and can inform the design of your courses, whether on campus or online.

Principal Schools of Learning Theory

The basic principles of instructional design are derived from learning philosophies, theories, and learning practices. Anyone who has been teaching for any length of time has a philosophy of teaching and learning, even if that philosophy is difficult to articulate. Very simply, philosophies of learning are important because how we think about learning and how we think about students affect how we design for learning.

A philosophy of teaching and learning includes a view of what learning is, how it happens, and what a student's role is in learning. The principal schools of learning theory each reflect their view of what learning is, what knowledge is, and how students come to acquire knowledge, skills, and attitudes.

The number of instructional theories available to instructional designers and faculty is impressive. One good general web resource for a summary of these theories is the Theory Into Practice Database (http://tip.psychology.org/), maintained by Greg Kearsley (1998-2003). This database lists 50 theories "relevant to human learning and instruction" and to "particular instructional settings." Most learning theories offer perspectives of interest to the instructional designer, depending on the goals and objectives of the instructional event to be planned. Another site that provides an attractive summary on the fundamental issues in three learning theories discussed below is at web.cocc.edu/cbuell/theories/.

The primary theories examined in this section are **behaviorism**, **cognitivism**, and **constructivism**. Your philosophy and theory probably share some views in common with one or more of these theories. With luck, a review of them will help you think about why you like to teach the way you do in the classroom and how you have changed or are thinking about changing in the online environment.

Behaviorism

The oldest of the theories, behaviorism is the learning theory that predominated in the early half of the 20th century. It holds that the goal of learning is to shape a learner's response to a set of stimuli. This theory defines learning as a change in observable measurable behavior. Behaviorists believe that the core learning process accustoms, trains, or conditions a learner to respond in a certain way, given a certain stimulus. The focus of the behaviorist is on the externals that can be observed in a person's behavior. As noted by the most prominent of the behaviorists, B. F. Skinner, this perspective allows researchers and teachers to avoid the problem of our inability to view mental processing before, during, or after learning. (Note: New brain-imaging capabilities that can measure the strength and location of mental processes in response to stimuli is causing a wave of interest in linking external stimuli and behaviors to brain activity.)

B.F. Skinner

Skinner believed that a learner would behave in a certain way by interacting with a manipulated environment (www.bfskinner.org). The interaction with the environment and the stimuli within the environment could cause an observable behavioral change in a learner. While Skinner is most remembered for his focus on the external stimuli and the ability to train behavior, one of his long-term research goals was to find ways to make the education of children much more efficient.

Essential Ideas

According to Skinner, the external behavior to be shaped and maintained in educational settings is usually verbal and is brought under the control of both verbal and nonverbal stimuli. A verbal behavior is acquired when either a verbal or nonverbal stimulus causes the verbal behavior to be ready and available. In many respects, a common example of this is the set of manners and customs that we all need to acquire to be successful in the full range of daily interactions with others. When people ask, "How are you?" they are issuing a greeting; rarely do they want or expect a health status report.

Skinner envisioned a learning machine that could serve as an environment for teaching a range of verbal and nonverbal behaviors. He did, however, distinguish such a teaching machine from a teacher. Examples of such teaching machines in the 1960s and 1970s were personal filmstrip-like machines and programmed instruction booklets. Skinner wrote:

> If our current knowledge of the acquisition and maintenance of verbal behavior is to be applied to education, some sort of teaching machine is needed. The machine itself, of course, does not teach. It simply brings the student into contact with the person who composed the material it presents. It is a labor-saving device because it can bring one programmer into contact with an indefinite number of students. (Skinner, 1958, p. 97)

With a little extrapolation, we might see the tutorials now available on the web for teaching a range of software applications as teaching machines. Similarly, the multitude of discussion boards and learning environments can be viewed as teaching machines because of their ability to bring students into contact with a teacher and with other learners and resources. Simulations might also be categorized as teaching machines. Simulations such as *SimCity* provide complete worlds or environments that enable students to interact with sets of programmed yet very complex options and consequences.

Implications for Teaching and Learning

Under a behaviorist theory of learning, a teacher defines and controls the instructional environment with which the student interacts and then assesses student progress based on a demonstration of the target behaviors that the environment is designed to elicit. In today's teaching and learning environments, the temptation is strong to dismiss behaviorism because of its focus on external control and stimulus. However, many skill-development activities can profit from behaviorist theory. Basic skills in math, reading, and language, or any skill whose mastery requires practice, can benefit from behaviorist environments. Skills that require complex integration of muscle memory and cognitive processing – surgery, piloting, or lab work – can benefit from thinking about the importance of environments.

Perhaps the best current example of teaching and learning environments that incorporate behaviorist thinking are the airplane simulators used to train pilots. Also, if we are to achieve efficiency in education, teaching machines as manifested in tutorial and simulation materials might be very useful for learning abstract and difficult core concepts in many disciplines. Thousands of hours of tutorials, simulations, and smaller objects will be more easily found and integrated over time as standards for learning resources are implemented. Disciplinary resources such as the MERLOT (www.merlot.org) database and standards supporting interoperability in learning technologies provided by the IMS Global Learning Consortium (www.imsglobal.org) are two movements that will support the use and reuse of learning content.

> **Thousands of hours of tutorials, simulations, and smaller objects will be more easily found and integrated over time as standards for learning resources are implemented.**

Instructional Design Principles

A fundamental principle of instructional design is to review and examine existing materials to see if they can be used to achieve stated goals and objectives. The following three instructional design principles can be derived from the behaviorist theory:

- Identify the goals and objectives to be learned.
- Create an environment for learning that assists the learner in acquiring these goals. The learning environment includes the stimulus or task that will engage the learner and provide practice in the desired behaviors.
- Review, examine, and consider adopting or adapting existing materials before developing new ones.

Cognitivism

Cognitivism as a learning theory is both a complement to and reaction to behaviorism. Behaviorism focuses on the function of external stimuli and observable behaviors in learning; cognitivism focuses on the internal mental processes of learning.

Cognitive learning theory posits that learning occurs when a learner processes information and acquires knowledge or skills by constructing nodes and linkages of knowledge structures. In cognitivism, the input, processing, storage, and retrieval of information are at the heart of learning. The learner takes an active mental role in planning and carrying out learning, and the instructor's role is primarily one of manager and director of the process, especially in the information input and processing phases. Instruction is not something that is *done to* learners; it involves learners by engaging their internal mental processes.

This cognitivist view of learning helped to popularize the transmission model of learning, whereby the act of learning involved moving knowledge from the instructor's mind, or from books or other resources, into the students' heads. A number of well-known philosophers and theorists, such as John Dewey, Jean Piaget, Jerome Bruner, Lev Vygotsky, and Robert Gagne, formulated and advanced many of the cognitivist ideas.

Jerome Bruner

A leading representative of the cognitivist school of learning, Jerome Bruner was one of the first to extend that theory to include the importance of interactive cognitive development. Bruner stressed social interaction as an integral part of information processing, and was also a strong proponent of discovery learning.

Bruner believed that mastery of the fundamental ideas of a field involved not only the grasping of general principles, but also the development of an attitude toward learning and inquiry, toward the possibility of solving problems on one's own (Bruner, 1963, p. 20). Discovery learning was not a random event for Bruner. He endorsed problem-solving strategies through structured searching strategies as an integral part of discovery learning.

Essential Ideas

> The first object of any act of learning, over and beyond the pleasure it may give, is that it should serve us in the future. Learning should not only take us somewhere; it should allow us later to go further more easily. (Bruner, 1963, p. 17)

The essence of this thought is twofold: Bruner emphasizes that learning should be purposeful – for example, developing skills to serve us in the future. And every time we learn something, we add to a cognitive structure upon which we can build more later; as we build, we are able to learn more and learn faster.

Implications for Teaching and Learning

The primary implication of cognitivist thinking on teaching and learning is the importance of structuring experiences that involve the learner as an active participant. The more instructional design can incorporate activities that require deep-level processing, thinking, and manipulating of content by the student, the more we increase the probability that effective learning will occur. In the online learning environment, this can mean giving students tasks that involve exploring and discovering goals and finding, organizing, synthesizing, and creating content.

Lev Vygotsky

Lev Vygotsky is a prominent cognitivist who developed the concept of the Zone of Proximal Development (ZPD). In the ZPD, the learner, teacher, and content interact with a problem that requires resolution. The ZPD represents the difference between what a learner can do individually and what the learner can do with the help of more experienced people, including other learners, experts in the field, and the instructor. The concept of the ZPD also reinforces the importance of the principle of readiness, often referred to in relation to a child being ready for reading. However, readiness as a concept applies at any age.

Essential Ideas

> The Zone of Proximal Development defines those functions (of a learner) that have not yet matured, but are in a process of maturation, functions that will mature tomorrow but are currently in an embryonic state. These functions could be termed the "buds" or "flowers" of development rather than the "fruits" of development. The actual developmental level characterizes mental development retrospectively, while the Zone of Proximal Development characterizes mental development prospectively. (Vygotsky, 1978, pp. 86-87)

In Vygotsky's description of the ZPD, learning is depicted as the budding or flowering of a particular knowledge or skill. This description also suggests that the window of learning for an individual learner might be fairly narrow and quite specific. This window of learning, or individual readiness, has always been a challenge for teachers, as a group of students is unlikely to share a particular ZPD. Because the lecture method might not ensure that all students are at the appropriate readiness point, learning activities may need to be customized to the individual learner.

Implications for Teaching and Learning

In Vygotsky's theory, the primary implication for the design of teaching and learning environments and materials is the importance of providing a range of content for any group of learners so that they can customize their own learning within a framework of the larger goals and objectives of a course. While all students will need to master a core set of concepts and principles in any unit, Vygotsky's ZPD suggests that we also provide ways for students to customize their learning within that framework.

Instructional Design Principles

The cognitivist theory suggests two additional basic instructional design principles:

- Design courses to include problem solving, and provide sufficient help and resources to assist the learner in solving problems. Such help can take many forms, from online tutorials to databases of questions or possible points of confusion. Structure the problems in steps so that learners can be successful in developing their own solutions.

- Analyze learner readiness for learning the core concepts, principles, and attitudes of a course. One traditional way of ensuring readiness for learning in higher education is by establishing prerequisites for a course. Other traditional ways of ensuring readiness include skills assessments in math, science, and writing courses. New tools and applications can provide for more specific and targeted testing than in the past. The challenge of readiness or appropriately meeting the ZPDs of students can be met either by admitting only those students who are demonstrably ready or by building sufficient preparation and support into the course.

Constructivism

Constructivism is an emerging learning theory, an extension of cognitivism focusing on what knowledge is developing in the learner's head. It differs from cognitivism in the nature of knowledge. In constructivism, the learner does not receive knowledge from a teacher, but rather constructs knowledge, growing and developing the body of knowledge that resides in the learner's mind. Knowledge is constructed by the learner and may or may not be what is in the teacher's mind. In fact, we know that everyone does know differently, but it does not follow that there is no knowledge that is the same for all.

Constructivism is influenced by the principles of information-processing theory as developed by Bruner and Vygotsky and by the work of philosopher John Dewey and adult-learning theorist Malcolm Knowles. As in cognitivist theories, the learner is an interactive participant in the learning environment; however, in constructivism, the learner is viewed as the creator and processor of the educational experience. Constructivism emphasizes teaching and learning strategies that get students interacting with other students, learning resources, experts, and the teacher. Another component of the constructivist-learning environment is that it is learner controlled or learner centered. The instructor is the manager and facilitator of the learner-defined environment; the learner is the builder of knowledge.

John Dewey

John Dewey is an American philosopher who did most of his influential writing and thinking about education in the first half of the 20th century. Dewey emphasized the importance of experience in the teaching and learning environments. With this emphasis on experience, he predicted the role that technology would play in the ability to customize learning for the individual.

Dewey foresaw an active and collaborative student experience that, almost a hundred years later, we finally have the tools to implement. He emphasized the individualized nature of interaction in the learning experience and believed, as do many constructivist theorists, that learners construct new knowledge based on previous knowledge, and that experiences are specific to each learner. Dewey promoted the active participation of the learner in defining the learning environment, and he conceived of the instructor as facilitator.

> **Dewey promoted the active participation of the learner in defining the learning environment, and he conceived of the instructor as facilitator.**

Essential Ideas

Dewey focused his ideas on developing the aims of education: the development of reflective, creative, responsible thought. In his 1933 treatise, Dewey said, "We state emphatically that, upon its intellectual side, education consists of the formation of wide-awake, careful, thorough habits of thinking" (Dewey, 1933/1998, p. 78). This quote captures the essence of Dewey's thinking. In this single sentence, Dewey sets forth one of the ultimate goals of education.

Implications for Teaching and Learning

A central idea in Dewey's work is that interaction and continuity are the two primary characteristics of effective teaching and learning experiences. The characteristic of interaction reinforces the importance of dialogue and communication underlying learning; the characteristic of continuity reinforces the perspective that the individual learner must be viewed as the main design element. In other words, we must design instruction so that learners can effectively build on what they know so they have the resources and assistance to learn or, in Vygotsky's words, to navigate the Zone of Proximal Development.

Malcolm Knowles

Malcolm Knowles was among the first to bring the concept of andragogy, or the study of adult learning, to the attention of American educators. Andragogy assumes that the strategies used to teach adults differ from the strategies used to teach children. From the andragogical perspective, the adult learner is self-directed and desirous of a very active learning environment, including actual experience to the extent possible. In adult learning environments, which include all of higher education, the instructor is viewed more as a facilitator of the teaching and learning process and less as the sole or primary source of information.

Essential Ideas

> Andragogical practice treats the learning-teaching transaction as the mutual responsibility of learners and teacher. In fact, the teacher's role is redefined as that of a procedural technician, resource person, and co-inquirer; more of a catalyst than an instructor, more of a guide than a wizard. (Knowles, 1980, p. 48)

Implications for Teaching and Learning

Knowles' philosophy strongly supports the move away from a focus on teaching to a new emphasis on learner-centered programs. The entire movement toward active and collaborative learning is supported by the theories of adult learning. The philosophy of adult learning has the following implications for instructional design:

- Learners participate in setting their own learning objectives. This encourages active and customized learning.
- Student-to-student dialogue taps into the current and expanding knowledge of most working and professional adults.

- The role of the faculty as mentor, manager, and facilitator is dominant. Students prefer a focus on problem-based learning, with help as needed.

Instructional Design Principles

With the constructivist theory, three additional basic instructional design principles arise:

- Design for continuity of learning at the individual level by providing options for students who are learning core material and by using well-structured content.
- Design for interaction. Include a balance of the dialogues between faculty and student, student and student, and student and learning resources.
- Design for student goal setting and decision making. Use a learning environment that puts the students in charge and makes them responsible for learning a set of objectives and skills.

Building an Active Learning Environment

A fundamental component of each of these learning theories is learner interaction with the learning environment. Whether responding to stimuli according to behaviorists, processing information according to cognitivists, or building knowledge collaboratively and constructively according to constructivists, the learner is an active participant.

Teaching strategies that include interaction and collaboration are rapidly becoming the norm in today's higher education environments. The traditional and comfortable pedagogical model of the instructor as the predominant source of information has hindered the incorporation of interactions beyond the dialogue between the instructor and the student. The instructor was the center of the communications structure for a class.

The online environment and the multitude of applications, such as email, discussion boards, and chat rooms, have changed all that, and changed it very quickly. Opportunities for interaction in an online environment are greater simply because time limitations and physical constraints are minimized, and because the applications and tools make it easier to collaborate and communicate.

> **Opportunities for interaction in an online environment are greater . . . because the applications and tools make it easier to collaborate and communicate.**

Today's technologies easily and almost effortlessly facilitate the three forms of dialogue mentioned previously. Moore and

Kearsley's (1996) notion of participation versus presentation nicely sums up the faculty perspective of the new pedagogical model. They state that "interactive teaching is really a mental set that requires teachers to think about inducing knowledge rather than instilling it... asking questions rather than giving answers... focusing on student participation rather than the teacher's presentation of information" (p. 133).

The ideal learning environment engages the learners and views learners as masters of their own learning. In this environment the instructor is the mentor to the student, serving as content consultant, motivator, and contextual integrator, as well as the leader and manager of the learning experience. Implementing an interactive pedagogy in the online environment enables faculty and students to use their imaginations to move beyond the constraints of the traditional campus classroom. Today's learning environments require using instructional design principles that focus on the learners' characteristics and the desired educational outcomes. Today's learning environments also require creativity to design meaningful experiences in a new context using a broader set of pedagogical strategies.

During a keynote speech at the 14th annual *Conference on Distance Teaching and Learning* in Madison, Wisconsin, Elliott Maisie conjectured that perhaps one day, learning would "be like air" in that it would be all around us. With the new online environments and ubiquitous communication devices, we are much closer to achieving that state. Learning, even formal structured learning, is no longer just anytime, anywhere; it can be everywhere and always, a continual, lifelong process.

Chapter 4

Envisioning, Planning, and Identifying Resources for Teaching Online

This chapter begins the how-to section of the book. We begin by describing a set of design decisions that faculty will usually want to consider before launching a project to move a course from the classroom to the web. The purpose of the questions is to define the project sufficiently so that the end product is clear, and to make it easier to estimate the amount of effort it will likely take to produce the desired results.

- What tools and resources, such as people, time, and money, are needed to support this project?
- What tools and resources are already in place to support a project of this type?
- If this course is planned as a fully online course, is it part of a certificate or sequence of courses that will be attractive to students?

Questions about courses to be offered in the fully online format usually involve a team of academic leaders. Here are a few of the questions to be considered by department chairs and deans:

- What resources should all faculty in a department have in order to support effective use of online environments for teaching, learning, and research?
- How should a department support the first set of web course projects?
- How much time and what types of resources are generally needed to design and develop an online web course, a webcentric course, or a web-enhanced course?
- What technical infrastructure needs to be in place at the faculty, department, and college levels?
- What institutional policies need to be in place?

Two layers of decision making and planning can help guide the design and development of online courses. These decisions segment the planning tasks and make the process more manageable. Many times, faculty or department chairs just want to get started and not do a lot of planning. With very innovative projects, this can often be a good strategy, but planning makes avoiding the potholes easier and helps to create more reasonable expectations. In fact, that might be the most important outcome of this chapter: helping to manage expectations about what *can* be done, how *quickly* it can be done, with what *resources* it can be done, and *where* web course models of delivery fit in the institution's programming of instruction.

In addition to planning, this chapter provides examples of types of faculty support and training programs, as well as ways of identifying and estimating resource needs. This is a readiness and planning chapter, designed to help you envision and build an action plan for moving teaching and learning to an online environment. This chapter will help you determine if you are ready, if your institution is ready, and if your college's digital infrastructure is ready to support online courses.

Decision Layer One: Envisioning a Course on the Web

The first step in the preparation phase is the visioning step. What does it mean to have a course on the web? Ask yourself, "What kind of an online course best suits my students, the content, and my teaching experience? What kind of web course fits the image and context of my institution?"

> The phrase "online course" means something to almost everyone, but it can conjure up very different images in the minds of academic decision makers, legislators, college presidents, and deans.

The phrase "online course" means something to almost everyone, but it can conjure up very different images in the minds of academic decision makers, legislators, college presidents, and deans. If we hear a technically savvy faculty member say, "Oh, I put my EXE 1401 course online last weekend," what does that mean? Some people may expect that all faculty can do this, and that the entire course is on the web. Often, however, only a few course documents, such as a syllabus, bibliography, and course calendar are online, and some of us may feel we will need a lifetime to put these few documents on the web!

Managing expectations is difficult, but considering the three major types of web courses might help:

- A **web** or **online course** is available anywhere, anytime.
- A **webcentric** or **hybrid** course combines face-to-face meetings with
- significant use of online tools and resources. Many webcentric or hybrid courses also have reduced the amount of classroom seat time. This type of course is also sometimes described as a **blended** course.
- A **web-enhanced** course is primarily a campus course that uses many online applications, tools, and resources.

It should be noted that we are still searching for the best vocabulary to talk about the different types of online courses. The description of the types of online courses that follows is one set of terms. The specific terms are not as important as why we want terms to differentiate these types of courses. Each has a different set of requirements, such as time, resources, and planning for their design and development. The three primary types of web-based or online courses are described in more detail in the following sections.

Online (Web) Course

A course that is truly and completely an online course can be accessed anywhere and anytime. A fully 100 percent online course has no place-based requirements. Many courses are called online courses if they have a few place-based requirements, such as initial launching face-to-face meetings and wrap-up or assessment or congratulatory events at the close of a course. A course with these types of place-based requirements might be described as a 90 to 100 percent online course.

The times and places for interaction and communication in an online course are flexible and generally asynchronous. There are few synchronous meetings, although newer tools that support synchronicity are rapidly developing and becoming widely available. Most online courses use course websites that are easily developed with course management-system applications. In online courses, the instructional experience begins and ends with the course website functioning as our 21st century equivalent of a classroom. All instructional strategies are planned and executed around the communication capabilities and content resources available online.

The primary characteristic of an online course – that it is fully available online – means that the faculty member teaching the course and the students taking the course can participate from anywhere in the world. Many campuses make use of another variant of the online course by focusing on students within a geographic area that enables students to gather for a one- or-two-day event in conjunction with a course. But a class that is fully online and is fully globally available includes no requirement for students to gather physically anywhere.

Another essential feature of online courses is the significant use of internet technologies and applications to support the teaching and learning that make up an educational experience. Some of the basic communication tools used in online courses include electronic mail, chat rooms, bulletin boards, and online seminars to support meaningful dialogue and social communication between and among course participants, including faculty and students. Online courses also use other internet applications to access electronic resources such as databases, simulations, current news sources, courseBook sites, and digital libraries. These tools and resources help support discovery learning by individual students and among groups of students. The use of all these tools supports the creation of a learning community.

Web or online courses are sometimes cohort based, involving a group of students who stay together throughout a series of courses. Online courses that are part of a series of courses have an additional instructional benefit if they are cohort based, because the community and the relationships created during one course can continue and deepen during subsequent courses.

Many online courses design "gathering" or face-to-face activities into the program to enable students and faculty to bond with each other in a learning community. Communicating with a person about learning content can be more comfortable in the digital environment if the participants have met and talked in physical space. The online synchronous and asynchronous communication activities support both social and intellectual networking and bonding.

Webcentric or Hybrid Course

How do you know if your course is a hybrid or webcentric course and not simply a campus course with lots of online components, *i.e.*, a web-enhanced course? A course is a webcentric or hybrid course if a significant part of teaching and learning experiences are online and the amount of classroom seat time is reduced. The paradigm shift away from the classroom as the primary site of organized instruction has occurred. A webcentric or hybrid course begins and ends on the internet, usually at the course website. Additionally, the course is designed using a rich set of online resources, seminars, and discussion experiences that take the place of experiences that would normally occur in a classroom setting.

The faculty member may introduce the course from the course website classroom and from that space specify the course requirements, procedures, and resources. Student testing and assessment is accomplished with examinations, projects, and reports, most of which are completed and submitted online. Like the fully online course, the webcentric or hybrid course makes significant use of internet tools and applications to create an online community.

A webcentric course may have a series of scheduled synchronous classes either on campus or at a hotel or conference center. To meet the needs and convenience of working professionals, however, the length, frequency, and content of the class sessions may be significantly different from traditional on-campus courses.

A typical campus class is designed with 45 hours of synchronous class time, usually distributed in one to three hourlong weekly sessions over a 15-week semester. Synchronous gathering activities for a webcentric course or hybrid course are generally in the range of 16 to 24 hours over a semester. A webcentric course can be designed with anywhere from one to eight or even more meetings, but each meeting is longer, ranging from between three to eight hours. This means that class time is concentrated, reducing the number of times students must travel, park, and gather in a physical space. It can also be cohort based, and can benefit from being so, but since it includes more face-to-face meetings, the cohort is not as critical a design factor. The impact of these longer, less frequent campus meetings suggests we need a fresh look at the design of classroom facilities.

Webcentric or hybrid courses were initially thought to be most applicable within a fairly limited geographic area because of the requirement for face-to-face meetings, but this has been disproved. Working adults will travel farther for occasional synchronous meetings. Courses may include use of gathering events such as intensive location-based launching activities, weekend seminars, and celebratory events. Depending on the frequency and length of class meetings, these courses can look a great deal like regular campus courses with heavy reliance on internet technology and tools.

A number of campuses are using webcentric courses to provide faculty and students more convenience and flexibility (Brown, 2002; Martyn, 2003); other campuses, such as the University of Central Florida, are finding that reduced-seat-time hybrid courses can reduce demands for campus classroom space during their critical growth phase (Young, 2002). Fairleigh Dickinson University, in New Jersey, instituted a requirement in 2002 that all first-year students take "at least one course online each year as a way of ensuring that students are experienced at online learning" (Young, 2002).

Web-Enhanced Course

A web-enhanced course uses the internet and tools such as a course website to support a traditional campus classroom-based course. Faculty use internet technologies to assist in the management and administration of a course, using a course website as a central distribution site for course components such as the syllabus, calendar, bibliography of resources, course and project requirements, and project consultation. A faculty member teaching a web-enhanced course also uses the course website as the central communication and collaboration site, supporting a range of communication exchanges and discussions about faculty-to-student dialogue and student-to-student communication. Traditional office hours are usually replaced with email communication and an online office discussion and consultation area. The website can also centralize announcements and access to content resources, including live guest experts.

As the range of course designs combining face-to-face and online tools and applications is infinite, many of these campus courses using online technologies are also often called hybrid courses. For planning purposes, it is recommended that a webcentric or hybrid course include activities or requirements in which online instruction is substituted for some amount of classroom instruction. As language is a living entity not known to subject itself to rules, however, *hybrid* might be used to refer to any course that uses a course website.

Designing, developing, and delivering a web-enhanced course can be an efficient and nonthreatening way for faculty to become engaged in online teaching and learning. It can be an evolutionary step for many faculty and students, as it removes dependencies on paper-based materials and increases student-to-student dialogue. Implementing a web-enhanced course model can also help faculty members migrate from dependency on a lecture mode of presentation to more interactive and collaborative learning strategies.

> **In 1999, the suggestion to a class of graduate students in educational administration that, by 2010, all campus courses would be a combination of face-to-face and online components was met with disbelief. By 2004, students were generally surprised if a course did not have online components and a website associated with the class.**

Moving to web-enhanced courses can be an effective change strategy for both faculty and administrators. For administrators, this way of moving to online teaching and learning can reduce the demand for a high level of instructional support by all faculty simultaneously. For faculty, it can reduce the stress and anxiety of expectations. In 1999, the suggestion to a class of graduate students in educational administration that, by 2010, all campus courses would be a combination of face-to-face and online components was met with disbelief. By 2004, students were generally surprised if a course did not have online components and a website associated with the class.

The use of course websites is moving faster than even many previous aggressive predictions. In the campus computing study results from 2002, approximately one-third of all courses had websites associated with a course. If an institution wants all of its faculty and students to move forward in the use of course tools and more student-centered learning, a good place to start is with mandating and then supporting the generation of websites for all classes. The generation of course management templates, such as

Blackboard and WebCT, made this quite clear, starting in 2001. Even if faculty don't use the course website, students use it for collaboration and communication.

If the web-enhanced strategy is used by technologically savvy and experienced faculty with departmental resources, it is almost free from an institutional perspective. For other faculty, deciding to develop a web-enhanced course requires a realistic look at the time and resources needed. Every campus has faculty who are reluctant to use technology. Starting with a web-enhanced course is an attractive, low-cost, workable strategy. At this writing, most of the required resources for web-enhanced courses will likely be the personal development area of the faculty member.

Envisioning the Outcome: One Course, a Series of Courses, or a Degree Program?

Over the last 20 years, the efficiency and effectiveness of the tools, applications, and resources for creating teaching and learning in the new online environment have almost kept pace with the increasing power and cost reductions of the hardware. Moving teaching and learning to a new format takes faculty time, skills, and effort. It also requires a new digital infrastructure of hardware, software, and support personnel.

All this means that moving teaching and learning online – particularly a certificate or degree program – represents a significant commitment of resources for any institution. It is wise to direct these institutional resources toward programs that are consistent with the institutional mission and goals and part of a larger, future-oriented set of goals.

If the course is to be redesigned for an online or webcentric course, it is likely that the course will be part of a department or collegewide effort, and thus be part of a much larger planning process. However, if a faculty member is an innovator in his or her particular setting and wants to get started, Design Layer One planning will be useful in estimating time and resource requirements for this smaller project as well.

In Design Layer One, a faculty member asks questions about the larger context for the planned web course. Is this course envisioned as an isolated pilot project, or is it envisioned as part of a larger department or college program offering? Will the course be part of a certificate program offered in the webcentric model for which students will be on campus a limited number of times, or will it be part of a redesigned core sequence of courses mostly for campus students? Will the new plan include delivery to a large percentage of off-campus students within a two-, three-, or four-year window? The type of online course or courses that faculty will develop, if well funded, will be determined by factors much larger than an individual faculty member's preference or, indeed, individual faculty readiness. The faculty in the program, the available resources, and the overall program and college goals will influence decisions about the course or program models. A program goal might be to update a set of courses that form a concentration within an existing degree program or to offer a certificate that might be part of a new or changing degree program or a self-contained program for upgrading skills of working professionals.

Beyond the Course Level

Just as faculty need to think about the larger context of individual courses, department chairs and deans find it useful to think about the larger context of the long-term mission and image of their institutions. Many colleges create committees to examine their priorities for developing flexible online learning programs.

Ideally, decisions about moving courses online should be made in the context of the mission of an institution and its goals over the next 5 to 15 years. While institutions often plan for physical infrastructure 10 and 20 years in the future, curricular and academic program planning also need to be refreshed continuously, but with a long-term view. Effective planning allows for flexibility to take advantage of opportunities that cannot always be foreseen.

Outreach programs should reflect and extend the desired image and mission of an institution; thus, decisions about outreach programs are best if the decisions are part of a campuswide planning process. A related question is a student-focused concern. One of the most common questions from students about online courses is, "Is the entire program of study – such as a certificate program, associate degree, baccalaureate degree, or master's degree – available in this particular format?" Students who are place-bound are particularly concerned with the availability of the full program of study in a format that makes it accessible from wherever they are. They want to be assured that they can complete all components of each of the courses, and that no location requirements are part of the program.

The two design questions, "What type of online course should be planned?" and, "Is this course part of a larger program of study?" are very interdependent. Answering these seemingly straightforward questions can shape and be shaped by an institution's mission, faculty, and students and significantly affect a department or college. The Design Layer One worksheet helps faculty determine the type of online *course* in which they are interested. Once this level of initial planning is complete, it is time to move to Design Layer Two.

Decision Layer Two: Envisioning Infrastructure and Context

Shifting teaching and learning to the online environment requires thinking about at least five areas clustered around campus infrastructure readiness, planning, and resources:

- Faculty readiness
- Faculty design and development time
- Types of faculty support
- Infrastructure support
- Mission and policy readiness

In examining these areas, we identify decision areas for each of these items that can help to determine whether the time is right for a faculty member to move teaching and learning to the online environment. Although everything need not be absolutely ready before starting the journey, thinking about these areas helps us identify potential and known trouble spots and helps to ensure that we are open to opportunities for addressing weak areas.

Faculty Readiness

Moving courses to the online environment requires a set of skills and resources on the part of the faculty member. The types of skills needed by the faculty member fall into two major categories: a knowledge of technology tools and a knowledge of the teaching and learning processes.

The technology skills recommended for all faculty members now include the following basics:

- Competence in the personal office suite of software: word processing, spreadsheet, and presentation tools. Database knowledge is a plus, but not essential.

- Competence in the use of a web browser such as Netscape Navigator, Internet Explorer, or Safari. This includes knowledge and use of plug-ins to support media players for streaming audio and video.

- Competence in the use of email applications and in dealing with spam and viruses.

- Competence in the use of a course management system template, or whatever tools are used by a particular campus for these purposes.

Worksheet for Planning and Envisioning Online, Webcentric, or Web-Enhanced Courses: Decision Layer One

Name:_____Date:_____

Discipline Focus: _____

Department: _____

Institution: _____

Scenario: *You are a faculty member interested in designing and developing some type of online course. Answering these questions generally helps to clarify your thinking about the when, where, why, and how of the course you are thinking about redesigning. These questions focus on the structural design of a course; the content design work is a different set of questions, examined in Chapter 6.*

1. What course or set of courses do you want to be part of this project?

_____

_____

2. If these courses are going to be part of a larger set of courses or a program in Phase One or subsequent phases, what is the name and size of that program?

Name of program _____

Number of credits/courses_____

3. What type of course do you envision?

❑ Online course, fully available anywhere

❑ Webcentric or hybrid course with reduced synchronous meetings

❑ Web-enhanced campus course

4. Is this project planned as

❑ an individual project

❑ a department project

❑ a college project

5. If it is a department or college project, how does this project fit within your department's plans?

❑ A single pilot course

❑ Part of a certificate program (3 to 5 courses)

❑ Part of an undergraduate major or minor (3 to 5 courses)

❑ Part of a graduate degree concentration (5 to 7 courses)

❑ Part of a full master's degree program (10 to 16 courses)

❑ Other

6. Where will the students be? How often will they be there?

Will the students be on campus regularly? _____

Will students meet synchronously in the same physical location for 16 or more hours? _____

Will students be within a single time zone, or across multiple time zones? _____

Will campus facilities be needed to support this class? If so, what types of facilities are required? _____

Other _____

7. Who are the students, and why do they want this program? What do you know about where, when, and with whom these students will be studying and working?

Working professionals who want to upgrade skills _____

Working professionals dependent on a new certification requirement _____

Lifelong learners_____

Other _____

8. What types of technologies will the students be expected to have easy or full-time access to?

_____

_____

_____

_____

Competence in managing an online course and in supporting student learning in the asynchronous environment, including use of chat and threaded discussions.

In addition to these technology basics, faculty should be open to developing skills in the new technology basics that include

- Knowledge of and competence in building and maintaining their own personal and course sites;

- Knowledge of online library resources and databases to ensure easy, reliable, and affordable access to content resources by students;

- Knowledge of search engines, how they work and how to search efficiently and effectively, and skills in what to do when search engines provide an overwhelming number of hits; and

- Knowledge of and competence in setting up and using synchronous audio-video meeting tools.

To develop and become proficient in these skills, faculty must have their own technology tools. We used to say that faculty required their own technology on their desktop; however, because faculty are mobile information-age professionals and consultants rather than stationary professionals, we now favor faculty members having their own portable laptop technology. While initial costs for faculty portable computing may look high, the cost reduction comes in eliminating duplicated equipment and software in classrooms, offices, homes, and libraries. Focusing on one good laptop for each faculty member can also provide a significant productivity boost, as the tools can be available anytime, anywhere.

Faculty need help and support in learning new technology skills and in rethinking the teaching and learning processes as they are used in the new online environment. Faculty programs that combine the learning of technology skills with the new and old research on teaching and learning are generally very well received. Faculty can learn these skills through a variety of training and support opportunities:

- One-day programs can be held as collegewide or small regional events.
- Hands-on, half- or one-day programs in the specific use of the various tools are a cost-effective and efficient way to learn. Hands-on activities can be very effective if people can be at the elbow of the faculty member, as needed.
- Brown-bag lunches are good for sharing stories. These lunch gatherings can also be used for learning a structured set of skills. One college

- scheduled a series of brown-bag events and invited trainers and speakers on various skills and topics for groups of 15 faculty members.

- Preconference sessions offer good opportunities for structured learning in technology issues and topics and for introductions to new technology tools

- Tutorials that accompany many software packages are remarkably effective, always available, and usually free.

- Online courses or workshops are offered by organizations such as the Learning Resources Network (LERN, www.lern.org), Capella University (www.capella.edu) and by system, campus, and college organizations. (See "Cyber Teachers' Institute," Chapter 8.)

- Other computer-based tutorials and synchronous and archived webcasts address many topics of interest to faculty and faculty support professionals.

Design and Development Time

Once the decision is made about the type of online course to be developed, the next question involves the amount of time a faculty member needs to redesign the course. Another question concerns other types of necessary resources and support. As might be expected, few hard and fast rules dictate the amount of time and resources necessary for preparing an online course.

Budgeting and planning for the redesign of courses is particularly difficult within the context of our current academic structures. When a faculty member is given the task of teaching a campus course, that faculty member is responsible for all phases: design, development, recruitment, and delivery. Often, these tasks are done within the time frame of one semester. This model is often referred to as the *bundling* of instruction design, development, and delivery.

With web course development it is generally recommended to unbundle the time and resources for each of the three major phases of instructional offerings. This means that the time for design and development is distinct from the delivery of the course. Design and development usually occurs prior to the semester in which the course is offered. This unbundling is particularly recommended if the course or series of courses will be marketed to a cohort of students and if the courses are delivered by a faculty member other than the designing faculty member or team. The only exception to this is the web-enhanced course. Because that course is an enhanced version of an existing course for campus students, many of the tasks of moving it online can continue to be bundled with the usual course responsibilities.

There is one big caveat, however: Time and resources are always needed to assist faculty in the first offering of a web-enhanced course.

To arrive at reasonable time and cost estimates, consider the distance learning program model of design and development. Many distance learning programs have been able to reduce costs by taking highly paid, highly expert research and development faculty out of the delivery phase of the program.

> we can say with some level of certainty that creating one hour of web instruction requires about 10 to 18 hours of faculty time.

Based on much anecdotal evidence from faculty plus experience of over 20 years of designing and developing content material for stand-alone computer tutorials and online teaching and learning, we can say with some level of certainty that creating one hour of web instruction requires about 10 to 18 hours of faculty time. This range is wide, as the time required depends greatly on the complexity and novelty of the technologies being used and how many new materials and new teaching strategies are being prepared. This time is needed to ensure that the instruction is structured and developed to be delivered independently of the designing faculty member, but the ratio quickly produces a negative reaction on the part of faculty, department chairs, and deans. Faculty who have done this kind of work either nod sagely, having known this all along, or nod vigorously as if to say, "That's about right."

These reactions should not be surprising, but the cost consequences are problematic. If we multiply 10 to 18 hours times the current 45 hours of classroom-based lecture and discussion time, we have an investment of 450 to 810 hours to design and develop an online course that can be delivered without the presence of the designing faculty member. And this only represents the time of the faculty member. If we assume some time for startup with learning technology and instruction in teaching and learning in this new environment, plus arranging for any copyright and other issues, we can rapidly approach the 1,000-hour mark for developing an online course.

Although release time for a course varies among institutions, the average amount of release time in a semester is about 198 hours. This figure assumes a 15-week teaching semester with a week before and two weeks after, for a total of 18 weeks, averaging about 11 hours per week working on the course. Using these figures, the resulting 198 hours of faculty time spent on developing a three-credit course represents less than half of the faculty time needed to create an online course.

The ratio of 10 to 18 hours of web development for every hour of instruction is supported by research on the design and development of distance learning programs and the development of computer-based programs. Using estimates from research done by J. J. Sparkes in 1984, Rumble (1997) shows estimates of the hours of academic effort required to produce one hour of student learning in different media forms (p. 79). See Table 4.1.

Table 4.1   Academic Work to Produce One Hour of Student Learning

Media	Hours of Academic Effort
Lecturing	2-10
Small group teaching	3-10
Teaching textbook	50-100*
Broadcast television	100*
Computer-aided learning	200*
Interactive video or CD	300*

*Requires support staff as well.

Note that the number of hours listed as the amount of academic work to produce materials for one hour of student learning refers to faculty time required. The amount of time for support staff to assist in the materials development is not included in these figures. Data suggest that if faculty are going to be successful in moving courses to the online environment, we need to look at how to support their effort.

The time requirements and the model for designing and developing a web-enhanced course are different from the traditional distance learning model. Faculty preparing web-enhanced courses have reported working 60 to 80 hours a week while moving a course from the classroom to the online environment. Some of these reports are from the days before the wide-spread availability of course management templates, before the ready availability of digital content resources and the improved technologies of the browsers and threaded discussion boards. Early innovative faculty members were usually motivated by interest, enthusiasm, and dedication. In addition, the materials they developed were generally not intended to be used by other faculty.

For web-enhanced courses, the number of hours required for designing and developing an hour of instruction for the online environment can range from 5 to 18 hours, again depending on how aggressive the faculty member is in making use of the new technologies and finding and developing content such as animations and simulations. Many faculty are using the bundled approach for designing web-enhanced courses, as it is much more affordable and both faculty and students develop new teaching and learning skills over time. However, the web-enhanced course in its current form results in little significant productivity gains for higher education, since very little is being changed.

Types of Faculty Support: Time, People, and Technology

The types of support faculty need for moving teaching and learning online fall into two broad categories: time and technical expertise.

The most critical success factor is time. If faculty members and department chairs expect faculty to move large blocks of teaching and learning to a new format, to a new environment, then faculty members need time to make this change. Part of this involves the time needed to learn new tools. Time is also required to review digital content resources. The internet is a rich source of content for almost every discipline, but just as a faculty member must review textbooks and journals for appropriate course content, they also need to review a portion of the available sources of digital content for a course.

Faculty members also need time to learn new web technology and to change their ways of conducting the academic work of teaching and learning. Incorporating and testing new teaching strategies and tools requires time to learn the tools, apply them, and implement them. Faculty must develop new habits of teaching and interacting with students.

Online learning is also new to students, and their questions, problems, and habits may require more time from faculty members and support staff. Obviously, as both faculty and students develop experience with new tools, some of these support requirements will go away. However, we can expect more and better tools to become available in the future.

A faculty member's gradual adoption of tools to support a web-enhanced course can be supported in several ways. Time and resources for the webcentric and the full online course will be proportionally greater, but the following suggestions are useful for all course design and development projects:

- Provide a semester of release time as a minimum. Two semesters of release time over the course of a year are recommended for a webcentric or fully online course. Or, consider dedicating a full summer plus a semester of release time.

- Provide time for training and learning. This can be one to two weeks of concentrated time in the summer or a semester of release time solely for the purpose of learning a subset of skills, such as basic productivity tools. Work to achieve a long-term goal of providing time for training into all faculty programs.

- Provide support for revising and updating course curricula to include new digital content resources. Look into the digital content, resources, and events now offered by many textbook publishers.

- Provide funds for hiring content researchers who work with faculty members to identify and review quality learning materials available on the internet. Students who have taken the course or are majoring in the discipline can be excellent content researchers.

- Provide training in course management tools that can smooth the process of the first online course experience.

  Assign support personnel to help faculty and students.

Infrastructure Support

Before beginning an online learning project, the faculty member should get support from the department or college administration. The online environment is a real physical space, even though a digital one. Common support structures for web-enhanced courses and programs include course management templates and systems, course management system support personnel, servers that are reliable and always backed up, student support help desks, and training. In addition to these support structures for web-enhanced courses, webcentric courses need support for flexible meeting arrangements and facilities and for learning-resources media access such as library materials. Support structures for the fully online courses and programs include those for marketing, recruiting, counseling, student advising, and library and media.

Faculty may decide to offer an online course without significant infrastructure or administrative support, but doing so takes time and arrangements for technology support and tools. Some faculty can do this by collaborating with other faculty on campuses in establishing infrastructure support.

Mission and Policy Readiness

Since moving teaching and learning to a new environment consumes time, talent, and resources, the full support of the institution is helpful. Faculty willing to experiment and work in these new environments and interested in helping to define and develop these new environments should have the explicit support of colleagues, chairs, and deans.

Worksheet for the Resources for an Online, Webcentric, or Web-enhanced Course: Decision Layer Two

Scenario: *You are a faculty member preparing a project plan for putting one or more of your courses online, either in a fully online, webcentric or hybrid, or web-enhanced mode. You are planning to do this more or less on your own, on a shoestring, and you want to be sure you are thinking ahead about the resources that may be essential for success. These questions can help identify potential software, hardware, or people support. If you are part of a team for designing and developing a series of courses, they can help in the building of a project plan.*

Tools and Support during the Design and Development of a Course – Phase 1

1. What is the state of your personal work technology?

❑ Do you need a new computer or any upgrades?

❑ Are your storage solutions appropriate?

❑ Do you need to update your major software applications?

❑ Do you need specialized discipline software

❑ Do you have access to printers, scanners, and digital cameras?

❑ Do you have access to email away from campus and at home?

List below the items and the cost of resources you need during the design and development process. It is always good to have a wish list ready if money becomes available.

Design-development resources and estimated costs:

_____

_____

_____

_____

_____

_____

_____

_____

_____

Tools and Support during the Design and Development of a Course – Phase 2

2. List infrastructure items you think you will need during the delivery stage of your course, including a stable, reliable server and support in case of difficulties. Also specify student and staff support needed during delivery and, if needed, campus meeting spaces and facilities.

Delivery infrastructure and support items:

_____

_____

_____

_____

_____

_____

3. List the training resources and time you will need to become technologically knowledgeable.

_____

_____

_____

_____

_____

_____

4. What other types of support are important to you? Prioritize and quantify the following items. Note that this support is highly variable and depends on the type of online course you are planning.

———————— Faculty   _____   Amount of time

———————— Content researcher   _____   Amount of time

———————— Technical support   _____   Amount of time

———————— Instructional designer   _____   Amount of time

———————— Graphic support   _____   Amount of time

———————— Editor, writer   _____   Amount of time

5. It is important to develop a plan for what you will do and when you will do it.

——————— Start of planning   ——————— Date

——————— Plan complete   ——————— Date

——————— Start of design   ——————— Date

——————— Design complete   ——————— Date

——————— Start of development   ——————— Date

——————— Development complete   ——————— Date

——————— Semester of first delivery   ——————— Date

6. When you are finished, what will the result look like? Be specific here about content of the course website and the general overall resources used by the student. Would another faculty member be able to deliver this course?
Deliverables: what type of course, how many modules, types of resources, goals, objectives, and syllabus.

_____

_____

_____

_____

_____

_____

_____

_____

_____

_____

_____

_____

_____

_____

_____

_____

_____

Major Constraining Factors and the Future

The major constraining factors for most faculty interested in moving teaching and learning to the web are a lack of time, technical assistance, and moral support, as well as the student factors of student readiness and access to technology. Academic administrators are constrained by the need for planning, vision, and faculty expertise and time. Teaching and learning take time, and the current faculty workload supporting the traditional paradigm is usually fully booked. We will continue to see many variants of the basic models of teaching and learning emerge to meet learners' needs and opportunities. This process means reconfiguring strategies to take advantage of the new paradigm and support efficient faculty teaching and student learning.

Chapter 5

Instructional Design Guidelines for Moving Teaching and Learning Online

This is the instructional design chapter. If a faculty member is going to design teaching and learning for the online environment, what will the course look like? How will it be similar to a traditional campus course? How will it be different? What will it have in common with and how will it differ from a traditional distance learning course?

Guidelines for designing courses for the online environment help to ensure that as we change the context for teaching and learning, we take care to design quality into the new environment. We want to make certain that the online environment is designed with sound instructional methodology and strategies.

This chapter begins by analyzing the structure of traditional courses. We describe the expectations for time and workload on the part of faculty and students and, given these expectations, what the learning outcomes will be.

One important design element for any course is the amount of face-to-face or seat time expected of students. Online courses that rely less on classroom meetings may run counter to state requirements and curriculum policies. Strategies for interpreting and changing these requirements are suggested.

What Is an On-Campus Course?

The core unit of academic planning for administrators, faculty, and students is the three-credit course. The three-credit course can be looked at in a number of ways. For design purposes, we examine the course from the perspective of student time or student competency. Another way of looking at the three-credit course is from the faculty viewpoint. How much time does it take to design, develop, and deliver a three-credit course?

From the administrative perspective, the question is one of managing space and resources for a three-credit course in return for the amount of tuition generated. On an institutional level, the question might be how any single three-credit course contributes to the development and maintenance of a quality institutional image.

A three-credit course typically requires 135 hours of student time. On-campus courses generally meet three hours a week for 15 weeks, for a total of 45 hours of contact time. In addition, students are expected to spend a certain amount of time working on the course outside of class. We have been asking faculty and higher education administrators about this practice for the last 15 years or so, and the most common belief is that students devote two hours outside of class for every hour in class. This 90 hours of study time can be accomplished in either individual or group study and using a variety of content resources.

As we design courses for more flexible environments, designing from a time perspective can provide a point of constancy and assurance that we are not changing things too dramatically.

In traditional distance learning course models, the decreased focus on time expectations is countered by a greater focus on competency, or whether or not students achieve a stated set of goals and objectives. Many faculty in traditional on-campus courses protest that their courses are not based solely on time expectations, but also require competency as demonstrated through assessment and observations.

Two perspectives for course design are worth examining in more depth. Given the difficulty of providing objective measures of achievement for all courses, many state regulations and accreditation models specify a certain number of required "contact hours" for a three-credit undergraduate course. The time-based model does have a certain amount of validity, because we know that learning requires time, but regulations based on time rather than student competency contribute to outcomes only indirectly and superficially.

When we know the desired outcomes of education, and when we can measure those outcomes, we are better prepared to require that individuals pass competency tests. However, when the desired learning outcomes are a set of complex cognitive, behavioral, and attitudinal learning, we have traditionally relied on a time-based model of education with competency exams at regular intervals.

Given the difficulties of assessment and accountability in higher education and professional arenas, we often rely on a time-based experience coupled with a competency-based demonstration such as a licensing exam. In other fields, we combine a time-based experience with a set of products, such as a series of innovative research projects or a portfolio of art or writings.

This analysis points to a recommendation for the redesign of on-campus and online courses. We should design instruction with the knowledge that while time for learning is necessary, time alone is not sufficient to ensure success. We also need to design instruction in such a way that we ensure a focus on the more important goals of learning. We need to design instruction by specifying a body of knowledge, skills, and beliefs that students are to learn in the specified period of time.

> **We should design instruction with the knowledge that while time for learning is necessary, time alone is not sufficient to ensure success.**

As we move to designing online courses, a viable approach is to combine a time-based model with a competency-based model. Future degrees, however, may be based on competency only, so it is probably wise to be thinking about approaches and methods emphasizing these.

Designing a Course from the Student Time Perspective

If we apply this analysis to a practical situation, we can imagine how an online course might look segmented into the expected course components of a traditional on-campus course (see Table 5.1).

Table 5.1   Example of Campus Course Components: Student Time-Based View

Hours	Student Activity
30 Hours Face-to-face time in classroom	Primarily time for faculty-to-student dialogue, often described as lecturing or faculty-led monitored dialogue
30 Hours Face-to-face time in classroom	Time required for general administrative and management tasks
30	Time for reading, study, project assignments using learning resources of all media types, including books, journals, papers, webcasts
30	Primarily individual and group project activities, study, and collaboration
30	Time devoted to testing and assessment and studying for testing
15	Time required for general administrative and management tasks
165	Total number of hours for a three-credit course

As we review the types of dialogue and activity that make up a course, we see that most hours in an on-campus course are outside the classroom. In fact, in the preceding analysis, 45 of 135 hours are contact time, leaving 90 hours, or two-thirds of traditional campus courses, as distance learning, if we define distance learning as time a student is learning outside the presence of the faculty member. Viewed this way, distance learning only becomes a matter of varying percentages and is not so different from what we do now.

The one traditional activity that may be difficult to envision immediately in the online environment is the faculty-to-student dialogue known as the faculty lecture. The lecture has been under review in the recent past as we search for data that support and validate lecturing as an effective learning strategy for students. The pedagogical research that encourages active rather than passive learning indicates that we may need to find ways to increase student mental activity during the lecture time. The active-learning movement suggests that lecturing may be effective part of the time, but that we need to link faculty talking to student learning more consistently.

> **As the web develops, a myriad of applications supporting different types of dialogue and communication are emerging.**

As the web develops, a myriad of applications supporting different types of dialogue and communication are emerging. One category of tool is presentation software, the tool closest to the lecture teaching strategy. The most recent releases of presentation software packages have made putting presentation slides online a fairly straightforward process. Other tools to support faculty-to-student dialogue include tools for review and response to students. New improvements allow audio of the faculty member in the form of a voice-over; new email packages have voice applications that allow users to send audio email messages, either as stand-alone messages or as complements to written messages.

The view of the online course from the perspective of student changes primarily in the amount of time devoted to independent inquiry, group study and inquiry, the types of assessment used, and the amount of time spent interacting with other students and faculty. Table 5.2 outlines student time use in an online course.

As described earlier, the core processes of teaching and learning are the communications between faculty and students, among students, and between the students and assorted content resources. Table 5.3 illustrates how an online course might be analyzed from the perspective of the amount and type of dialogue. From a design view, all three dialogues are important, and a balance of these types of dialogues can contribute to effective and delightful learning experiences.

Table 5.2 Example of Online Course Components: Student Time-Based View

Hours	Student Activity
40	Reading, study, and project assignments using books, journals, papers, webcasts, and other digital resources online.
20	Primary faculty-to-student dialogue, often described as lecturing or faculty-led dialogue. The tools that can be used are a mix of asynchronous online seminars with faculty, guided problem solving, faculty interaction with small groups of students, and group activities guided by faculty.
30	Primarily individual and group project activities, study, and collaborations.
30	Time devoted to testing, assessment, and studying for testing. This is done via self-check tests and participation in online seminars and conferences. Final evaluation can be via projects or proctored testing.
30	Time required for general administrative and management tasks
135	Total number of hours for a three-credit course

The very nature of an online course will shift the balance toward student-to-student dialogue and to asynchronous dialogue. Tools for asynchronous dialogue are much more advanced and readily available than the tools for synchronous dialogue, although we shouldn't forget about the effectiveness of older technologies, such as the telephone, and physical meetings for campus-based courses.

Designing a Course from the Content Perspective

Consider the types of content goals and objectives that make up the 135 hours of study. For every body of defined knowledge, a set of core concepts and principles needs to be learned. These core concepts are the building blocks of knowledge. This view of knowledge structure is very consistent with the constructivist theory of learning. The foundation of knowledge has to be built in an area, since some concepts are essential to understanding a multitude of

Table 5.3 Example of Online Course Components: Dialogue Focus

Type of Dialogue	Faculty to Student Hours	Student to Student Hours	Student to Resources Hours	Total Hours
Synchronous dialogue in various size groups. The tools used can be chat rooms, telephone conversations, small group meetings online or in physical places, study groups.	20	20	NA	40
Asynchronous dialogue in various size groups. This includes email, online groups, threaded discussions.	25	35	NA	60
Individual dialogue, study, analysis, practice with content resources	NA	NA	35	35
Total hours	**45**	**55**	**35**	**135**

other related concepts. One way to think about the course content from this building-block perspective is to think of the content as residing in three concentric circles (see Figure 5.1).

The innermost circle holds the essential concepts that form the stable core of a field of knowledge. For students to learn these core concepts and related principles, they need to think actively about, manipulate, and use these concepts in some meaningful way. This is also the layer in which students must memorize, repeat, rehearse, and process deeply.

The next circle of knowledge is the first application layer of the discipline. At this level of knowledge, learning begins to be applied in simulated scenarios. To integrate this layer of knowledge, students actively build and create their own networks of knowledge, linking concepts and principles to existing knowledge. This application level, for example, might be the first math

Figure 5.1   Content Design Model

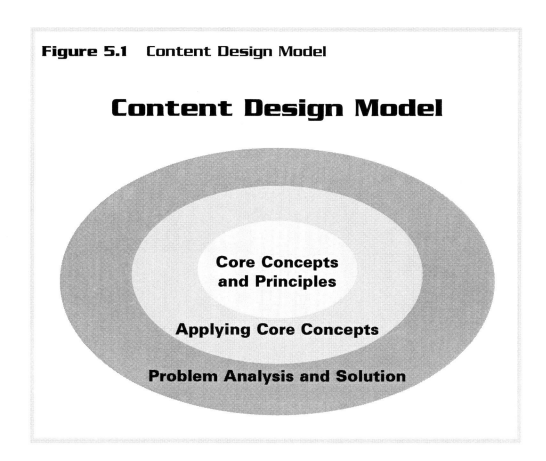

problems that a child solves: simple, straightforward, and easily solved by application of a basic rule or theorem. At this level, students can solve problems by following procedures and known formulae. This stage of knowledge can also be compared to the skills developed by following directions in a strange city. A stranger accomplishes the goal of getting from point A to point B, but can't necessarily retrace his or her steps, serve as a guide for someone else, or go from point B to any other point. This is also referred to as a novice stage of knowing.

The third circle represents a student's active use of core concepts and principles to solve problems of increasing depth and complexity in a selected area. At this level of knowledge, students often can and should customize their own learning and pursue their own paths of inquiry, often using materials of their own choosing.

The core concepts and principles of even a stable field of knowledge can change rapidly in our information age. Remember the rapid appearance of cloning, for example. We need to plan the content of our courses to allow for dynamic content changes. This is an area where the dynamic nature of the internet and globally accessible resources can be invaluable.

Thinking Outside the Three-Credit Course Boundary

The need has arrived to think outside the boundaries of a three-credit course when we are preparing and identifying content resources to support online learning. Rather than thinking only of building a rich environment to support one course, we might do well to pursue developing comprehensive databases of resources that can support a set of related three-credit courses. Well-structured linked databases might support introductory, intermediate, and graduate courses in disciplines such as online biology, chemistry, and math. A comprehensive geography project might support general education students and majors, all with many of the same overlapping materials. Online reference materials, CDs, and databases, in addition to books, are needed for learning the basic concepts in all disciplines. Comprehensive, multilayered disciplinary and interdisciplinary databases could support many levels of content interaction and application.

Students often need realistic scenarios and situations to develop complex problem-solving skills. In many areas, this means costly simulations; in other cases, we need learning that will include internships addressing complex problems and building professional networks. These educational needs may coincide with societal needs for additional skilled resources to solve real problems. The conservatory approach to learning has been a grand tradition in the arts; we now are at a point where we may want to incorporate regular internships and conservatories in other fields as well.

Course Hours: The Content Perspective

Table 5.4 illustrates the approximate number of hours in a course that might be devoted to the three levels of knowledge in a field: core concepts, structured predictable applications, and unstructured complex applications.

Table 5.5 provides a look at the number of hours that might be needed to develop learning materials for an online course. This table shows two types of online courses and can help provide a basis for planning the amount of resources, time, and support needed for moving a course online. One type is a web course that redistributes the 45 hours usually spent in class meetings into 15 hours dedicated to general administrating and testing and 30 hours of planned interaction in the online environment. The 30 hours of online interaction and instruction need to be planned and developed carefully to promote the interaction that will build and nurture a community of learners.

The webcentric or hybrid course model redistributes only 30 of the 45 hours usually spent in class meetings: 15 hours to general administration and testing and 15 hours to planned interaction in the online environment. This reduces the

Table 5.4 Example of Online Course: Content View

Hours	Type of Content
45	Core concepts and principles; stable, predictable content focus; enhanced with links to current events
45	Structured practice and manipulation of core concepts and principles in discussions, exercises; predictable problem solving, check tests, weekly summaries. Content in this area can be dynamic and unpredictable as students attempt to integrate it into existing knowledge base.
30	High-level problem solving or projects; content can be even more customized to student interest
15	General administration
135	**Total number of hours for a three-credit course.**

challenge, as many of the course management systems support moving the general administrative tasks online quite efficiently. It means faculty can focus the redesign of the equivalent of 15 hours of teaching and learning.

These instructional hours online can take advantage of the interaction tools and resources now available online. Students can be more active, and the faculty member can recede further into the background, monitoring and supporting students doing more of the real work of learning. These hours can be allocated to the desired objectives of a given course in a great variety of ways.

In planning, consider that the real number of hours that need to be shifted or redesigned for a traditional campus-based course refers to the 45 contact hours. The other 90 hours are usually already in place, another good reason to focus on taking existing instruction online before designing totally new courses for the online environment.

Building an online course also means making build-or-buy decisions for the three levels of content resources. The majority of faculty have usually chosen to buy a textbook as an efficient way of providing core content resources. When going online, decisions need to be made about how much and how many of the resources are digitally available and how many of the new interactive and collaborative activities will need to be designed.

Table 5.5 Example of a Web Course and a Webcentric Course: Materials Design and Development View

Online Course Student Hours	Webcentric-Hybrid Student Hours	Faculty Work	Type of Content
60 Hours	60 Hours	Review and identify primary and secondary learning resources; prepare assignments, projects, and rubrics for assessment.	Course materials that a student is to purchase or access through a license or subscription
30 Hours	30 Hours	Prepare directed activities for students.	Course materials that a student is to search, depending on personal choices

Note: The sections above are for the 90 hours generally dedicated to "study time outside of class time." The type and amount of work can be almost equivalent for campus courses and all types of online courses. However, instructions must be very clear and feedback processes and tools in place, as students can't rely on asking the faculty in class.

Online Course Student Hours	Webcentric-Hybrid Student Hours	Faculty Work	Type of Content
30 Hours	15 Hours	Prepare materials for the web that direct students' experience and content learning.	Course materials to support the learning experiences that a faculty member will teach, guide, and direct
0 Hours	15 Hours	Prepare materials for synchronous meeting times and activities.	Course materials that a faculty member will use to support synchronous interactions, generally specific to course requirements and students
0 Hours	0 Hours	Develop advanced designs for the communication tools and systems to be used.	Dynamic response to students' needs and interests during course delivery
15 Hours	15 Hours	Prepare testing and grading and general course assessment plan.	General administration and testing

Note: The preparation time for these online or a webcentric courses needs to be multiplied by the standard planning and preparation factor of 10-18 used in Chapter 4. Using the high range of the factor (18) to be conservative, the planning time for a fully online course is 30 times 18, or 540 hours; for a webcentric course, it is 15 times 18, or 270 hours. In delivery mode, more students equals more faculty time.

| 135 Hours | 135 Hours | Total Hours for a three-credit course | |

Developing Content for the Three Web Course Types

Developing content that is essential for good teaching and learning has always been costly. In the 1980s, when full sequences of computer-based education (CBE) courses were being developed for a lower-division science and engineering curriculum, the cost of a three-credit course averaged about $1 million. This covered all aspects of the development process, including an advisory board, content selection, course design, development, and testing. These costs have been gradually dropping, although providing excellent content is still quite expensive. We have been seeing content costs decline in direct correlation to the availability of improved and easy-to-use design and development tools and environments. Course management systems put much of the control back in the hands of faculty; however, designing high-end simulations, interactive environments, and sophisticated high-quality content learning objects will no doubt continue to be expensive. It helps to analyze just what percentage of a course depends on existing packaged content and how much of the course depends on dynamic spontaneous interaction and transactions.

Table 5.6 estimates the amount of packaged content and the amount of dynamic course material in traditional and online courses. Estimates of the amount of customized content plus amounts of planned dialogue and transactions are also provided. One way of describing the difference between a traditional distance learning course and a traditional campus course is in the varying amounts of a course that are prepackaged. In the case of distance learning courses, almost 100 percent of the course is preplanned and prepackaged. A traditional distance learning program plans and packages the course materials in advance of the course delivery time. A traditional campus course, on the other hand, is generally less than 50 percent prepackaged. So to move a course from the traditional campus mode to a totally online course can be daunting in terms of time, skill, and resources. As distance learning courses and campus courses each begin to incorporate online communication transactions into their courses, these differences start to diminish. Both types of courses are shifting to be closer to a webcentric model. As these versions evolve, we need to move forward wisely so we retain the benefits of various learning models.

A look at these types of courses from the point of view of what can be available to students in the anywhere, anytime mode may be helpful. Table 5.7 shows the distance learning model at the top and the campus course at the bottom, with the three types of online courses in between. The two columns show the relative percentage of teaching and learning that requires synchronous meetings in physical space and learning that requires synchronous meetings in physical space.

Looking at courses from this perspective, we may be surprised to see the small difference between a traditional campus course and a web-enhanced campus

Table 5.6 Relative Percentage of Developed and Dynamic Course Content Elements

Type of course	Percent (%) Predeveloped Materials	Percent (%) Dynamically Generated Materials	Percent (%) Student Choice	Percent (%) Dialogue and Interaction
Traditional distance learning course	92% to 100% Often delivered in a fully developed course package	0% to About 5%	About 5%	About 3%
Online course	70% to 80% Prepackaged content such as textbook, plus online communications	5% to 10%	10% to 15%	10% to 15%
Webcentric course (also called hybrid, blended)	50% to 75% Use of textbook plus additional online communications, resources, and events	5% to 10%	20%	15% to 20%
Web-enhanced course (also called web-supplemented)	About 50% Use of textbook plus additional online communications, resources, and events	15%	20%	20% Dialogue often can increase beyond 100%
Traditional campus course	35% predeveloped, using a textbook	20%	20%	25%

course. A faculty member teaching a traditional campus course can change it to a web-enhanced course by altering only 10 percent of the content and interaction. The easiest way to do this is by making three major changes:

- Use an online tool, such as a CMS, for distributing all the documents for a course.
- Use the online tools for email communications, discussion boards, and online seminars.
- Use online resources for providing content and events.

Table 5.7 Relative Percentage of Course Content Elements Online

Type of course	Online content and interactions plus other asynchronous resources, such as books, webcasts, and tutorials	Synchronous requirements in same physical place or other gathering requirements
Traditional distance learning course	90% to 100%	0% to 10%
Online course	90% to 100%	0% to 10%
Webcentric course (also called hybrid, blended)	75% to 90%	10% to 25%
Web-enhanced course (also called web-supplemented)	65% to 75%	25% to 35%
Traditional campus course	50% to 65%	35% to 50%

Given this simplicity, it would seem more colleges might require all faculty to use course sites. Institutions that require all students to have 24-hour access to computing resources are close to this requirement. However, this type of change often produces unexpected or unforeseen consequences. Moving toward online learning at any level means a great deal in terms of faculty skill and knowledge and accessible, portable tools. Such changes also have ripple effects in increasing the requirements for an effective teaching and learning infrastructure. Moving teaching and learning online is not an isolated activity; it has impact throughout campus structure and campus practices.

Instructional Design: What Is It?

With a move toward wide-scale use of interactive strategies and materials in higher education, and the offering of courses online, instructional design becomes more critical to ensure quality of outcomes. However, the meaning of instructional design may not be well known. Simply, instructional design is the process of designing the environment, methods, and resources for effective learning of specified goals and objectives by students.

As we move teaching and learning experiences to the online environment, instructional design is critical. We have literally hundreds of years of tradition to support much of what we do in our campus-based courses. As we move online, we should refresh ourselves on the principles of learning, teaching, and instructional design. We know more about how students learn now than we did hundreds of years ago, and the new environments give us an opportunity to design anew, using this knowledge. This can be a very exciting time.

Fortunately, most faculty who enjoy seeing their students succeed readily embrace instructional design principles. In instructional design, the answers to the four core questions (See Fig. 5.2) guide the design of the instructional experience:

- Who are my students?
- What do my students need to know, to feel, or to be able to do as a result of this course or experience?
- Where, when, and with what resources will my students be learning?
- How will I direct and manage the context of the learning experience and how will I mentor my students?

After these questions are answered, an instructional designer or faculty member considers additional questions:

- What types of experiences and interactions will facilitate the students achieving the stated goals and objectives?
- What types of assessment tools will help to determine whether the students have achieved the goals and objectives?
- When and how should these assessment tools be used?

Another way of helping to remember these four key questions is to link back to Vygotsky's four-element model and think about the learning experience as theater. In this view, each instructional experience is designed around a Learner (Le); a faculty member doing the managing and mentoring (M); the problem to be solved or Knowledge to be learned (K); and the context for the Experience (E). This view can be remembered as the LeMKE structure. In designing courses, it can be useful to envision these four variables as actors on a stage, with the faculty member either onstage or offstage directing, planning, coaching, and assessing the learners. Thinking about a course in terms of a series of instructional events, with each of these variables needing to be planned for, helps to envision and support desired learning. This view of learning events can also be used to evaluate tools and consider if these systems address the actions and responsibilities associated with each of the roles played by these four variables or actors (Boettcher, 2003).

Instructional Design Checklist

Following is a checklist of instructional design guidelines intended for use by faculty designing a specific course. They include consideration of the importance of design, the environment, and the support infrastructure in teaching and learning.

1. Know your students. Who are your students? What do your students already know? As constructive learners, we can only build knowledge on what we already know. Students who have an established foundation in a field can learn more, and learn more quickly. Remember: The more you know, the more you can know.

2. Determine the goals and objectives of the course. What will students know that they do not already know? What are the core concepts they must learn? What are the students' zones of proximal development? What will students be able to do that they do not already know how to do? What will students think about the content and the possibilities of the content?

3. Visualize the environments in which students will be learning. Will students have their own tools to customize and store content and interactions? Will students have 24-hour access to computers? Will students' computing resources support a standard set of productivity software, *e.g.*, word processing, browsers, pdf formats? Do students study most often surrounded by children, in a car, or during late-night or early morning hours? Will students be doing joint projects with other students in the library, over the phone, or online? Will they have their own learning resources, books, CDs, and subscriptions to online services? How, when, where, and with whom will students be learning?

4. Plan the learning assessment and visualize the environments for assessment. How will students know what they are learning? Will there be regular, short self-checks, reports, and postings? Will there be practice activities? Will students be evaluated weekly? In what ways will students be graded?

5. Plan for the types of learning activities that will take place. Design activities with a balance of dialogue of faculty to student, student to student, and student to resources. Design with a balance of types of resources available in print, audio, and web format, if possible. Plan for activities that introduce, apply, reinforce, and extend concepts. Plan for activities that are controlled and led by learners.

6. Effective communication and interaction requires planning; it doesn't just happen. This statement is particularly true in the online environment. All course-management systems and many internet applications are designed for specific types of communication and interaction. A discussion of some examples follows.

- **Mail and discussion list tools.** These tools are effective for general communications to one or more people, and particularly good for faculty-to-student communication, such as announcements, reminders of upcoming events and deadlines, and answers to general questions. This application is also good for students to communicate with each other. The faculty member does not need to answer all the questions. In fact, students can be assigned to moderate and answer questions on a weekly basis and to direct questions to a faculty member only as needed. Some type of mail or discussion list tool is essential in an online course. Fortunately, all course management systems have such tools. An important timesaving and increased-learning strategy is for the faculty member to step aside in many communications.
- **Online seminar and conference tools.** Online seminar tools are designed for extended discussions of a focused topic. For example, in an American history course, a student might convene a seminar or conference on the beginning of the Vietnam War. In a computer science course, a conference might be held on breakthroughs in chip technology. With these tools, faculty can assume or delegate a variety of roles, and then monitor the discussion and solicit summary statements.
- **Team projects.** Simple tools, such as chat rooms, telephone meetings, and physical meetings, can support group work.

7. All media require infrastructure. In the instructional design process, effective decisions on the use of media are among the most important. When selecting media for a course, we need to address two major questions:

- What is the minimum set of media needed for an effective teaching and learning environment for this course?
- What are the distinct educational characteristics of a medium that can best support the teaching and learning experiences in this particular course?

In planning online courses, we may be tempted to use many new media tools and applications. But because every type and choice of media requires access and familiarity with the media and support, the best rule is to keep it simple.

- **Textbooks are media, too.** Assigning a textbook to students can cause numerous difficulties if your institution doesn't have a process whereby students can easily purchase books and other resources without coming to campus. Over the last few years, the challenge of providing textbooks for online students has been eased significantly with online bookstores, both campus-owned and commercial vendors, such as Amazon, Borders, and Barnes & Noble.

- **Course management system and course website.** Use of a course management system or course website requires technical support to ensure stability and reliability of the site. Use of a course website also requires that students and faculty develop habits for using the various media. A course site also needs to be maintained over the life of a course and possibly beyond, depending on the role of the course in the department or program. A course site is not a book, and a web page is not a printed page. A course website is a resource that is best when it is nurtured and updated.
- **Classroom or teleconferencing room.** Any place that a class meets is part of an infrastructure somewhere. It needs to be designed, scheduled, maintained, and easily accessed.
- **Online resources and databases.** Faculty and students need to have access to required and recommended materials that are online. They also need to know how to use the resources and develop effective skills.

8. The more hours of teaching and learning to be designed and developed, the more time and resources will be needed. The preceding statement is the basic principle of instructional design. The instructional design of a program impacts the budget of a project, and the budget of a project impacts the instructional design.

In corporate training courses, one goal of instructional design is effective analysis of the goals and objectives of learning so that the program can be condensed into the shortest possible time. When instructional designers are trying to maximize learning while trying to reduce the number of hours devoted to learning, the cost per hour can increase. Well-designed materials can take more time and resources to design and develop. For companies paying their employees' training time, however, the higher cost per hour of development can quickly be offset by fewer hours of employee training.

Reducing the amount of time for learning is not generally one of the goals of higher education learning. For campus courses, planning should include a certain amount of time required for every hour of teaching and learning that is shifted from the classroom environment to the online environment. A good estimate for planning is that for every hour of teaching and learning to be moved online, a faculty member should plan to spend between 5 and 18 hours, with a standard of 18, in design and development. Building a webcentric or hybrid course and moving 30 hours of instruction to the web takes at least 150 hours. This assumes familiarity with the tools and applications for online teaching and learning.

9. Course delivery requirements affect design and budget. Many of us are familiar with the cartoon showing a person rolling on the floor, laughing out loud, and saying, "You want it when?" This cartoon is great at conveying the fact that delivery time can be a critical piece of design. If a program needs to be launched quickly, it will cost more than it will if availability is less important.

Another common saying in the instructional design and training field is, "Good, fast, and cheap. Pick two!" Quality instructional programs generally cannot be built quickly with limited budgets.

In translating these guidelines to higher education campus courses, this means that if a provost, dean, or department chair wants a degree or certificate program to be launched within 18 months, a serious commitment of resources will be needed. If there is time to move the program gradually to the online environment, fewer resources will be needed. So, important questions need to be asked:

- When is the program needed?
- What human and infrastructure resources can be allocated to this project?
- What financial resources can be allocated to this project?

10. Instructional goals and objectives affect design, media, and budget. This principle of instructional design has two main corollaries. First, complex hands-on skills programs are generally more time consuming and expensive to design, develop, and deliver than are traditional seminars or lecture courses. It is more expensive, for example, to run a lab course than to run a traditional seminar or lecture course. Second, if the skills and knowledge to be acquired can only be taught by highly trained and compensated individuals, the cost of resources will be higher. This is easily seen, for example, if the skills to be taught are those necessary for success in piloting, surgery, executive business management, or scientific research. In some cases, learning environments need to be sophisticated simulations, also requiring expensive equipment and highly skilled mentors and teachers.

Additional questions need to be asked for designing instruction:

- What kinds of learning need to be developed?
- What instructional strategies will be used in the learning experience?
- What are the specific educational characteristics of the technology?

Summary Instructional Design Principle: Match the instructional goals and objectives to the students and to the best media and processes that can be used within time, budget, and infrastructure constraints.

This summary principle combines the instructional design standards of goals and objectives, media, budget, time, and infrastructure capabilities. Instructional design is not simple or straightforward. This principle reinforces the importance of up-front planning and course design using a variety of media and infrastructure support structures. When a teacher is not easily accessible, the infrastructure and the media must have backups. These basic guidelines for designing instruction have been developed from the training field and from the field of higher education. They contain a wealth of wisdom. These instructional design guidelines should be applied as part of any project planning process before submitting proposals for materials or course development.

Models for Learning Design

Two models for designing learning help encapsulate these ideas. The first is a model of program planning from Tony Bates, author of many books in the field of distance learning and one of the founding members of the Open University in the United Kingdom. This framework for making decisions about learning programs is from his 2000 book, *Managing Technological Change*. The items and questions in the Actions Model are from Bates; the annotations and descriptions have been expanded and updated.

ACTIONS Model

The ACTIONS model provides a practical decision-making framework for designing a new program on campus or online.

Access. **How accessible is the technology for the students?** This question of access is particularly important in designing learning experiences for the web. If all students and faculty have their own computers and easy, fast, reliable access to the internet, faculty members can assume easy, convenient, and usually unlimited access. This can greatly affect the design of requirements, communication activities, and research recommendations. On the other hand, if students must go to an on-campus lab to share in the email, discussions, and learning experiences, the number of hours and the type of access requirements will need to reflect this condition.

Costs. **What is the cost structure of the technology?** Any technology needs to be affordable for the three partners in a teaching and learning experience: the faculty, the students, and the institution. Questions of support and infrastructure need to be considered unflinchingly.

Teaching and learning. **What kinds of teaching and learning are required for the program goals?** The types of goals and objectives and the types of learning activities need to be considered.

Interaction and user friendliness. **What kind of interaction is enabled? How easy is it to use?** The quality of interaction, as we have discussed, is fundamental to the dialogues that make up an effective learning community. Different types of dialogue and interaction need to be enabled and supported.

Organizational issues. **What are the organizational requirements and barriers to success?** Delivering courses and learning experiences to students online requires a supplemental infrastructure to that existing on campus. Systems and processes need to be in place to recruit, admit, support, evaluate, and counsel students. These support structures are critical to students' success. Similar support structures are also needed to support the faculty and the teaching and learning environment. Campuses today have a strong physical infrastructure; we now need campuses with fast, reliable data networks and internet infrastructures.

Novelty. **How new is this technology?** New technology is often difficult to deploy and support effectively. Some designers of distance and online learning programs tend to be too conservative in their use of media by staying two or three media generations behind. Decisions regarding media selection have been greatly oversimplified by the widespread availability of the internet. Still, design decisions need to weigh assumptions about network speed and the ability to use asynchronous and synchronous tools, including video and audio technologies. By the time a course is deployed, assumptions may change. The question is not what the level of knowledge and access is today, but what the level of knowledge and access is likely to be when the course is delivered to student populations.

Speed. **How quickly can the courses be developed and delivered?** Quality courses can take a significant amount of time to design and develop. The design and development of a complete online course can easily take 18 months, even with the sophisticated tools now available. However, a web-enhanced course can be designed and developed fairly quickly. Distance learning courses that used to arrive in students' mailboxes in a course-in-a-box form have taken three years for a team of faculty to develop. How quickly can a course be developed and delivered? It depends.

This ACTIONS model can be used effectively at the beginning of the design of a program and as a checkpoint during the design process. It is a good guide for making practical decisions about an instructional program.

ACCEL Model (Characteristics of Interactive Web Learning)

We propose another model, ACCEL, for designing teaching and learning experiences in the online environment. The characteristics of the online paradigm have been evolving for over 10 years now and will continue to evolve as improved tools and applications become widely available.

We already know that one of the fundamental characteristics of online teaching and learning experiences includes the role of the learner as active, involved, and collaborative, and a role for faculty as guide, mentor, facilitator, and framer of knowledge. ACCEL provides a summary of how these characteristics of the new paradigm may interact in the new environments and in the design of new educational experiences.

Active. Learners participate in a variety of learning experiences that require thoughtful, engaged activity and guided discoveries.

Collaborative. Interactive online course environments support and facilitate discussion and exchange between and among students, with the faculty member monitoring, directing, and planning.

Customized and accessible. Interactive online learning fits the needs and requirements of many students in terms of time, access, career goals, levels of preparation, and learning styles.

Excellent quality. Courses are designed with a learner focus, enabling learners to achieve desired goals and objectives. This type of learning generally includes communication with faculty members and other students and quick, easy access to high-quality instructional resources.

Lifestyle-fitted. Interactive online learning accommodates the lives of students, affording cost-effective educational opportunities at a reasonable speed anywhere, anytime. ACCEL learning experiences are nurtured within the context of a mentoring relationship among faculty and students. The model also assumes access to extensive digital libraries with databases, electronic journals, and interactive, high-quality instructional resources.

Instructional design keeps the learner, the content, and the environment in focus at all times, while applying the knowledge of how learners learn and how knowledge is nurtured and grows.

Instructional design keeps the learner, the content, and the environment in focus at all times, while applying the knowledge of how learners learn and how knowledge is nurtured and grows. We now have an opportunity to design a teaching and learning environment that maximizes time, the joy of learning, and the satisfaction of teaching.

Chapter 6
Steps in Developing Web Courses

n today's higher education environment, a bundled strategy is the predominant method of course preparation. This means that the design, development, and delivery of a course is the responsibility of one person, usually the faculty member assigned to the course. This bundled approach has a long tradition, and is one with which we are comfortable. Under this model, the faculty member is expected to have an appropriately deep and rich knowledge of course content as well as knowledge about how to design and structure the learning experiences for the course. The faculty member is also expected to effectively and efficiently deliver the course.

The technologies for delivering a course generally consist of synchronous and asynchronous meeting places, communication tools, and learning resources. The predominant instructional strategy is the lecture enhanced with visual communication tools. When presentation software and tools are used to develop and deliver the lectures, the educational experience for the student is mainly in the category of teacher-to-student dialogue, occasionally integrated with student-to-student dialogues. This is the model for the standard 45 hours of class, or a regular 15-week course of a semester.

Internet and communication technologies are changing almost everything in this model, from student and faculty expectations to the design of teaching and learning strategies. Courses delivered in online environments require additional design and development support. A totally online or web course be comprehensively planned in advance. Developing and delivering an online course requires more coordination than does delivering a traditional face-to-face campus course. No longer can a lecture be finalized or developed in a few hours before a class, although newer tools are changing this. Additionally, changing an activity that is not working as planned cannot happen as quickly online as it can in a classroom.

Effective online courses use a variety of technologies and resources. They use a variety of learner-centered instructional strategies to help the instructor manage the dynamics and interaction of the course once it is under way. The infrastructure to support this variety must be in place prior to delivery, and tools to help the instructor manage the course must be intuitive and user friendly.

Building an online course means constructing a complete teaching and learning environment. Just as a physical plant is needed for campus courses, a digital plant is needed for online learning. Fortunately, many commercial and open-source software applications are now available. These systems, combined with campuswide administration systems and portals, support and create an online classroom comparable to the physical classroom.

This chapter looks at the kinds of expertise needed to design and develop course materials and activities for an online course. It is good to be specific about what materials and content are developed and prepared ahead of time, and what materials and instructional activities might be developed during the delivery of a course. An online course completely designed and developed prior to the beginning of course delivery usually consists of a course website that serves as a guide to direct and coordinate student activities and experiences. The website contains links and access to a set of digital materials. It serves as the communications center for the students' learning activities. And the site also serves as the online meeting place for students of the faculty member who is the manager or mentor for the course experience.

Preparing a fully online course is usually best done with a systematic instructional design process and a team approach.

Preparing a fully online course is usually best done with a systematic instructional design process and a team approach. This type of systematic design and development approach is especially important when the course will be offered many times to a large number of students and will be delivered by faculty who may not have participated in its design and development.

Designing and Developing an Online Course

This section describes a systematic step-by-step process that can be used to design and develop an online course, whether individually or as part of a team. In practice, there are as many ways of designing and building a course as there are faculty members and courses. In the bundled approach, the design and development of courses is similar to a master craftsman approach. Each faculty member designs, redesigns, updates, and modifies constantly, and no course is quite like any other. This is a benefit and a drawback of the current models. Faculty can quickly adapt to a particular group of students and maximize the fit between what the students know and what they want to know. In the unbundled approach, using a systematic design and development strategy, the members of a team generally design and develop a series of courses, making up a certificate, degree, or professional program, and customization is done at the point of delivery by a tutor.

Viewed simplistically, an online course can cost as little or as much as we want it to cost. However, the basic consumer principle that we generally get what we pay for usually applies. If we spend little or nothing, the course is ephemeral, unable to be used beyond the moment or the semester. If we spend money systematically and wisely on design and development, the course might be used for thousands of students over a period of years, and may even be sold or licensed to other institutions. This is not unlike writing a textbook that can be used by many students and faculty over a period of time; a course program that is developed also contains a database of digital content, instructional activities, assessments, and delivery designs.

An online course can be effectively designed and developed by following the eight steps below.

Step 1. Identify a course to design and develop by completing the Decision Layers One and Two worksheets in Chapter 4. Determine if the course will be designed with a team guided by a project manager or if it will be designed and developed by an individual approach.

Step 2. Describe the particular assumptions of the course environment and accompanying support infrastructure, including the tools and media that will be in the hands of faculty and students.

Step 3. Determine the learning goals and objectives for the students, the course content and structure, and the assessment of student learning. This includes the specification of the core content that students will interact with to achieve the goals and objectives.

Step 4. Search for, select, gather, and ensure access to the core content resources and course materials. Make sure that communication tools are in place.

Step 5. Define and plan unit activities and interactions.

Step 6. Build, populate, and organize content in the course website.

Step 7. Deliver the course, assess student learning, and evaluate the course.

Step 8. Revise based on feedback and analysis.

Although the steps in the design and development process are described in a neat, linear fashion, this is never exactly how it works in practice. Many of these steps are best done concurrently and iteratively, cycling back as needed.

For example, Step 3, specification of learning goals and objectives, course content, and assessment, must consider the availability of appropriate materials and the availability of course management tools, which is part of the work in Step 4. Since cost and availability influence the choice of materials, it means revisiting Step 3 once access to materials is determined.

What about Course Management Systems?

Instructional courses and programs find course- or learning-management systems (CMSs, LMSs) very useful for managing online and distance courses. In fact, the growth of these systems has been so rapid that few online courses do not use some tool for these functions. These systems support moving online for all types and components of online learning experiences. Even for campus-based courses, faculty find these systems to be useful for the following functions:

- Distribution and storage of course resources and materials
- Providing easily accessible locations for essential content resources
- Supporting communications and dialogue between faculty and students, between students, and between students and external resources
- Supporting the managerial and administrative functions of online teaching and learning

The number of courses using these systems is rapidly growing (Green, 2002), but the complexity and expense of the systems are also increasing. Knowing what level of resources is needed and at what point the resources are needed is an important part of the planning process.

Step One. Determine Your Strategy for Moving a Course Online: Individual or Team Approach

The choice of a design and development strategy is important. If a complete degree or certificate program is the anticipated outcome, some variation of the team approach is recommended. This approach requires all the planning and funding preparation discussed in earlier chapters. The first part of this section describes this team approach and the people and functions needed for this type of development.

If you are preparing a web-enhanced or even a webcentric course on your own and are ready to begin, you may want to go directly to the second part of this section, "Developing an Online Course On Your Own." However, you may want to quickly skim this first section to see all the various hats you will be wearing as you develop your course.

Faculty innovators or early adopters of technology should be aware that the support structure on campus might not be as ready as they are. Support for students might not be in place, either, and the institution may be struggling with ways to provide support for the online environment. Plan on being flexible and patient in the face of these obstacles.

The on-your-own approach is a low-cost strategy, and the one to use when there is more time for transition, and when the designing faculty member will probably teach the course.

The Team Approach

The team approach involves support from two groups of individuals: one team to support design and development, and a different team for the delivery phase. Each of these phases has its own distinct budget and timeline.

Table 6.1 lists the primary team members for the design, development, and delivery of online degree or program offerings. The development team is responsible for the design and development of the learning environment, the course materials, and their production. The delivery team is responsible for tasks associated with the effective marketing and delivery of the course. In some cases, members of the development team, such as the project manager and instructional designer, stay involved as informal consultants to the delivery team. This practice supports the marketing and planning for the students who take the course. Marketing and planning for the delivery of the course needs to occur concurrently with the design and development phases.

Table 6.1 Team Members

Design and Development Team	Delivery Team
Project Manager	Program/Degree Manager
Faculty Member(s)	Instructor/Faculty Member(s)
Instructional Designer	Course Assistant(s)
Infrastructure Support Staff	Infrastructure Support Staff
Content Researcher(s)	Administrative Coordinator
Graphic Artist/Videographer	

The Development Team: Roles and Responsibilities

The number of team members may be surprising. For some development efforts, the team members might assume more than one of these functional roles; for example, the instructional designer might also serve as the project manager. In other cases, as in the case of a graphic artist, an individual might be subcontracted for certain well-defined development tasks

Project Manager. The project manager coordinates project tasks to ensure that a quality degree or program offering is completed on time and within budget. As project managers are not usually part of the traditional bundled approach, it can be tempting to try to do without one. This is almost always a bad idea. A project manager creates schedules and plans; conducts project status meetings; coordinates the availability of people, infrastructure applications, and support; ensures the readiness and availability of instructional materials; and handles the interface with the delivery organization. A project manager may also plan and coordinate the evaluation of the completed course during initial delivery to students. For small projects, such as a single course or a short program, the function of the project manager might be effectively handled by partial assignment of a faculty member or other personnel.

Faculty Member. The faculty member is the content expert of the development team and maintains overall responsibility for the content selection, framework, and instructional strategies of a course. The faculty member is responsible for determining the goals and objectives of the students' learning, the overall course requirements, and the student assessment processes. The faculty member works collaboratively with the instructional designer and the other faculty in the program to ensure content consistency and student competencies across courses.

Instructional Designer. An instructional designer provides a blueprint for the overall learning environment based on established learning. By using a systematic process to analyzes the basic components of instruction, the designer recommends instruction strategies, assessments, media tools, and course management techniques that will effectively meet the needs of the learner, the course goals, and performance objectives.

The designer begins by matching the learning goals and objectives with the characteristics and lifestyles of students and with the constraints of the delivery environment. For example, an important design decision focuses on the choice of media. For fully online programs as well as campus courses, every media choice has a ripple effect because all media need to be supported. The basic principal that all media require an infrastructure must be included in an instructional designer's plan.

The designer is responsible for recommending instructional activities that engage the learner and provide opportunities for interaction with information sources such as the instructor, online resources, and experts in the field. The designer also often helps in the preparation of instructional materials. Other responsibilities might include researching online resources, developing the components of the course website, and evaluating the instructional effectiveness of the produced materials. In a large team in a corporate training environment, many of these responsibilities might be assigned to specialty personnel.

Specialty skills such as instructional design can be outsourced or subcontracted. Institutions with degree programs in instructional design or educational technology might have a ready resource of student experts who can be effectively tapped for some of the smaller projects or as assistants in larger programs. Full-time instructional designers may appear costly, but on larger curricular projects and full degree programs, they can produce great gains in efficiency, content effectiveness and development, and student learning.

Infrastructure Support Staff. The staff to support the online learning environment has changed dramatically in the last 10 years. When the first large-scale online programs were designed and developed in the mid-1990s, the webmaster's was a principal role. At that time, the webmaster worked with the program team to ensure a user-friendly environment for both faculty and students. Now that course management systems are into their third and even fourth generation (Boettcher, 2003), the definition and support of the online learning environment is generally part of the overall campus information technology (IT) organization and infrastructure.

> The staff to support the online learning environment has changed dramatically in the last 10 years.

The responsibility of the infrastructure support staff for large degree programs now generally consists of a representative from the IT organization meeting with the project team, soliciting the requirements for teaching and learning capabilities for the planned degree program, and then working to ensure a match between the design of the program and the capabilities of the infrastructure. In some cases, this means that existing tools can be modified to meet the design of a program, or, alternatively, that the design of the program or instructional strategies might be adapted to fit the existing tools and applications.

One goal of program planning is to strive for structural efficiencies in a curriculum offering. Every discipline, particularly a tightly structured degree program, can benefit from curriculum planning that identifies core sets of resources and processes that may be common across the program.

Other personnel from the IT organization support faculty and students in their use of the overall campus infrastructure. Ideally, students should be able to inquire about online programs, register for class, and gain access to networking, library resources, consulting, and other resources without coming to campus. Some campuses now boast automatic account generation for students as soon as they register for a course. Technical support personnel can also advise a team on how to make the most of what is available on campus and work around limitations. Technical support is definitely needed for general infrastructure resources such as the help desk, access to computers, web hosting services and backups, oversight of the course management system, and arrangement for the use of technology for on-campus meetings.

Content Researcher. A content researcher assists the faculty member by identifying effective and well-structured content resources available in digital form. One longstanding issue in online programs is how to best provide student access to required and recommended content resources. A way of managing access issues to content resources is to categorize content resources into (1) core resources, (2) highly recommended resources, and (3) resources for customizing learning.

Most courses now rely on content material that is available in digital format and can be linked to or accessed from websites. Generally, if content materials can be made available via the internet, then student study, dialogue, and inquiry can happen anywhere, anytime. Digital content can greatly increase access for students and possibly reduce costs. In the university environment, a graduate student can often serve as content researcher; in other environments, contractors might play this role. Another option is to select a textbook from a publisher that has an established website for that course, or to use a service such as XanEdu (www.xanedu.com) or University Readers (www.universityreaders.com) to design coursepacks.

Graphic Artist or Videographer. A graphic artist or videographer may be needed for a degree program. For programs where large segments may be faculty-to-student dialogue or lecture, a videographer might be a real asset. A graphic artist might be desirable if the course content is highly visual. Some of the work originally done by graphic designers has been integrated into well-designed course management tools and content from publishers. Input of a graphic artist can be most valuable at the beginning of a project, when decisions about the look and feel of a course or degree program are being created. Graphic artists are often freelancers and work on many projects at the same time.

Other Personnel. Large-scale projects designed as by-many-to-many programs will probably need a team member to shepherd the coordination, production, and packaging of instructional materials into a master-course database resource. In some projects, a commercial content publisher might be a partner to whom such a resource database or any printed and digital materials would be handed for final editing and production. In other projects, where no new materials are produced, there may be little or no need for development and production assistance. As part of the course design process, faculty identify instructional materials to be purchased from existing content producers.

In addition to development work, other personnel are often needed to support the project team. Clerical support personnel can assist in the acquisition of resources and general daily communication. Review personnel can ensure that the materials are accurate and complete for the specified goals and objectives. These review personnel may be faculty, students, or other experts.

The Delivery Team

Degree Manager. The degree manager manages the scheduling of courses in the degree program and helps to ensure that they are full and that the teaching and learning environment and support structures are in place for students and faculty. This person may be in a college or in a continuing education organization.

Faculty. The faculty member manages the teaching and learning experiences and communications with the students and monitors, challenges, and assesses student learning.

Course Assistant. To maintain a high level of interaction in the learning environment, a course assistant is recommended when more than 25 students are enrolled. The course assistant answers some of the email from students, facilitates online conferences, and generally assists in the course delivery. In distance learning physical sites, course assistants can be the face of the faculty and encourage engagement (Riffee, 2003).

Infrastructure Support Staff. The infrastructure support staff ensure that the course website and support services are available to students and faculty 24 hours a day, 7 days a week. Course websites are now mission critical and need to be mirrored in other sites. Services required, including email and network access support, often do not differ from the support services for hybrid or web-enhanced campus courses. Adequate technical support is particularly critical during the first few weeks of the semester, when online learners are becoming familiar with new media or teaching and learning environments. It is also critical at midterm and during the last few weeks of the semester, when technology problems can impact the submission of assignments and, in turn, the determination of final grades.

Administrative Coordinator. The administrative coordinator assists in the marketing, recruiting, and admission processes of students for the online certificate and degree programs, and ensures that all the student services are available to provide a stable, reliable, and productive educational experience. Depending on the environment, this role might be absorbed into the normal operating business of a college or university. In fact, this is the goal, since many online courses are used by students on campus as much as by students off campus.

Developing an Online Course On Your Own

> The team approach is definitely the preferred strategy for development of an online course that is part of a certificate or degree program or that will be delivered many times.

The team approach is definitely the preferred strategy for development of an online course that is part of a certificate or degree program or that will be delivered many times. In the case of a single course or a sequence of two or three courses being prepared for online delivery, the general strategy is that faculty members will develop the online courses in the same manner they design and develop a face-to-face course: in the bundled approach, over time, as part of their normal load, and making changes from semester to semester. In the early years of online teaching and learning, many institutions provided small grants and some release time to assist in this transition. This type of support should be provided whenever possible, because getting the first version of a course online is a significant commitment. A major part of the commitment can be the faculty's own learning of the new tools and environments and developing new habits of working.

How do faculty manage the design, development, and delivery of a course for the online learning environment? The first two steps include the completion of Design Layers One and Two worksheets from Chapter 4. These tools help clarify what hardware, software, support, and time might be needed for a particular project. They also help clarify expected outcomes to deans, provosts, department chairs, and faculty. All should agree on whether the outcomes are the content and materials for a fully online course, a webcentric course, or a web-enhanced course.

Other questions that should be addressed include, "How and for whom will the course be developed?" and, "When will it be delivered?" Without support from a project team, it is good to be flexible about expectations, as it will be a new experience for the faculty member and a new environment for students. One successful strategy is to enlist the students' help in designing the course. Ask for feedback concerning what is working and what is not, and what additional resources might work for a particular concept.

Without the support of a team, the faculty member must perform many of the functions or find the resources to have functions performed in other ways. Preparing a course for the online environment is more complex than teaching a course for the first time, so additional release time during the first semester of delivery is recommended. If possible, enrollment in a faculty member's first online course should be kept low to provide the opportunity to learn to manage online communication effectively.

With some provisos, the recommendation is that faculty not attempt to become online designers and developers. A faculty member who is fairly technical, is an early adopter of technology, has access to a good course management tool, or has a technologically adept student at hand can serve this role. The tool sets for teaching and learning online are now available and generally affordable; thus, the recommendation is to use these available tools unless the faculty and the institution are part of content development projects.

Most academic computing centers also provide training programs to help faculty get started. If the organization does not provide support for faculty converting to online courses, the internet itself is an excellent resource. Good courses are available online and at conferences, and faculty can earn certificates in Online Teaching and Learning from many colleges and organizations.

The internet is also a great resource for content materials. Many faculty have put their courses online, and many of these courses are freely accessible. The OpenCourseWare project at MIT (ocw.mit.edu) is in the process of publishing the materials used in MIT courses online as "free and open educational resources for faculty, students, and self-learners." Content from over 500 courses are already available, covering disciplines including architecture, biology, chemical engineering, and urban studies. Fellow faculty also can be great resources, as are the many publisher websites. Some of these resources are free; others are fee-based or linked to consortia memberships.

Developing an online course alone should be a planned and communicated project. Designing, developing, and delivering a quality online course of any type is a time-consuming yet creative and rewarding task. For the individual approach, examining the time requirements early and deciding how much of the course will be converted in a single semester or year is essential. If the plan is to convert gradually, then proceed. If the plan is to convert quickly and support and time are needed, seek prior approval for these efforts. Once you obtain approval, manage well the expectations of *what* can be done, *when* it can be done, and with what *resources* and *time commitment* it can be done.

Step Two. Select Your Course Environment

Selecting a teaching and learning environment is one of the most important steps in the process of moving a course online. This single decision will have an impact on every other part of the process. For institutions that have a standardized course or learning management system, the decision may be already made. These systems are quite competitive, so while they are all different, most have all the basic capabilities and sets of communication tools.

Course management systems have evolved rapidly from simple templates built by one or two faculty to large-scale commercial software with links to the campus administrative systems. They now require support and maintenance by IT staff and multiyear planning budgets for licensing, support, upgrades, and enhancements. Many design decisions are made for you, and this is good. The commercial companies behind these systems are upgrading and continually adding features so that any flexibility and choices that are not available today will probably be available later. And most institutions have training classes and personnel to help faculty use these systems.

If your institution has a standardized course management system, your task is to get acquainted with the system, get an account and start using the system for campus-based courses. More on course management systems, their history, and their future is in the Chapter 8.

Table 6.2 lists features common to both commercial and open-source course management systems.

Step Three. Redesign a Course

Moving a course to an online environment provides an opportunity to reassess the course's strengths and weaknesses. This is a good time to update content and to apply research on new teaching and learning strategies that increase active and collaborative learning.

Table 6.3 provides a Course Design Guide, a tool to guide the development learning objectives and the linking of each instructional component to a course objective. For example, if one of the objectives is a knowledge objective – such as being able to reproduce the structure of a human brain cell or being

Table 6.2 Desirable Features in Course Management Systems

Faculty Tools	Student Tools
• Syllabus	• Access to current grades
• Course announcements	• Student presentation areas
• Customized course look and feel	• Student biography information
• Course backup	• Student self-evaluation
• Connections to external references	• Student management
• Questionnaire and testing delivery and support	• Peer-critique tools
• Grading tools and systems	

General Tools for Faculty and Students

• Calendar	• Capability to upload information easily
• Chat tool	• Searchable and linkable glossary
• Discussion lists	• Automatic indexing and searching
• Electronic mail	• Progress tracking
• Online conferencing and seminar rooms	• Timed online quizzes

able to provide a definition of a complex concept – then the instructional strategy used by the faculty member, the content resources, the learning context, and the assessment process should be linked to that objective.

For skill objectives, the instructional strategies may well include presentation and hands-on practice, followed by a student project or demonstration of that skill. The Course Design Guide provides a set of ideas for all three types of objectives: knowing, doing, and thinking (attitude).

This Course Design Guide is best used twice: once when determining the course goals and objectives, and then again for developing activities at every unit level within each course. For example, learners may individually read a chapter from the text, complete a thoughtful response or analysis based on their reading, and then share and discuss those conclusions in a group of three to five peers. Or the discussion may occur while preparing a group response. After the activity is planned, the description and instructions for each activity can be part of the course website.

During the process of redesigning a course, the faculty member should examine the course's various components. The following list may be helpful when moving to online environments, updating courses, or targeting a different group of students.

Course Goals and Objectives. What are the overall goals of the course? What instructional objectives should be achieved? What should learners know, be able to do, or think about a particular topic at the end of the course?

Type of Dialogue. What type or types of dialogues support the learning of the course objectives: instructor-student, student-student, or student-resources? When is each dialogue most effective?

Teaching and Learning Strategies. What teaching and learning strategies will be used? Based on the type of dialogue desired, several instructional strategies are available. For example, instructor-student dialogue can be accomplished through such strategies as lecture, discussion, mentoring, feedback, and questioning.

Technology. What technology will be used to support the course objectives? Based on the types of dialogue and instructional strategies selected to accomplish an objective, various technological resources are available. For example, an objective that requires instructor-student dialogue and mentoring might best be served by online office hours, one-to-one email, or video meetings. This component may require assistance from technical support personnel to determine what is possible in your existing campus infrastructure.

Assessment. How will each course objective be assessed? In the past, a multiple-choice exam might have been used. However, you may now choose to have students complete a final project that demonstrates their knowledge and skill level. With the proliferation of online courses, the development of e-portfolio software and related tools has expanded dramatically. If an objective is change of attitude, you might want students to keep a reflective journal of their thoughts over the course of the semester. Consider creative options to assess students who are now taking an active role in their learning and who are working online.

Table 6.3 Course Design Guide

Type of Learning Objectives	Type of Dialogue	Teaching and Learning Strategies	Technology	Assessment
Know This type of objective is useful for core concepts and principles. It is also important for student-generated knowledge objectives. One of the knowledge objectives for the course is _____	Instructor-Student	Lecture, Discussion, Consultation, Group Mentoring, Feedback on Assignments, Note Taking, Summarizing, Questioning,	Videoconference or Videotape, Audio Webcasts, Online Office Hours, Email, Chat Room, Online Seminars, Online Content	Online Self-Check Tests, Problem Solving, Written Critiques, Questions and Analyses
	Student-Student	Synchronous and Asynchronous Collaborative Discussions and Projects	Study Groups, On and Off Line Audio or Videoconference, Chat, Email, Database of Concepts Built Collaboratively, Online Seminars, Discussion Lists	Individual or Group Projects, Journal, Portfolio Project
	Student-Resources	Readings and Experiences, Interviews and Discussions With Experts, Exercises and Experiences in All Varieties of Digital and Analog Resources	Online or Printed Course Guide, Books, Journals, Visiting Experts, Digital and Analog Resources (Simulations, Databases, Tutorials)	Concept Mapping, Media Projects, Paper, Film, Internet Problem Solving

Table 6.3 Course Design Guide - Continued

Type of Learning Objectives	Type of Dialogue	Teaching and Learning Strategies	Technology	Assessment
Do This type of objective is best for skill objectives, such as "What do I want the student to be able to do as a result of this instruction?"	Instructor-Student	Demonstration, Consultation, Group Mentoring, Summarizing, Questioning, Problem Solving, Hands-On Activities, Interactive Simulations and Scenarios	Videoconference, Audio Webcasts, Online Seminars, Postings and Critiques, Online Office Hours, Email, Chat Room	Projects and Problem Solving, Hands-On Skill Development
	Student-Student	Collaborative and Experiential Activities or Projects	Interactive and Collaborative Experiences, Hands-On Problem Solving and Analyses, Online Seminars	Project and Scenario Experience and Analysis
One of the skill objectives for the course is _____	Student-Resources	Simulations of Authentic Experiences, Field Trips, Internships Interviews and Discussions With Experts Exercises and Experiences	Interactive Resources, Online Discussions With Experts, Electronic Field Trips	Demonstration of Skills, Portfolio Additions

Table 6.3 Course Design Guide - Continued

Type of Learning Objectives	Type of Dialogue	Teaching and Learning Strategies	Technology	Assessment
Think This is an attitude objective answering the question, "What do I want the student to think regarding this content, this skill?"	Instructor-Student	Lecture, Discussion, Consultation, Group Mentoring, Feedback on Assignments, Note Taking, Summarizing, Questioning, Problem Solving	Threaded Discussions, Online Seminars, Conferences of All Types	Summary Papers and Projects, Including All Types of Media Projects
	Student-Student	Role Plays, Collaborative Activities, Value Activities	Threaded Discussions, Online Seminars, Conferences of All Types	Discussions, Joint Problem Solving, Problem Solutions
One of the attitude objectives for the course is	Student-Resources	Reflective Journals, Internships, Community Services, Real-World Problem Solving	Interactive Resources, Online Discussions With Experts	Case Studies, Community Service Feedback

Step Four. Find, Gather, and Ensure Access to Course Resources

It is a good idea to begin the search for digital and online resources as early as possible in the design and planning process. There are two reasons for this: (1) The materials available online may significantly influence decisions about what objectives are appropriate for students, and (2) highly desirable or essential materials may require copyright permissions and subscription access arrangements before they can be available to students in an online environment. As mentioned, the process of design and development has many interactions and interdependencies and is not a linear one. The sooner the process of ensuring resource availability is begun, the less stress is involved.

Step Five. Define Unit Activities and Interactions

In a face-to-face environment, interaction often happens spontaneously. We may plan a particular activity, but as it unfolds, we may change it in response to what is working and what is not. However, spur-of-the-moment inspiration does not work as well in an online environment as it does in a face-to-face learning environment. Therefore, it is important that course activities be developed in detail before the first class session.

Step Six. Build, Populate, and Organize Content in the Course Site

During this step, all those yellow pad notes and miscellaneous pieces of digital documents – syllabus, bibliography, project descriptions, and handouts – are brought together. Course management systems and other application tools provide a real yet virtual space for putting it all online. With a course management tool, the process can be very much like word processing. But the course templates do not do the course redesign yet. This is where the real work of faculty comes in. A course site can be as distinctive as the course and the faculty member's philosophy allow it to be.

This is also where the power of the campus infrastructure makes a difference. The instructor, through discussions with other faculty members and an instructional designer, can determine the needed features and discuss them with the course management systems support person, who will suggest ways in which various features can be incorporated into the course site. Although several people are involved in the process, the instructor is the one who makes the instructional and content decisions.

Step Seven. Deliver the Course and Assess Student Learning

You should now be ready to launch your online course delivery. Very simply, your job is to create a welcoming, interactive and instructive environment for your students. You will want to set the ground rules, just as you do in the face-to-face environment. Set the tone for the environment and explain how student and faculty roles are evolving. Discuss how students will be expected to take charge of their learning and customize their learning perhaps to a greater extent than they have previously. Discuss guidelines for setting up a study schedule so that they participate in the synchronous and asynchronous activities.

Managing any online course will have its distinct set of challenges based on the personalities in the course, just as with the face-to-face classroom. The web-based environment creates a perception of 24-hour instructor availability, so it is helpful to set expectations about your availability. Provide guidelines concerning your methods for responding to email, facilitating discussion groups, and giving feedback on activities and assignments. Students should also know who to turn to for technical assistance and with questions on course content.

It is a good idea to have contingency plans for times when the technology is unavailable, such as when the server goes down. Remember that you have alternative technologies, such as the phone and fax, to use when the computer fails. As failures do not typically occur everywhere simultaneously, it can be possible for students to continue on their own.

Step Eight. Evaluate, Revise, and Redesign Based on Feedback and Analysis

Evaluation is one of the most important steps in a course, whether online or on campus. Although you have carefully designed and planned the course, you will no doubt want to change some features after seeing the course components in action. Students can also provide insights into the course experiences from their perspectives. If a course evaluation tool is not readily available, companies such as ECurriculum (www.ecurriculum.com) provide evaluation tools for online courses.

At least six course components should be evaluated, either by you or your institution:

- Organization of the course website
- Clarity of course materials
- Quality of activities
- Adequacy of technical support
- Level and methods of communication
- Overall satisfaction with the course

Institutions often provide a means to evaluate at least four of these six areas. You may wish to administer a separate evaluation that provides a means for learners to suggest improvement for the design level of learning activities, as this design level is seldom addressed with the more holistic evaluation tools. This type of evaluation can be done with a simple wrap-up discussion question that asks them to share aspects of the course they think should be continued, discontinued, or added to enhance effectiveness.

A Final Word on Instructional Design and Planning

At first glance, instructional planning may seem too time consuming to be worthwhile. Certainly the up-front development time of an online course is more time consuming than face-to-face classes may have been. However, it helps to remember that the better a course is planned, the more time will be available to handle unforeseen events that go wrong while delivering a course online. And inevitably, *something* will go wrong! You will be better able to handle it if you are not developing the course at the same time you are implementing it.

Moving a course online, if done in an organized, systematic manner, can result in a quality course that delights the teacher and the learner and minimizes the frustration of both. It will allow you, the instructor, to manage learner interaction and respond in a timely manner to the needs of the learner once the course is under way.

Here are a few excellent resources on online instructional strategies and activities:

Engaging the Online Learner (Conrad & Donaldson, 2004)
Teaching Online (Draves, 2002)
Building Learning Communities and *Lessons from the Cyberspace Classroom* (Palloff & Pratt, 1999, 2001)
Facilitating Online Learning (Collison, Elbaum, Haavind, & Tinker, 2000)
Learning Networks (Harasim, Teles, & Turoff, 1997)

Additionally, Chapter 9 provides stories from faculty about their experiences preparing for and teaching online.

Chapter 7
Creating and Sustaining Community

When instructors first began moving courses online almost a decade ago, they were the pioneers of the online environment. They faced the challenge of determining what aspects of a classroom-based course they would take with them as they crossed the mountains of technology and established their new homesteads on the wide-open prairies of the web. Once there, they faced a myriad of questions. What important elements should they bring to the new environment, and what look should they try to achieve? How should they convey course content? How would they establish their presence and motivate learners to participate? How would learners and instructors relate to one another? What were the expectations of the inhabitants of the online world, and by what rules should it be governed? In this new world, faculty had to determine how they would establish a cohesive learning environment.

Current communication tools support types of interaction among the students and between students and faculty that were never possible before. But how should these tools be used? What types of applications made sense? How were they best used for instruction? Once the learning environment is in place, how does one ensure that worthwhile communication exchanges occur?

> **What types of applications made sense? How were they best used for instruction? Once the learning environment is in place, how does one ensure that worthwhile communication exchanges occur?**

Stories from these online pioneers have been encouraging and inspiring. Best practices and core principles for teaching and learning online are now available. We have guidelines for directing and managing a cohesive learning environment. Consistently noted as major contributors to an effective online course are substantive course-planning and development processes focused on effective content delivery and the creation of a learning community in which instructors and learners interact to generate knowledge based on core content, complemented with newly generated content (Palloff & Pratt, 1999, 2001; Lynch, 2002; Salmon, 2002; Moore, 2002).

Upon entering the online world, it helps to move from faculty-centered to learner-centered instruction, or to what is often called learning-community-centered instruction (Hanna, et. al, 2000). In embracing this change, traditional faculty and student roles are often redefined. Faculty become facilitators, mentors, and guides, rather than being the primary or sole sources of information. Students become active knowledge generators instead of passive knowledge absorbers. In the online environment, learners assume more responsibility for their learning and even begin recognizing their role in the learning process of fellow students. Some traditional faculty responsibilities, such as identifying and generating course resources and leading discussions, are being shared with learners. At the same time online learners face the challenge of learning new content, they are also learning new technology, communication methods, and instructional strategies, and assuming new roles.

Collaborative learning is one instructional strategy faculty have found useful in encouraging students to take responsibility for learning in the classroom. With this strategy, group members are responsible for discussing and explaining course content, solving problems, providing feedback, and ensuring mutual success. Learners depend on one another as knowledge providers; the faculty help validate students' mutual knowledge building. The online environment is well suited for this type of strategy.

The challenge facing faculty in the online environment is the effective establishment and management of community building without face-to-face cues. A faculty member who has used collaboration strategies in the traditional classroom has an advantage, but the web-based environment has slightly different dynamics and management considerations, so we are all learning how to best teach and learn in the new online space.

The Continuum of Community

Interaction, collaboration, cooperation, and community are terms whose definitions seem to blur when we talk about small group work. While these terms are similar, each has a discrete meaning in teaching and learning environments. Each level of communication exchange can be a distinct stage in establishing a learning community; it also can be differentiated by the learning goal and duration of the activity, and by the structure and complexity of the learning experience.

When discussing community, it is important to remember that "learning is in the relationships between people" and that "there is an intimate connection between knowledge and activity" (Smith, 2003). The connection among learners usually deepens as interaction time, task structure, and complexity increase. As they spend more time interacting on increasingly complex, higher-order thinking activities, an online community of multiple, interdependent perspectives begins to form.

Interaction

Interaction is a communication exchange between two or more learners. It is not a prolonged exchange, so there is no lasting affiliation established between learners. When students exchange answers or discuss their ideas with the people near them in a face-to-face classroom, interaction occurs. It is short in duration and does not require that learners maintain or build a lasting connection.

Interaction is used to increase learner communication and participation, to enhance the processing of content by learners, and to give and receive feedback (Wagner, 1997). In a classroom, a faculty member usually leads the interaction process and is a visible figure in it. When learners are interacting, the faculty member is in the background, but learners still have a tendency to look to the instructor for answers instead of relying on each other for guidance and interpretation.

The major drawback of interaction is that it does not necessarily promote the team-building process. For team building to occur, we need to use the next stage of community building: collaboration.

Collaboration

Collaboration is the act of students working together in small groups on a particular activity during a finite time period. One example of collaboration is to form student groups to complete a single activity or a set of activities during a single class. The purpose of group collaboration is usually to analyze a situation, solve a problem, or brainstorm ideas. Learners are connected through the joint activity and the common short-term goal. But due to the short duration of the activity, learners may not become interdependent or look to each other for mutual support as the course progresses.

The faculty member provides less guidance and is less the focal point in collaboration than in an interactive activity. At this collaboration stage, the group may turn to the faculty member to resolve group negotiation problems or to validate certain facts or processes: "They say the answer should be this, but I think it's that. Which is right?" Overall, however, the group operates more independently than students do during simple interaction.

Cooperation

A fine line separates collaboration and cooperation, which is why the two terms are often used interchangeably. The difference between the two terms, as they are used in the continuum of community building, lies in the complexity and duration of the activities. In cooperative groups, learners work together with minimal guidance from faculty in order to achieve an outcome or goal that can only be achieved collectively and interdependently. Cooperative groups work together throughout a course to complete a series of problem-solving or peer-learning activities that culminate in a product, such as a project report, or an action, such as leading an online conference.

Two significant attributes of a cooperative group are that the members are interdependent since all group members must succeed in order for the group to succeed; and that the members are individually accountable since each member's performance is individually assessed in some manner. In a cooperative activity, the faculty member may monitor the process and provide guidance as needed or requested by the group. As learners become more dependent on each other, they become more responsible for their learning and move closer to being a learning community.

Community

A learning community consists of learners who support and assist each other, make decisions synergistically, and communicate with peers on a variety of topics beyond those assigned. Community goes beyond cooperation; it is a self-managing entity. In a learning community, the faculty member is a community member with a consulting role. Although the faculty member may introduce some activities and discussion topics, the community members also determine additional activities and topics. Learners turn to each other first for problem resolution and knowledge building before they seek information from the faculty.

Why Create Community?

Larocque (1997) summarized the sentiments of many faculty members in his paper's title: "Me, Myself, and . . . You? Collaborative Learning: Why Bother?" Creating community often seems to take more time and effort to plan and administer than other instructional strategies. So it's worthwhile to ask, Why do it? What are the benefits? During the last three decades, collaborative learning has been used throughout all levels of traditional face-to-face education, from elementary to higher education. More than a decade ago, studies of its effectiveness concluded that achievement, productivity, self-esteem, peer interaction, and group cohesion are higher in collaborative groups than in individual or competitive learning environments (Johnson & Johnson, 1993), and critical thinking is enhanced. In addition, Johnson and Johnson (1993) found that "a dialogue with peers promoted more higher-level reasoning and ability to apply learning than did a dialogue with a computer" (p. 147).
In an online environment, collaborative learning techniques have been

implemented through the use of computer-mediated communication tools such as email, chat rooms, and conferencing software. Computer-mediated communication tools support the small-group interaction, peer collaboration, and teamwork that Pea (1994) found lacking in satellite and other videoconferenced distance learning environments. Studies analyzing computer-mediated communications indicate that online collaboration can increase participation and decrease student isolation in distance learning courses (Harasim, et al., 1996; McCormack & Jones, 1998; Collis, 1996). Collis further reports that online collaboration increases the likelihood that different perspectives will be introduced, and supports quick and easy communication and interactive instructional strategies. The most recent work of leaders in online learning indicate that interaction and community building are the "heart and soul of an online course" (Draves, 2002) and that it is essential "for the learning process to be successful" (Palloff & Pratt, 1999).

> In an online environment, collaborative learning techniques have been implemented through the use of computer-mediated communication tools such as email, chat rooms, and conferencing software.

Building community can also assist in the management of the course. As an online community grows, learners become more self-directed and can take responsibility for tasks such as facilitating discussion, ensuring access to content resources, and providing technical assistance.

Technology Tools that Promote Community

Many web applications and tools support each of the types of interactions that promote community building. Email and chat rooms are tools that fit the short-duration characteristics of the interaction stage of community building. Both are good one-to-one communication tools, and they are also useful in collaborative activities. Conferencing tools support collaboration because of the longer duration of the activity and the increasing interdependencies; they support cooperative and community activities. Video and audio tools help build community by infusing some of the usual face-to-face cues into the online environment.

In these cooperative and community interactions, virtual environments such as Multi-User Dungeons (MUDs), MUD Object-Oriented (MOOs), Multi-User Simulations Environments (MUSEs), and Multi-User Adventures (MUAs) support community building through online simulations and problem-solving activities. These are "imaginary worlds in computer databases where people use words and programming languages to improvise melodramas, to build worlds and all the objects in them, solve puzzles, etc." (Rheingold, 1993, p. 145). Table 7.1 illustrates the relationships between tools and types of interaction.

Table 7.1   Tools and Types of Interactions

	Interaction	Collaboration	Cooperation	Community
Email	X	X	X	X
Chat	X	X	X	X
Conferencing		X	X	X
MUDs/MOOs			X	X
Blogs			X	X

One of the newer web applications on the scene is the weblog, more popularly known as a blog. Tansey (2003) defines it as "a site that contains the personal thoughts of the blogger," and explains that blogging activities are being incorporated into the educational environment as a collaborative project tool. Examples of blogs are diaries, research journals, news digests, or commentaries on a particular topic. Tansey also comments that because the tool is easy to learn, the uses for blogs are expanding rapidly and are beginning to be used for class web pages and assignment portfolios. For more information, see the Weblogs Compendium at www.lights.com/weblogs/.

Are all of these tools needed for online communication to be effective? No! In fact, the simplest approach is sometimes the best, particularly when starting an online course. If you are using a course management system, use the tools within it and add others as you and your learners become more comfortable with the tools. Throwing too much technology at learners in order to facilitate community building can have the opposite effect, where learners are so consumed by learning the technology that the quality of the communication suffers. Community cannot be developed unless learners feel technologically competent.

Drawbacks to Community Learning Online

Quite honestly, online learning environments generally require more time, effort, and commitment on the part of every member of the community. We have identified the following challenges presented by increased interaction in online learning environments.

• *More faculty time.* When learners are new to an online learning environment, online communication encourages an expectation of increased faculty availability and may increase student dependency on the faculty (Eastmond, 1995). Faculty have reported that teaching distance learning courses "is a demanding proposition for professors . . . an enormous amount of work, much more than teaching in a classroom" (McKinnon, 1998). However, conflicting studies were published by Visser (2000) and DiBiasi (2000). Visser's study indicated that more faculty time was required, but DiBiasi stated that while a distance course "requires more frequent attention," the data did not indicate that "teaching an online course requires more effort than teaching a comparable synchronous classroom course." Visser suggested that the level of instructor experience and institutional support affected the faculty time required as his study involved a first-time online instructor.

• *More student time.* Learners must face the challenge of interacting without the usual physical and vocal cues of face-to-face communication. They must also overcome the difficulties of the asynchronous nature of online discussion as it relates to negotiating consensus. Communication is not instantaneous in many cases, and the spontaneity that can be helpful when solving problems is lost. This can slow the group formation process as well as group discussion. Brainstorming, for example, is best done synchronously. Even the lowly, ubiquitous, and familiar telephone can be a good tool of choice for some activities, and the technologies supporting voice over the internet will make this type of synchronous tool even more useful.

• *Technology comfort level.* Comfort with technology is fundamental to community building. However, discomfort with technology can promote community when a learner reaches out to the community for help. Identifying peer consultants or providing a peer communication space such as a cybercafé can encourage this reaching out.

• *Less self-paced.* Another drawback to community building is that sometimes it can appear to interfere with the positive aspects of time independence and self-pacing. The class must stay together in some manner to communicate on the same topics during a particular time frame. A person falling behind can be detrimental to the community when the situation causes frustration or resentment on the part of those who respond in a timely manner and wish to move to the next topic.

• *Late Posters and Lurkers.* Learners can develop negative perceptions of collaboration if all members of the group are not fully engaged in the process or do not contribute in a timely manner (Muirhead, 1999). While those who post late in the week are not considered as detrimental to community as lurkers – those who never contribute – both late posters and lurkers disrupt the flow of dialogue. Some learners remain community lurkers if collaboration is not perceived as a valuable or essential part of the learning experience. While lurking has traditionally been discouraged, some learners may argue that they are learning just the same, and this may be true (Swan, 2002), but for the overall good of the community, it should be discouraged.

• *No emotional cues.* Students may not feel comfortable disagreeing with one another in text-based communication. Sometimes a student can disagree in a joking manner in a face-to-face environment, and peers do not take offense. In an online environment, misunderstandings occur more easily and often take longer to resolve than they do in face-to-face environments.

• *Inexperience with collaboration.* Many adult learners have not been taught how to collaborate with and critique their peers' work. Adult learners may also discount a critique that comes from a peer they do not perceive to be an expert in the same sense that a faculty member is an expert. Learners may look to the faculty member to referee the discussion. They want to know they are on the right track with their thoughts and may want faculty validation before they accept the opinion of a peer.

Techniques for Developing an Online Community

Techniques for structuring collaboration are not necessarily obvious. One faculty member, asked how to structure collaboration, said, "Well, I give the students the activity and tell them to form groups." While this strategy might work in a physical environment where students have met each other, online learners will not automatically group. The anxiety with which learners begin to interact and collaborate online with peers they have never met is similar to going on a blind date. How will I get to know this person? What will we talk about? Will we be compatible? Will we have similar interests? How well will we work together? Given the choice, many online learners will avoid interaction; therefore, it falls to the faculty member to design and implement effective interactions.

> ... learners usually require an orientation to their more active and responsible roles as online learners.

Palloff and Pratt (2001) underscore that careful management is needed to cultivate community in online learning environments. In an online learning environment, "it cannot be assumed that students will engage with one another in the learning process; this must be taught" (p. 107). Many of today's learners have received much of their education in a lecture-based, traditional classroom. Therefore, learners usually require an orientation to their more active and responsible roles as online learners. Increasing the time, structure, and complexity of collaborative activities as the course progresses can encourage this shift of focus for the learner.

The Community Development Plan (CDP) illustrated in Table 7.2 is one tool for faculty to use in planning and analyzing the level of community development in a course. Creating community, or at least incorporating some level of it, must be a planning goal. As Palloff and Pratt (2001) state, "It is the interactions and connections made in the course that students will remember as the keys to learning in an online course" (p. 153).

The Community Development Plan provides a means of planning activities for each learning objective in the course on a week-by-week or unit-by-unit basis. Each activity can be categorized based on the interaction type – Learner-Resource (L-R), Facilitator/Faculty-Learner (F-L), Learner-Learner (L-L), and continuum point (interaction, cooperation, collaboration, community). A time estimate for learners to complete the activity should also be included to make sure that there are not too many activities planned. The technology tools to be used can be indicated as well for implementation considerations, such as whether peer partners or groups need to be formed.

The overall purpose of the CDP is to determine whether there is a balance between the types of activities and the timeframe for those activities. If activities are too heavily weighted toward faculty-learner interactions, learners are more likely to remain dependent on the faculty member as the source of all knowledge. If the majority of activities is too learner-to-learner oriented, particularly in the early weeks of the course, learners might feel lost and perceive lack of faculty presence in the course. If the activities lean toward being predominantly learner-to-resource, learners may feel they are in an independent study course, and community will not developed.

It's also important to look at the continuum point of the interaction, so that learners are not dumped in the deep end of the pool prematurely. Requiring a community-level activity such as a group presentation in the first few weeks of the course nearly guarantees failure, unless, of course, the students are experienced online learners who have had an opportunity to form a community in some other venue or are part of an ongoing cohort of learners.

The estimated completion time must also be balanced from week to week; to achieve this, some activities may need to run across a longer time frame than usual. Most online courses have activities that run for one week. But, in some cases, it may be necessary for an activity to run longer in order to fully explore a particular topic.

How much interaction and community building is enough? That is limited by the time and objectives of the course. Activity should not be done for its own sake. We must never lose sight of the fact that the ultimate goal of the course is to help the learners achieve the planned performance objectives within the timeframe of the course.

Class Activities that Build Community

More than a decade ago, Johnson and Johnson (1993) found that cooperation among students would not occur unless the students were trained in cooperative strategies. Providing adequate training can be a challenge when a course is limited to one semester. However, the following suggestions for ways in which cooperation can be gradually developed in an online course can help overcome obstacles. With these activities, students can learn collaborative techniques while they learn course content.

• *Space for interaction.* Before any interaction can occur, the appropriate interaction spaces must be established on the course site. The basic spaces should include a faculty office, a student lounge or cybercafé, an academic discussion area, and perhaps a web-logging area for student reflections.

• *Initial communication guidelines.* It's important for learners to understand the basics of communication in the course. The minimum number of interactions required, as well as the definition of a quality contribution, should be provided by the instructor, with the understanding that learners can add to this.

• *Student introductions.* Begin with an introduction activity. This can be done through an online profile, via a conference posting, or in a more informal area such as a café or student lounge.

Provide examples of topics learners might like to mention in their introductions. Encourage them to post pictures or a representation of themselves or their location, to provide visual cues to their peers. These profiles can be used to get a sense of which community members might work well in a group together, based on their careers, learning interests, and time commitments.

Follow up with an email or survey concerning student experiences with technology, online learning, and collaboration. Individual email messages to students might be appropriate with some students to determine personality and work ethic. Appropriate grouping of compatible individuals will move the learners more quickly toward successful collaboration.

• *Pre-interaction activities.* Begin the content activities with tasks a learner can accomplish individually such as a nongraded introductory icebreaker discussion, online lectures, readings, and reflection assignments. These activities give students time to become familiar with the course site, get to know one another through the introductory exercise, and become familiar with the basics of the technology before adding the stress of coordinating activities with a peer or group. If students are not confident in the use of the technology, they will be slow to participate or may not use the tools at all. Provide a space on the course website where technology problems can be posted for peers to read and assist with resolution.

• *Interaction activities.* It is good to plan about two weeks for new learners to become comfortable with the online course environment. Once students are comfortable, introduce an activity that requires interaction between two peers, such as having each one review the other's reflections or allowing them to question each other on factual or core content. This can be done via email, chat rooms, or online discussion exchanges. Be sure to allow three to five days for this activity to occur in order to accommodate scheduling difficulties between the two learners.

• *Collaboration activities.* At this point, two or three dyads can be merged to form a recommended group size of four to six students (Harasim, et al., 1996). Balancing expertise within each group as much as possible is a worthwhile practice. Small group discussion is a good strategy for the groups to learn consensus building and begin forming interdependency by focusing on resolving a problem or dilemma.

Set netiquette standards, or manners, for the community and allow members to amend or appeal the rules as the community builds. See Harasim (1996) or an online site for helpful examples of netiquette rules. Keep after the lurkers who are not participating by assigning roles and responsibilities, such as summarizing a discussion. Call on them just as you would in class, by asking questions in the conference area addressed specifically to the lurker.

• *Cooperative activities.* Effective face-to face cooperative techniques such as a jigsaw also work in an online environment. Jigsaw is a cooperative activity in which each group member has a piece of the knowledge content needed to solve a puzzle. Other small group strategies include roundtable discussions, role plays, and team projects that result in the creation of strategies for complex real-life challenges.

In cooperative activities, assigning and rotating roles to team members throughout the semester is an effective strategy. Varying roles can assist learners in organizing themselves and developing self-direction.

- **Group manager** helps set group goals, tracks group progress, and manages group activities.
- **Facilitator** starts the discussion and keeps it going. This individual can also serve as the alternate summarizer.
- **Summarizer** brings the team to consensus and posts the summary in the discussion area.
- **Resource generators** search the web for resources to recommend to the other community members.
- **Resource generator coordinator** refines the list of resources to be recommended to the community.
- **Peer coaches** review the work of others, as needed. Each peer coach serves as a consultant and is responsible for asking questions and sharing ideas,

suggestions, and resources that might help the peer improve and complete work.

- **Peer coach coordinator** assigns work reviews to the various coaches as peers request them.
- **Negotiator** eases or resolves conflicts
- **Pacesetter** encourages the cooperation and participation of lurkers
- **Challenger** encourages critical thinking by introducing questions or engaging group members in a debate.

• *Online community activities.* Large group conferences and seminars are effective online community activities. Student teams can be responsible for researching topics, presenting ideas, and soliciting feedback and ideas from the other learners. Many of the book sites mentioned in Chapter 8 offer synchronous events with experts. One community activity could be to participate in one of these online events and integrate that experience and information into the conference. The student team presents and facilitates the conferences. Sufficient time needs to be provided for planning these types of conferences.

> Once a community is formed, it should be predominantly self-managed, meaning that community members take responsibility for initiating and coordinating activities.

The time that a faculty member spends managing the online interaction should decrease as the course progresses and learners become more experienced with collaborative and community activities. Once a community is formed, it should be predominantly self-managed, meaning that community members take responsibility for initiating and coordinating activities. The faculty member is then able to step into the background and allow the community to govern itself.

• *Ask well-constructed questions.* No matter what the phase of community development, asking the right question in the right way is central to promoting discussion. Brookfield (1999) lists several types of questions that are useful in any type of learning environment:

- Open-ended
- Hypothetical
- Cause and Effect
- Asking for more evidence
- Asking for clarification
- Linking or extending comments
- Summarizing and synthesizing

It is best to begin with questions that are either open ended, hypothetical, or related to cause and effect. Instructors and learners should follow up initial postings with questions asking for more evidence or clarification, if needed, or comments that link the posting to others' or extend the initial posting. Either learners or the instructor can close the discussion with a summary or synthesis question.

The opening question is the most critical. If it is too narrow, one learner will provide the definitive answer and the other learners will chime in with agreement. End of discussion. Brookfield offers several examples of strong opening questions:

- Numerous course design models have been developed over the past few decades. Why do you think so many have been developed? Why might more be needed?
- How might online courses differ from classroom-based courses if audio and video tools were more accessible to learners?
- How might a new design model impact the design of online courses?

Learners should be instructed to provide part of the answer they are thinking of and leave room for others to reply. In contrast to the classroom environment, instructors should not be looking for one learner to provide the answer, but rather for a community answer to be developed over a specific time frame. Of course, there may be specific instances where one correct answer is appropriate. In an online learning environment, specific questions are best asked in self-quizzes.

• *Provide opportunities for choices.* In some cases, learners may choose to ignore additional questions from the faculty or their peers during the course of a discussion. This can occur because students feel as if they have met the interaction requirement for a discussion and do not feel compelled to continue the discussion. In other cases, we have begun to see the phenomenon Collison, Elbaum, Haavind, and Tinker documented in 2000: *too much* interaction, which can cause some learners to be overwhelmed by the amount of information that must be processed to meet the minimum discussion requirements. It is better to require deeper discussion on fewer questions than to require responses on multiple questions. One solution to both lack of depth and too much discussion would be to post several questions and allow learners respond to two out of three, which they can continue discussing throughout the week.

Additional ideas for online activities are provided in *Engaging the Online Learner: Activities and Resources for Creative Instruction* (Conrad & Donaldson, 2004).

The following stories by online instructors illustrate the power of community and provide additional tips based on their experiences. The first story is from a faculty member teaching World Regional Geography in a fully online mode at Moraine Valley Community College (IL); it includes hints about the use of a journaling assignment. The second story is about developing community in an online course in college composition at Monroe Community College (NY).

Around the World in 80 Clicks: Teaching World Regional Geography Online

Contributed by Dawn Wrobel

When I am not in the classroom, I live on the internet. So, when Moraine Valley Community College offered me the opportunity to transfer World Regional Geography to the internet, I was ecstatic. When not in the geography classroom, I alternate between teaching web design and programming courses and running a small internet catalog, so this was a great way to combine my skills in both geography and information technology. I thought it would be an easy transition because the internet links students to such a wonderful array of geographic information: satellite imagery, dynamic population pyramids, online field trips, live webcams from around the world.

The World Regional Geography course covers physical and cultural content for 11 regions and almost 200 countries. It is a tough course for students in the classroom and has proven to be tough for online students as well. There is a tremendous amount of material to cover. The class I teach is entirely online, but I offer optional help sessions once a month on campus. Thirty-six of the 44 students in the online section at the end of the first week are still actively participating in the 11th week. The class includes six graduate students in education who need the course in order to complete their teaching credentials.

Now that I am nearing the end of my first semester facilitating a completely online course, I am more realistic about its demands. Even with years of internet experience, I was surprised at the technical limitations I encountered, both in Blackboard and with the internet in general. Questions that might take 30 seconds to answer in the classroom require many minutes to write a response. But my enthusiasm for the internet as a learning medium has not diminished.

The reason for such continued optimism is primarily the element of communication using asynchronous discussion boards. Over the first 11 weeks of the semester, 38 to 54 percent of the traffic to the Blackboard site has been in the communication areas. The discussion boards are being used for three distinct purposes: communication between students and instructor, guest speakers, and discussion of geography journal submissions.

The Blackboard site for the course contains three discussion areas. The first is a question-and-answer board on which students can discuss assignments with each other and review for exams. I monitor this board but do not post to it. The one criterion I instituted was that students could not post complete answers; hints, however, are fine. Students have also used this area to recommend supplemental material. One student posted thorough summaries of each help session for her classmates who did not attend, so the board is used on a regular and continuing basis by many students.

The second communication board is for questions to the instructor. This forum is for any question that might be useful to other students in the class, as long as it does not concern a grade for a specific student. Approximately 30 percent of the students post to this board on a regular basis.

The third communication board is called Breaking News. We use this area for current news topics applicable to the course. The topics tend to fall heavily in the natural-disaster category, but the discussions offer an opportunity to ask students to think about how the magnitude of each disaster is influenced by human activity and policies.

The most popular use of discussion boards is for hosting guest speakers. The kickoff guest was a Moraine Valley staff member who had grown up in Argentina. Guests are available to respond to student questions for a three-day period. Questions are open ended. Initially, the students were tentative, but their questions steadily improved. They asked questions about climate, tourism, the educational system, politics, diet, immigration, women's issues, and family life.

Additional guest speakers included a young woman who described herself as a "Russian army brat," living in places not on many maps; an American living in Indonesia; and a local resident who served in the navy in Vietnam, and who is now actively involved in missionary work in that country.

I offer participation in the discussion with the guest speakers as an elective assignment. My purpose in providing guest speakers is to offer students a glimpse into what life is like in other parts of the world. More than half the students actively participate in the discussion boards; others choose to read the material but not post. I've received enough positive comments from students to know that the guest speakers are one of the two most popular aspects of the course.

The third use of discussion boards, and the second most popular aspect of the regional geography course, is for posting submissions for geography journals. I require geography students in all my courses to complete journals. In the classroom, students read and analyze two articles per week for inclusion in their journals. I review the journals on a regular basis and occasionally share articles with the class. In preparation for translating the journal into an online assignment, I tapped into the expertise in Moraine Valley's Library/Learning Resource Center and worked with a librarian to adapt the journal assignment. Online students are required to post a summary of one article for each of the 11 regions covered, plus one article on globalization. The student must include a citation for the article, a summary or abstract, the reason the student chose the article, and the branch of geography the article covers. The student then poses a question about the topic to fellow students. Students are required to respond to at least two posted topics for each region. In addition, the articles have to be chosen from a mix of sources: academic journals, professional journals, popular magazines, newspapers, news magazines, and websites.

The library provided students with worksheets on determining the credibility of a source. I adapted two additional documents, one to assist students in selecting sources and the other, a checklist to make sure that students followed the guidelines. The library also participated in the mandatory orientation for the course, providing students with a training session on how to use the online databases most appropriate to the journal assignment.

I'm very pleased with the outcome of the journal assignment. Students have found that the opportunity to share information is actually much greater than they have in the classroom. A separate board is set up for each of the regions; I monitor the boards, but only occasionally participate or redirect a discussion. Sometimes the discussions wander from pure geography, but they do give students a chance to compare life experiences, to share, and to learn from each other.

One education major decided to research quilts after attending a program on the connection between quilts and slavery. Along with an article summarizing quilting, she posted ideas on how she planned to use this material in her classroom, which benefited other education majors in the class. In the traditional classroom, there would not have been time for the in-depth discussion of the topic that occurred online.

Another student posted an excellent article on the disappearing coral reefs in the Caribbean. The initial post was strong, but the discussion rapidly took a nongeographic turn and continued for weeks, eliciting posts about students swimming with dolphins, rays, or barracudas at a variety of locations. A post on Mexico yielded a discussion of vacation destinations and bargains. These were not on topic, but they generated a great deal of discussion from a large group of students. Again, while we might have discussed the coral reefs in a classroom setting, the students would not have had an opportunity to share their vacation stories with each other. The result: The class became an online *community*.

A number of my students have suggested increasing the journal assignment to two per region and dropping some of the other required assignments in favor of additional discussions. I'm amazed because the journal assignments, done well, are more time consuming than many of the other assignments. When was the last time you had students ask for *more* work? Now, if someone can just help *me* learn how to translate the rest of the course into discussion boards, I'm all ears!

Stories From the Field

Fostering Community in Online College Composition

Contributed by Jay Keith

Monroe Community College (MCC) in Rochester, New York is a leader in online education, offering over 90 online courses per semester. To many in the MCC community, online courses have become so much a part of the college's academic landscape that it's hard to remember a time when there were no online classes. However, there is a long history of online learning at MCC, and that history begins with Cathryn Smith.

Professor Smith taught the very first online course, College Composition, at MCC in 1997, before the widespread availability of course management systems such as Blackboard, WebCT, and the SUNY Learning Network (SLN). Inspired by an online graduate seminar at the New School for Social Research in 1996, Smith taught herself HTML, then painstakingly revamped and posted her course as an extension of her faculty website. Her class was an experiment, to say the least, and she regarded her first 15 online students as fellow experimenters. Together, they explored the powers and limitations of online learning. Smith has been teaching College Composition, as well as other English department online courses, ever since.

Smith was initially inspired to teach online because she was interested in the effect the web would have on the way students were willing to communicate, both among themselves and with their professors, especially through their writing assignments. Like many English professors, Smith noticed that students are often more candid in print than they are in person, and wondered if the guise of anonymity offered by the web would free students from their inhibitions and help them grow as both writers and critical thinkers.

Moreover, once Smith delved into the work of writing the content for her online class, she found that this process helped her become a more organized and more consistent educator in every delivery mode. She noticed that planning an online course demands that the instructor have a very good view of the whole picture from the outset. While Smith, a poet, always prided herself on her creativity, she sometimes struggled to align her inspirations along a single thematic thread. For her, online courses helped her to focus her creative energies in ways that reinforced consistent messages for students. In short, according to Smith, online learning stresses above all consistency, clarity, and repetition. These three elements gave her the grounding that she needed to become a whole-picture educator.

After more than seven years of online teaching experience, Smith is neither a zealous advocate for online education nor a zealous opponent of it. Instead, she regards online learning in much the same way as many in the MCC community do, as a learning tool. Although she continues to be at the forefront of online learning at MCC, she also recognizes a need to reflect on and reassess the value of online experience, particularly in the following two areas.

Students: Who is your audience, and why are they there?

When Smith began teaching College Composition online, her students were enthusiastic, innovative, adventurous, intellectually savvy, and independent. They wanted to experiment with the asynchronous delivery mode for many of the same reasons she did: Her classes shared an enthusiasm for the possibilities the new media had for writing, creativity, and written communication. Recently, however, Smith has noticed that her audience is changing. She finds more and more students sign up for online courses under the flag of convenience, believing that an online class might somehow be easier or less work than a traditional class.

Smith also finds increasing numbers of adult learners in her online classes. While adult learners often make great online students because of their abilities to learn independently and manage their time effectively, she has found that online courses are most suitable for adult students who have already established themselves in their academic communities. Older students who have just returned to school may not be served as effectively by online courses because they often lack confidence in themselves, their teachers, and their abilities, which develop when connected to a community of learners.

Overall, Smith is convinced that online learning can be of great value to students who are ready to capitalize on its strengths. Independent learners and self-motivated, disciplined students will excel, while students who lack self-assurance may feel isolated or lost.

Fostering community: Can there be an us in cyberspace?

According to Smith, the humanities offer a challenge peculiar to online education, because effectively teaching the humanities requires shaping and maintaining relationships with students through ongoing dialogue. Producing such dialogues online can seem a daunting and almost impossible task. To foster a sense of community in her online classes, Smith has developed the following techniques:

- Log on every day, even if you don't do any work. One of the beneficial illusions fostered by web-based teaching is that the teacher is always online. The sense that the teacher could at any moment be present can serve to make students feel more tightly connected to the class. Posting short announcements and answering questions every day helps to foster a sense that you are paying careful attention to your students.
- Use private folders frequently. Private folders (one-on-one conversation between teacher and student) are the most important way to prevent students from getting lost in cyberspace. Smith feels that many online instructors underuse private folders and instead attempt to cultivate community only through postings to larger groups. Although group discussions are important, the teacher can't possibly respond to everyone in the discussion. By contrast, private folders provide the most direct link between teacher and individual student; they are often students' primary connection to the class, and their most important indicator that their teacher is indeed paying attention to their progress.
- Put students in small groups. Group discussions and assignments are often much more effective when they are run with smaller numbers. Groups of five or six students can have more meaningful discussions online because there is a more manageable amount of material to respond to. Moreover, small groups tend to encourage in students the sense that they are part of something tangible and intimate rather than something faceless and anonymous.
- Use technology to create visually exciting feedback. When Smith uses rubrics to grade essays for her online College Composition course, she frequently uses the technology at her disposal to make the feedback she is giving her students visually exciting. Students often find the look and feel of her comments motivating even when the message she sends them is, "There's a lot more that you need to do here."

In the future, Cathryn Smith hopes to continue to be a pioneer in online education. She is particularly excited about hybrid courses, because she sees in them the possibility to give students the anchor that a face-to-face class provides, while at the same time promoting increased access and greater opportunities for independent learning.

Smith would also like to see more online collaboration across both department and college lines. At MCC, faculty members from different disciplines often collaborate in the traditional classroom. What might the online environment add to interdisciplinary learning? Similarly, Smith feels that the potential for online learning to cross institutional boundaries has only just begun to be tapped. The nature of the web, after all, makes it possible for faculty at two or more institutions to co-teach a class.

For Smith, online education continues to be exciting to the extent that we can use its strengths to bring out the best in our students. Moreover, we will continue to be successful as online educators only to the extent that we are willing to critically assess this evolving learning tool.

How Does Building an Online Community Work in a Hybrid or Blended Course?

Using the online environment to build community is beneficial even when learners have an opportunity to meet in person. The online environment *can* extend discussions initiated in the classroom, and additional discussions can be conducted online to extend and expand related knowledge exchanges. An online faculty office can provide additional access to an instructor. An online resource repository can enhance the knowledge generation of a course. Online lectures can provide an opportunity for instructors and learners to focus on active knowledge exchange in the classroom as opposed to passive lecture listening.

One caveat: The online environment should not be used for activities that are better done synchronously, such as brainstorming and consensus building. Requiring these activities to take place online when a face-to-face option is available will only frustrate the learning community.

The Bottom Line

An online community is not something that simply happens. It must be developed and nurtured through diligent planning by the faculty. It also requires the commitment of the class community to make it work. However, the outcomes are well worth the effort. Similarly, effective collaboration and cooperative learning activities also must be developed and planned. These types of activities nurture student learning and are useful tools in creating effective online teaching and learning environments. Collaborative activities may also be among the best ways to help manage the time commitment of faculty for online courses.

Above all, it is crucial to remember that community building is a balancing act. Activities must not consume so much learner and faculty time that the course becomes a burden rather than a learning adventure. There are still time boundaries in online learning. Online courses are no longer bound by the *when* of time, but they are still limited by the *how much* of time.

While research on the topic of community building techniques and tools has grown, more is needed to help make significant differences in future learning environments.

Table 7.2 Community Development Plan

Week or Unit	Topic or Learning	Activity Description	Continuum Level of Activity	Estimated Completion Time	Media Tool Selected	Implementation Considerations
1	Introduction of Subject	Icebreaker	Interaction	2 hours	Discussion area of CMS	Course familiarity with CMS
2	Determine objectives for a unit of instruction	Peer partner discussion and critique of individually developed unit objectives	Cooperation	1 hour	Email	Textbook received

* Continuum Level = Interaction, Cooperation, Collaboration, Community

Chapter 8
Tools and Resources for Creating Online Courses

Tools and resources to support faculty and students with the tasks of teaching and learning in the online environment have grown almost exponentially with the growth of internet and web applications. This chapter provides an overview of the evolution of course management systems (CMS) to an integrated part of the teaching and learning environment, followed by a look at some of the newer categories of tools and applications that faculty and students are using. These newer categories also provide a glimpse of how the online environment is changing the roles of teachers and students.

Early Development of Course Management Systems

The development of course management systems and tools was a real boon to faculty and staff. Just as word processing applications made it easy for everyone to write and edit papers, course management systems made it easy for all faculty members to have a course website. In fact, some campuses generated websites for all the courses being offered during a semester. In cases where faculty didn't know how or didn't want to use their course site, the students often used the class communication tools.

Many of us remember the early efforts of faculty and staff who used HTML editors and web tools such as Adobe's PageMill, Claris HomePage, Microsoft FrontPage, and Asymetrix ToolBook. Even earlier, the really committed faculty innovators spent hours learning and using animation and presentation tools such as Apple's HyperCard and Macromedia Director. Almost before we knew it, Word and PowerPoint within the Microsoft Office Suite offered the option of saving text and slides as HTML, in spite of significant problems. The faculty who were putting courses or materials on the internet in the early years (1994-1997) did so by using a combination of these tools plus email lists, bulletin boards, and other homegrown tools. Over time, fewer technical skills were needed to use these individual tools, but putting all of them together into an integrated online course – along with finding suitable digital content – often took more time and energy than most faculty could muster.

Teaching faculty development workshops at Penn State, we encouraged faculty to start with just one or two tools, to ignore all the other hype and possibilities, and yes, to ignore their well-meaning early-adopter and innovator faculty colleagues, if necessary. Focusing on one new tool or one new competency can be very calming and rewarding, because one can move forward without feeling panicked or stressed, and then feel good about developing a new competency – proving once again that learning is its own motivator. This strategy continues to be a good one!

The wonder of the new generation of CMS tools is that they enable faculty to learn just one competency and reap the benefit of a comprehensive set of capabilities. These systems now provide the full range of basic administration tools: syllabus and class information; course design tools; collaboration tools; content resource sections; and tracking, grading, assessment, and management features. Newer generations of tools are beginning to reflect a sophistication of thinking about teaching, teaching philosophies, and an expanded set of choices in teaching and learning strategies.

What is a Course Management System?

A course management system is application software that makes it easy for faculty to manage a course online and for faculty and students to communicate and share knowledge and experiences in the online environment. Another definition from the Educause Evolving Technologies Committee is that a course management system is a software tool that provides an instructor "with a set of tools and a framework that allows for the relatively easy creation of online course content and the subsequent teaching and management of that course, including various interactions with the students" (Meerts, 2003).

Who Should Use These Tools?

Use of course management templates or systems is now recommended to all faculty, whether or not they are teaching in an online environment. These tools are now the de facto standard for the communication and management of most campus and online courses. They also support the full range of courses, whether the courses are web-enhanced, webcentric or hybrid, or fully online courses. CMS and related tools are now as important to faculty as word processing tools, spreadsheets, and email applications. If a website for a particular course does not exist, students often ask for one.

Any of the systems now available can help faculty and support staff with the design, development, and delivery of online offerings. CMS tools are now flexible and sophisticated and can be used by technologically novice or experienced faculty. They provide built-in guidance in the design and development of effective instruction and support the use of all three dialogues:

faculty-to-student, student-to-student, and student-to-resources. Support of these three types of basic interactions is essential to designing a course with a balanced set of instructional strategies.

In Chapter 6, we looked at the types of skills and functions important in building a quality online course. Many of these skills, as embodied in people, are expensive and scarce. Course management tools now provide rich teaching and learning environments that have been designed and constructed by professional application developers drawing on input from faculty and higher education staff. These systems now have the capability of guiding faculty through the planning of an online course by providing a wide choice of application modules that support the range of teaching and learning activities in a course. The power of the CMS is that the capabilities are built in as part of the environment; faculty can choose whether or not to use them.

> **Course management tools now provide rich teaching and learning environments that have been designed and constructed by professional application developers drawing on input from faculty and higher education staff.**

We don't want to oversell these, as they are still just tools, but they are instruments that we did not have at our disposal in the first years of experimentation in online teaching and learning. They remain far from perfect – and we recognize that perfection is elusive and ever-changing – but many of these tools are quite good. The early versions often were not sophisticated enough for some of the faculty innovators; there is always a trade-off between simplicity and flexibility. However, most are now well structured, with excellent interfaces that make them easy to use for faculty and students alike.

A 2003 report (Morgan) from the Educause Center for Applied Research surveyed more than 700 faculty and instructional staff from institutions in the University of Wisconsin system. Faculty reported finding course management systems useful for helping in "the more mundane tasks of teaching." They used the systems "to help communicate easily with students, to give students access to class documents, and for the convenience and transparency of the online gradeBook" (p. 2).

Since these tools incorporate much of the design and development work that normally accompanies the preparation of online courses, they can speed processes of course design and development and significantly lower barriers to offering online courses or enhancing campus classes. In the same Educause survey, it was noted that 80 percent of faculty surveyed used the CMS in their regular classrooms; 27 percent used the CMS to teach fully online. This may or may not reflect how many fully online courses are being offered. Faculty also reported using a CMS to enhance distance education courses primarily taught using other media such as compressed video, and for other hybrid classes (p. 4).

The Waves of Course Management Systems

We are now in the third or perhaps fourth wave of course management systems. Our use of these systems followed the three-phase pattern of technology innovation and dissemination. In the first wave, we used the technology to do what we always were doing, such as using a simple course template application to (1) organize the elements of a course; (2) communicate with and among students; (3) transmit basic information about courses, requirements, and resources; and (4) tracking, grade, and assess student learning. The landscape of the early course management systems included systems reviewed in the first edition of this book: Convene, Course Info (now Blackboard), eCollege, First Class, Learning Space by Lotus, and WebCT. Nearly all of the early course management templates and systems have evolved and are now much larger and more complex.

The second wave of CMS focused on using the technology to make our old processes more efficient. This wave saw the rise of the now-common hybrid or web-enhanced campus courses in which the best uses of the web space were integrated with the best of the classroom. The third wave of CMS provided integrated systems that supported efficiency in administration and delivery at the infrastructure and enterprise level. These systems, representing the cusp of a fourth wave, are complex and usually expensive, requiring ongoing support, upgrade, and maintenance for integration with other campus systems. At the same time, they provide features and capabilities that support a totally online campus.

The enterprise systems of the third wave are now being widely deployed, and the number and types can be overwhelming. Selection of a campus CMS is now often organized and directed by a campus IT group advised by an IT committee and involves input from large groups of faculty and staff. The evolution of the systems is easily seen in the names: Angel 6.0, BlackBoard 6, FirstClass 7.0, Jones e-education v2003, WebCT 4.1 Campus Edition, and WebCT Vista 2.1. Many colleges and universities have generated an evaluation form to streamline the review process. When your campus is ready to make a campuswide decision, this is a good model to follow. Other resources to assist in the selection of a course management system are listed later in this chapter.

The fourth wave of CMS includes design standards from the Open Knowledge Initiative (OKI, web.mit.edu/oki/) and spinoff open-source systems such as Stellar (stellar.mit.edu) from MIT, CHEF (chefproject.org/index.htm) from the University of Michigan, and CourseWork (aboutcoursework.stanford.edu) from Stanford University. Much of the research and development for this new wave of open-source systems is supported by the Andrew W. Mellon Foundation, and the commercially supported systems are all using or planning an architecture and design based on industry standards. The evolving learning-industry standards include the specifications for interoperability learning technology from the IMS Global Learning Consortium (www.imsproject.org) and the Sharable Content Object Reference Model (SCORM) standards distributed by the Advanced Distributed Learning Initiative (www.adlnet.org), plus the Application Programming Interfaces (APIs) being specified through the OKI project. The Advanced Distributed Learning (ADL) Initiative is a collaborative effort between government, industry, and academia and sponsored by the Office of the Secretary of Defense.

The fourth wave evidences a focus on content and learning objects, responding to the need for good digital content and teaching strategies in addition to the management and administration of teaching and learning. Some of the high-profile initiatives include MERLOT, the Multimedia Educational Resource for Learning and Online Teaching (www.merlot.org), the Open Courseware project at MIT (ocw.mit.edu), and the work on learning objects at the University of Cambridge. MERLOT is a "free and open resource designed primarily for faculty and students of higher education. Links to online learning materials are collected along with annotations such as peer reviews and assignments." MIT's OpenCourseWare project is a "free and open educational resource" for faculty, students, and self-learners around the world.

These waves of development are happening rapidly and represent a set of developments, rather than a single technology capability. Innovators in charge of early e-learning initiatives had to worry a great deal about who had access to equipment and how much was available for teaching and learning experiences. While the digital divide still needs to be considered, access to the internet and to computer applications is in most of our students' hands now.

> **These waves of development are happening rapidly and represent a set of developments, rather than a single technology capability.**

The following observation by Economics Nobel prize-winning computer scientist Herbert Simon sums up how our society – and our teaching and learning environments – are evolving and changing before our very eyes: "The point is that when technology reshapes society, it is not the result of a single invention but of a host of additional, completely unanticipated inventions, many of them of the same order of magnitude as the first one in the chain (Simon, 2001 p. 30).

As for the role of the CMS in our new digital learning environments: One of our visionary instructional-technology pioneers, the University of Michigan's Carl Berger, expects the next killer application to be "a ubiquitous system for students, faculty, and support to carry out learning, instruction, and research" (Berger, 2003).

Course Management Systems — Getting Started and Finding the Tool for You

After taking a new look at these tools, many experienced faculty have chosen to use them to prepare new online courses and to renovate their existing courses. The best advice for faculty just starting to use the online environment is to pick an application and go with it, and don't look back for at least 12 to 18 months. Keep your course simple for the first offering. Creativity and an individual style for teaching and learning online will gradually develop.

It is also helpful to use the tool provided by the infrastructure support group at your institution. Another system might be a little better for your particular needs and ways of teaching and learning, but established support in the infrastructure for you and your students usually outweighs potential advantage from any other benefits. Often, if a specific feature is missing, the next version of the software may provide it.

Basic Features and Functions of Course Management Systems

Almost all course management systems, also called learning management systems, are really management systems, primarily designed to address the third D of the bundled design, development, and delivery course strategy. At their best, these systems provide support for faculty in the administration, testing, tracking, and communications functions of course delivery and also support the three dialogue and interaction models for students, faculty, and content resources. Ideally, the tools provide support for faculty at all stages of technology expertise, from novice to more experienced, sophisticated, and innovative users, and will evolve over time to help transform and support the new teaching and learning environment. An effective system is easy to support, requires minimal administrative and technical resources, and is available at reasonable cost. The best tools are integrated, linking and talking to the back-office operations of the college, including portal integration.

The EduTools site (www.edutools.info/index.jsp) describes course management systems according to more than 40 different features and functions. Features are organized around the three main categories of Learner Tools (16 features), Support Tools (16), and Technical Specifications (10). Each of these three categories is subdivided into groups as well. For example, the set of Learner Tools is organized into Communication Tools (7 features), Productivity Tools (5) and Student Involvement tools (4). The full set of features described for each course management system is listed on pages 145 and 146.

COURSE MANAGEMENT SYSTEM FEATURES
Category One - Learner Tools

Communication Tools
- Communication Tools
- Discussion Forums
- File Exchange
- Internal Email
- Online Journal/Notes
- Real-time Chat
- Video Services
- Whiteboard

Productivity Tools
- Bookmarks
- Calendar/Progress Review
- Orientation/Help
- Searching Within Course
- Work Offline/Synchronize

Student Involvement Tools
- Group Work
- Self-assessment
- Student Community Building
- Student Portfolios

Note: The communication and collaboration tools, such as email, file sharing, bulletin board, and asynchronous and synchronous discussion tools help faculty and students collaborate and communicate with each other and with experts and resources not on campus. Remember the rule of keeping it simple; choose and become familiar with one or two collaboration tools for the first course, and then as you and students develop expertise and new habits of teaching and learning, gradually add other tools as appropriate. Just because the tools are there doesn't mean you have to use them.

Category Two - Support Tools

Administration Tools
- Administration Tools
- Authentication
- Course Authorization
- Hosted Services
- Registration Integration

Course Delivery Tools
- Automated Testing and Scoring
- Course Management
- Instructor Help Desk
- Online Grading Tools
- Student Tracking

Curriculum Design
- Accessibility Compliance
- Content Sharing/Reuse
- Course Templates
- Curriculum Management
- Customized Look and Feel
- Instructional Design Tools
- Instructional Standards Compliance

Note: Features such as student assessment tools, timed quizzes, grading, and tracking should help reduce the amount of time faculty spend assessing and tracking student progress. Because of difficulties in assuring security on quizzes and exams, many faculty members design student quizzes as competency-based or use online quizzes simply as practice tests, graded for completion rather than for comparison with other students.

COURSE MANAGEMENT SYSTEM FEATURES
Category Three - Technical Specifications

Hardware/Software

- Client Browser Required
- Database Requirements
- Server Software
- Unix Server
- Windows Server

Pricing/Licensing

- Company Profile
- Costs
- Open Source
- Optional Extras
- Software Version

Note: Administrative features such as security, integration with administrative systems, and technical support features must be carefully considered as they help to achieve efficiency in delivery. These features provide assistance in using the tools, answering the inevitable questions that arise, and addressing the unpredictable responses that can happen when dealing with complex and interdependent systems. Some features that protect the course site can make getting copyright permission easier and increase the likelihood that the principle of fair use can be applied to some of the content. Other administrative and support issues to be considered in the choice of course management systems include compliance with industry standards, upgrade policies, training, and support.

Finding and Using the Right Course Management System

Choosing a management and administrative system while balancing the need for flexibility in instructional philosophies and teaching strategies is a task that can bring a campus community together to discuss what is important in teaching and learning to their college. This section provides some websites that can serve as starting points for assisting with the selection process. Additionally, friends and colleagues, particularly those who may have recently chosen a system, are excellent sources of information. They may be willing to share their decision-making processes and tools, including their request for proposal (RFP), if they had one.

Some well-known course management systems are used by hundreds of colleges. While change happens very quickly with these systems, many of them have evolved from templates originally designed on higher education campuses. The number of tools and systems has been increasing rapidly, despite a good deal of merger activity during the second wave. A good rule of thumb with technology is always to do a current search for applications and tools, since features and products change with each release of software and even within releases. Even the category name for many of our teaching and learning tools is still in flux. Some reviews call these products LMS for learning management systems; others call them WBI, for web-based instruction; still others refer to them as course management systems (CMS), as we have called them here.

Because your college will be investigating current evaluations, we include a beginning list of resources. The many articles and resources available that describe and compare CMS tools are most helpful in the decision-making process. Once the decision has been made, these resources are still useful to answer the question, "Can our current system do *X*? Many times these descriptions can give faculty more ideas about how they or their students might use the systems.

The Future of Course Management Systems

Course management systems are likely to evolve in three dimensions, mapping to the design, development, and delivery components of teaching and learning. The evolution of the delivery component, which is furthest along, may evolve such that it is hardly recognizable to the learner as a separate application.

Lois Brooks, one of the members of the CourseWork team at Stanford, theorized at the 2003 *Seminars on Academic Computing* (SAC) conference that the future of CMS systems may be full integration with the portal technologies that institutions are developing. In this scenario, the CMS becomes simply another channel on the portal.

The current open-source wave is in one sense research and development for how to identify and integrate effective teaching practices based on the science of learning. Integrating tools to support research-based activities and making them easy-to-use elements of the environment will support effective and efficient learning. The development D, which includes the implementation of instructional events and their associated content resources, will be supported by standard-developing initiatives such as IMS and OKI mentioned earlier, as well as content initiatives that are gathering, digitizing, and producing well-structured learning objects, content resources, and more complex discipline resources.

There are working groups within the many higher education organizations that interact with and provide feedback to the CMS vendors. The National Learning Infrastructure (www.nlii.org and www.educause.edu) has working groups focused on CMS. These are good structures within which to work to provide feedback on what we might want the future CMS to offer. Some of the features already on a wish list were discussed in an article on next-generation course management systems (Carmean and Haefner, 2003). The list of desired features included

- Ability to share materials and modules across course containers (CMS);
- Ability to export CMS materials to standard formats;
- Greater speed in loading of web pages;
- Tying student work directly to the assignments in the gradeBook;
- Improvement of assessment tools; and
- Expanded tools for collaborative teaching.

Resources for Comparing Course Management Systems

EduTools
www.edutools.info/index.jsp

One of the most comprehensive of current resources, this site provides independently reviewed analyses of selected course management software, including product comparisons, reviews, and automated decision-making tools. Reviews are available for 64 course management systems, including both commercial and open-source systems. Each product is analyzed according to 40 product features. The site also provides a review of student services products and a repository of eLearning policies.

EdTechPost
www.edtechpost.ca/mt/

This site provides a listing and links to course management systems distributed under open-source licensing arrangements. The listing has over 45 worldwide systems, including 21 based in the U.S.

EDUCAUSE
www.educause.edu

Be sure to investigate the Information Resources Library at this site and its related research initiatives program, ECAR, on frameworks for examining course management systems. Some of these resources are fee based; others are publicly available.

Syllabus
www.syllabus.com

Check for the newsletter on system-related issues and for articles in *Syllabus* magazine. The July 2003 issue focused on course management systems and included an interview with Carl Berger, discussing the development of the open-source system, CHEF (www.syllabus.com/article.asp?id=5938). We also recommend the CREN *TechTalk* archives on the syllabus site, for an interview with Stanford's Charles Kerns on systems and learning tools, "Where Are We at the End of 2002?"
(www.syllabus.com/techtalks/events/021107coursemgmt.asp).

While all resources on course management systems do become outdated, these resources are still good places to start.

Remembering that we shape our tools as much as our tools shape our teaching and learning behaviors and experiences reinforces the importance of members of our community to contribute ideas about what we want in the next generation of CMS. We hope that a future CMS will be able to easily identify and assess a student's zone of proximal development, and then potentially link our students to a holodeck offering instructional events that combine a student's current knowledge with emerging internal and external knowledge.

Content Resources and Learning Objects

While we are waiting for the next generations of course management systems and tools, here are a few resources on content and learning objects in addition to content initiatives such as Merlot and the MIT Open Courseware initiative. Content resources – including publisher textbooks, digital libraries, and content initiatives – support the development component of teaching and learning.

It is not easy to talk about content resources at this time, as we are in a transformational stage of our content technologies. Content resources, however, can be categorized according to a number of dimensions. The most important of the dimensions include the following four continuums:

- *Fee to free continuum.* Fee-based services include the content resources available from publishers of textbooks, journals, magazines, newspapers, and online libraries. The fees can be either purchasing or subscription licensing arrangements. Free content resources include the many resources available on the internet, which can range from the comprehensive MIT Open Courseware initiative, to daily news from well-known magazine and print publishers, to local and academic libraries and government and nonprofit organizational resources. This continuum includes content resources that provide a combination of free access, subscription to selected archives, and per-article fees.
- *Comprehensive resources to learning objects continuum.* Comprehensive resources can be course- and curriculum-level resources, textbooks, discipline websites, databases, and simulations, while learning objects can be instructional event descriptions, single animations, problem sets, or lab experiments. *Note*: The definition of a learning object is in flux. This is one of many areas to watch.
- *Well-structured to ill-structured continuum.* Structure is a characteristic of the content resource that makes content user friendly, attractive, and easy to navigate, use, and understand. Well-structured content supports the learning and understanding of concepts, ideas, and knowledge without undue pain and suffering. Much content is freely available, but its usefulness for teaching and learning may be very limited.

- *Format accessibility and flexibility continuum.* The continuum includes traditional physical formats such as magazines and books and embraces all the evolving digital combination formats using personal computers, PDAs, CD players, and so forth.

Other Tools and Resources

The next sections of this chapter provide a quick overview of other resources and tools that faculty teaching online find useful. The specific tools and websites mentioned here are examples of the types of tools and resources that may be available. Online tools and resources are subject to the speeding up of technologies and tools that we discussed in the first chapter. What doesn't change as quickly are the guidelines, principles, and hints about when and for what reasons the tools and resources will be helpful for teaching and learning. The following sections will focus on the hints and guidelines and provide the names and websites of tools and resources as starting points.

Content Resource and Learning Objects Websites

Some of these sites are really lists of lists, so once started on an exploration, it is easy to get distracted. But prepare to be amazed at the resources that are out there. The ready availability of all this content reinforces the need for structure, selection, and focus.

- World Lecture Hall (www.utexas.edu/world/lecture/). The World Lecture Hall at the University of Texas publishes links to pages created by faculty worldwide who are using the web to deliver course materials in any language. Over 80 discipline and content areas are listed here, containing links to content from universities around the globe. A click on the neuroscience discipline, for example, leads quickly to a sheep brain dissection guide from the University of Scranton and an extensive neuroscience web ring, and to a course website on "Computing for Neurobiology" from Cornell University.
- Technology Enhanced Learning Research Center at the University of Ohio (telr-research.osu.edu/learning_objects/). This Ohio University center is exploring and researching the definition, structure, and use of learning objects (Acker, 2003). This center is funded with grants from the Ohio Board of Regents, The Ohio Learning Network, and the U.S. Department of Education. Publications such as *Learning Objects: Contexts and Connections* and related white papers are freely available.
- The Office of Instructional Technology Site for the Minnesota State College and University System (www.oit.mnscu.edu/pages/learningobjects.htm). This site provides resources for those using and supporting technology in

teaching and learning. It includes links on conferences and online technology training.

- Wisc-Online Resource Center (www.wisc-online.com/index.htm). Here is a searchable database for hundreds of reusable learning objects and resources.
- University of Wisconsin System Institute for Global Studies Learning Object Database (www.uw-igs.org/search/index.asp?viewall=1). A resource called GEODE focuses on multimedia instructional resources with a global focus.
- Electronic Text Center at the University of Virginia (www.etext.lib.virginia.edu/). This site contains 70,000 online and offline texts in 13 languages.
- University of Texas at San Antonio (elearning.utsa.edu/guides/LO-repositories.htm). This is one of the more comprehensive learning-object repositories.
- Listing of Selected Digital Libraries (www.syllabus.com/article.asp?id=8578). This article lists 21 digital library sites, most of which are publicly available. Here are the sites that might be of most interest to faculty and students.
- Online Book Page (onlineBooks.library.upenn.edu/). This site links to thousands of online books, wherever they may be housed.
- Highwire (www.highwire.stanford.edu/). The site contains 618,000 free articles from 344 science journals.
- Humanities Text Initiative (www.hti.umich.edu/). This is a diverse collection that includes religious and secular texts, Lincoln's speeches, and medieval poetry.
- Internet Classics Library (www.classics.mit.edu/index.html). Sponsored by MIT, the site houses over 400 works by more than 50 classic authors.
- JSTOR (www.jstor.org/). This is a source for archived scholarly journal articles.
- Perseus Project (www.perseus.tufts.edu/). Humanities texts from the ancient and modern world are featured here.
- Project Gutenberg (www.gutenberg.net). This site provides 10,000 public-domain light and heavy literary and reference works, and is now branching out into music, audio, and video.
- Visible Human Project (www.nlm.nih.gov/research/visible/visible_human.html). Here you can find complete, anatomically detailed, 3-D representations of the human body.

An article in *The Chronicle of Higher Education* in May 2001 provided a list of electronic library companies, textbook publishers, and other textbook tools. The library companies mentioned included Jones E-Global Library, Questia, NetLibrary, and XanEdu.com.

It is impossible to predict which of these sites and services will be available in five to seven years, but the movement to e-libraries is certain to continue and accelerate. Even Amazon.com's recent opening of its archives in a searchable database opens the potential to "make connections hitherto unseen" and providing a "new kind of map" of our knowledge (Wolf, 2003).

The Part Played by Publishers

Combined with course management systems and the wealth of content resources available online, publisher resources and sites can be major elements in a workable strategy for moving teaching and learning online. A brief discussion on audio and video tools follows. Lastly, we take a look at a popular question relating to the problem of plagiarism and some techniques that faculty find useful in dealing with this issue.

Textbook Publishers, eBooks, and the Online Environment

Strategic planning has not been easy for textbook publishers recently. It is clear that students are buying, reading, and carrying fewer and fewer physical books. But it is also clear that the infrastructure to support digital content resources is still developing and evolving. The cost of publishing comprehensive textbooks keeps increasing, and faculty often think twice about the adoption of large, expensive textbooks. With the internet as a readily accessible resource, some faculty have chosen not to adopt textbooks at all for certain courses, choosing instead to assemble a set of course resources from other print, video, and digital materials, combining strategies such as custom publishing, selecting smaller books, preparing coursepacks, and assembling lists of online resources.

In the first edition of this book we listed a few major higher education textbook publishers who had launched new digital initiatives, building interactive animations and simulations packaged on CDs as well as launching companion websites for their most popular textbooks. Publishers have continued down these paths, making more and more of their content available in digital form.

Publishers' Content Resources and Tools Overview

As the publishing industry expands from print formats into digital multimedia formats, new content and pricing models are emerging. These new formats bring unparalleled flexibility and richness, offering access to dynamic, current, and relevant content and to well-known national and global experts.

The new electronic content formats are known by a variety of names. McGraw-Hill Higher Education has resources that it calls booksites, powerwebs, online learning centers, and case studies. Houghton-Mifflin has websites and a Smarthinking live online tutoring service; Prentice Hall, Addison Wesley, and Benjamin Cummings of the Pearson group have companion websites, and some offer online labs.

Generally, these websites are designed to complement their primary business of physical textbooks. The websites often contain materials that earlier had been distributed on standalone CDs. This content is now generally available on the web, behind login security. A search of the publisher websites, some of which are listed below, enables faculty members to explore how these new formats might help support their particular discipline.

It is hard to evaluate many of the materials without working through their sales representative. Logins and passwords are required to access these sites, as they. are designed to be used by faculty and students who have adopted specific textbooks. Most of these new online book sites share common features, such as links to other websites, student self-assessment resources, and instructor networking spaces. Some publishers also offer a service or product that is a course management system. If you are a lone faculty member with little infrastructure support, this might be a useful choice.

Following are brief profiles of some major publishers in this area. Many additional publishers offer complementary tools and resources, such as collaborative writing software and Harvard case studies. This list is intended only as a starting point to illustrate the different types of content resources that a faculty member might find in specific discipline areas.

Addison Wesley and Benjamin Cummings (www.aw-bc.com/home and www.pearsoned.com)

The Addison Wesley and Benjamin Cummings publishers, within the Pearson Higher Education Group, provide textbooks and content resources for the major areas of mathematics, computing, and economics, as well as for the life and physical sciences of anatomy, physiology, biology, and physics. The biology resources include the Biology Labs Online, a set of online learning simulations produced by collaboration among biologists throughout the California State University System, the CSU Center for Distributed Learning, and Benjamin Cummings. One of these labs is the original and very popular Virtual Fly Lab. Other labs in this series include the DemographyLab, the LeafLab, and the HemglobinLab. The popular A.D.A.M series for anatomy and physiology has its own website at http://education.adam.com/products/p_edu.htm. Textbooks accompanying this content are offered by Benjamin Cummings.

Houghton Mifflin College Division (www.college.hmco.com)

Houghton Mifflin publishes textbooks and other educational materials for elementary and secondary schools and colleges. Its college division focuses on subject areas of business, humanities, mathematics, science, social science, student success, and world languages. Some of its textbook sites are called Insite. These sites each contain four areas: (1) Course Resources, (2) Field Experiences, (3) Class Applications, and (4) Share Knowledge and Experience. Houghton Mifflin also offers an online tutoring service in chemistry called Smarthinking as well as a customized publishing service, BiblioBase® (www.bibliobase.com), that features historical documents and chemistry experiments. The company partners with eCollege for access to content. Most publishers do have partnership programs with the major course management systems.

McGraw-Hill Higher Education (www.mhhe.com/catalogs)

McGraw-Hill publishes instructional materials in over 80 disciplines, including humanities, social science, business, economics, sciences, engineering, and math. Its website is designed for both instructors and students. It includes product information, multimedia demos, downloadable ancillaries, and other interactive features. One of its online learning centers is an integrative biology site featuring regional perspectives in marine biology, with case studies categorized by world oceans.

Prentice Hall (www.prenhall.com)

Prentice Hall, another Pearson company, has strengths across major segments of higher education textbook publishing. The website features a companion gallery listing the imprint's major textbook areas on most of the main academic disciplines plus cutting-edge topics in business, computer science, engineering, and information technology. The development direction that Prentice Hall is pursuing appears to be similar to that of the other publishers: providing companion websites and CDs for its most popular textbooks. Prentice Hall's leading textbooks are supported by Course Compass, which is CMS Blackboard technology with Prentice Hall content.

The Prentice Hall textbooks are also supported by companion websites with online study guides, reference materials, communications tools, and faculty resources. Following the links, for example, of the chemistry series by Brown, Lemay, and Bursten leads to the Central Science Live Ninth Edition site, which is organized by chapters corresponding to the book structure. Chapter 2, on atoms, molecules, and ions, has nine different types of resources, including a list of web resources, a problem-solving center, current topics, and student activities. A section on visualization molecules links to demonstrations of molecules that make up water, oxygen, and hydrogen.

Thoughts on Content Websites: Digital Twins and Icebergs

Content websites offered by publishers continue to grow. These websites were launched as the digital twin of the physical textbook, with resources to help faculty deliver courses. Just as course websites made it easy for faculty to distribute resources to students, these textbook websites made it easy for publishers to distribute instructor resources to faculty. The expense of printing and inventorying all the instructor materials went away; the ability to distribute via the web arrived. These faculty resources often consisted of overheads, computer-enhanced presentations, test banks, student problems and challenges, and other planned activities.

Companion book sites have been adding digital resources such as interactive tutorials, animation, simulations, and real audio and video content. The sophistication of website lockdowns has also been growing. The number of publisher sites that can be casually reviewed is quite small. Websites now seem to share the characteristics of book publishing, in which materials are developed, reviewed, edited, and packaged for thousands of students. Book cycles are well defined, with new editions being released every two or three years. And websites associated with the books now appear to be experiencing similar life cycles.

Websites are becoming increasingly dynamic and multimedia, requiring all the media and Flash plug-ins. They have links to related web resources, hosted events, and contributing editors. The sites can offer virtual spaces for faculty networking. Rather than waiting for annual conferences, for example, faculty who are teaching in similar disciplines can network and share resources online.

These evolutions will soon lead to another, more revolutionary mode of content publishing: sharing content, materials, and events across the usual course boundaries. Rather than a database for one general geography course, for example, a geography site may have components that are available for faculty who are teaching any one of a multitude of related courses. Rather than course resources, we will have discipline resources that provide a rich environment for motivated students and an abundant and intriguing environment for students who only want to do the basics.

The current publisher websites are like the larger internet; only a small tip of the available resources can be seen with a quick glance. We are accustomed to taking quick measure of textbooks, but taking a quick look at the various book sites is not so easy, since only a small portion of the richness of the content can be easily seen at one time. These sites are like icebergs, accessed only a tip, a node at a time. While these book sites can save time, they can be very time consuming to review. Rather than spending days, weeks, or months examining the various websites, this may be a time simply to adopt the website of the textbook that best fits your course for now and use it for a while. As faculty and students use the sites, a more informed decision will be possible. The best piece of advice here is to do something. Get started, but don't sign multiyear contracts!

What Next for Textbook Websites?

Predicting what will come is often foolhardy. The following predictions were made in the first edition of this book, and we believe most of them are on track. See what you think.

Future textbook content websites are likely to include the following features:

1. More content organization by topic than by course. When this happens, we will need tools to help identify levels of content, types of learning objectives and associated content resources, and relevant activities and assessments.

2. More synchronous and current events, and greater access to experts, student networking, and faculty networking. Content resource sites will begin to leverage daily and weekly news events to provide relevancy to learning. Experts will be available remotely, and their comments and interviews will be archived and searchable. Some of these capabilities are already in place, with students monitoring and participating in a series of major national events. These events will help to stimulate the networking of faculty and students.

3. Resources that are mixable and flexible by faculty and students for interdisciplinary programs. It is likely that book sites will evolve into larger databases of resources in response to more interdisciplinary programmatic requirements and the increased use of digital materials. Value will be added to teaching and learning by publishers with related and complementary resources that make the barriers between the "courses" and the "textbooks" more malleable.

As the pace of knowledge creation continues to accelerate, the importance of learning core concepts and principles, and learning how to apply those core concepts in a discipline, will increase. Publishers may want to segment and package their resources into three layers of content, including core concepts and principles, application of core concepts, and problem analysis and solving.

4. Pricing models of all types. Pricing access to the content will be in flux for some time, but the availability of multiple options for access and pricing, including individual subscriptions, will be constant. Students and nonstudents, for example, may want to access a biology or international finance site, whether or not it has been recommended by a faculty member.

5. Expanded role in education by content publishers. If faculty move courses to the online environment and adopt the textbook and other resources provided by the content publishers, it is possible that the increased use of materials developed by publishers could enhance the productivity and accountability of higher education. Faculty might be able to spend less time designing and developing their courses. Students might have access to multiple and interactive ways of learning difficult content. However, if the materials are expanded, subscription costs may increase. The life cycle of content prepared by publishers will likely change, and that can result in more centralization of relevant up-to-date content and higher costs.

What About eBooks and the Future of the Book?

A 2002 study of 91 graduate students at Ball State University (Bellaver and Gillette, 2003) examined the usability of eBooks as well as learning performance using eBooks. The Human Factors class provided many recommendations for improving the navigation and user interface of eBook software, including a way of "ensuring that page numbers remain constant regardless of the font size or text orientation."

A hardware-user interface recommendation involved the size of the screen. Students recommended a screen size of 6 by 8.5 inches for easier readability. In the study, some students used a color version of an eBook with a screen size of 5 by 7 inches; other students had a black and white version that was only 3 by 4.5 inches. However, students found the eBook format difficult to navigate and use. As for achieving learning objectives via eBooks, the format of the content did not affect student performance on a series of text-oriented quizzes administered in class.

The authors of the study concluded that the eBook has some potential as a device to be used by college students. They felt that as an "easy to carry, relatively inexpensive, and completely reusable storage device, the eBook could fit into the hardware-software spectrum between the full personal computer and the PDA." It will be interesting to watch this category of personal tools. Perhaps we will increase the number of choices of PDAs with different screen sizes, or we will see the evolution of PDAs with flexible and expandable screens.

For a baseline examination of the myriad issues surrounding publishing, copyright, rights management, distribution, access, and archival issues, a 2001 article by Cliff Lynch titled, "The Battle to Define the Future of the Book in the Digital World" is an invaluable resource (Lynch, 2001). You might want to jump to the end and see how Lynch predicts the printed book will fare!

Audio and Video Tools: But How Do I Lecture Online?

From the very beginnings of teaching and learning online, the most persistent question faculty ask is, "But How Do I Lecture Online?"

The word *lecture* may be the next word in the teaching and learning vocabulary to bite the dust. Other words that have lost their meaning or have been redefined during the digital revolution are *course*, *book*, *campus*, *classroom*, and *seminar*. It is now time to re-examine what a lecture is; what a faculty member does before, during, and after a lecture; and what students do in their heads before, during, and after a lecture.

One of our colleagues has been searching, inquiring, querying people for years as to when or where a tool might be available that would support lecturing online. Secretly, we were pleased that there was no effective tool to do this, as we were convinced that lectures, as generally conducted, are great for faculty learning their own content thoroughly, but less effective for student learning. Not being able to lecture online was a good thing, as it served as a forcing agent to rethink what a lecture is and what purposes it does and does not serve.

But now, for good or for ill, we see a new generation of tools that come close to making it easy to provide asynchronous and synchronous lectures online. Here are a few of the tools that are available and what they can do at this time. As this is another area of rapid evolution, this section is intended to serve only as a starting point for exploring audio and video tools and for providing a few hints, guidelines, and questions to consider when thinking about using them.

A lecture is most frequently described as a transmitter of knowledge. Yet we know from the science of learning that knowledge cannot be transmitted. In the movie, *Matrix*, a support team downloaded a module of helicopter-flying skills to one of the leading characters. Well, we can't do that yet. For now, we know that knowledge can only be constructed by learners. We also know that a learner's attention span is limited. Listening only takes up a portion of our brain channels; thus, we have room for backchanneling of other activities. Think of listening to the radio while reading the newspaper, or preparing for the next class while sitting in a lecture.

The best lectures are designed so that students need to process information, answer a question, manipulate information, and take notes, to build and construct their knowledge structures. As for appropriate length of an online lecture video, consider how often you give your full attention to a video lasting more than 15 minutes.

One principle we have learned is that online video and audio events, such as webcasts and videoconferences, lend themselves to the concept of "learning anywhere," or learning while doing something else. This is not such a strange concept: Multitasking is the norm rather than the exception for most of us. The CREN webcasts that were available online from 1997 to 2003 were designed for a professional audience who used them only occasionally in the foreground, depending on interest in a particular topic.

Given the reality of the normal lengths of a sustained uninvolved attention span and the lures and often the necessity of multitasking, how will we use new tools that will make lecturing online easy? Here are a few ideas. As a community, we will refine these guidelines as we use the tools and combine our experiences with learning research.

- Online lectures need to be short. Terms used to describe short lectures include *minilecture*; *demonstration*; *concept overview*, *object*, or *process*; *problem solution*; and *research* or *project presentation*. We suspect that within five years, we will see a glossary with a whole list of substitute words for *lecture*.
- We suggest that the best time length for an online lecture is two to five minutes of well-structured content. It is good to think of longer segments as multiples of this shorter time. How long does it take to describe a concept and to give an example, and for learners to apply that concept to an experience? Also useful are concept maps showing the relationships and influences of ideas to guide the practice and application of concepts. Online interviews are popular, and the best interview segments consist of groups of no more than four or five questions. As students learn, each student's mind might be triggered by a different comment or concept. For students to efficiently build their knowledge structures, it may be helpful to structure content so that students can customize their learning experience by following their particular trains of thought. Short lecture segments arranged for easy maximum navigation can support this customized train-of-thought learning.

- Online lectures should include requirements for students to respond and interact with the concept, knowledge, or process. This can contribute to length, but with each meaningful interaction, the clock can start again within certain parameters. Including interaction can help students work through solving a problem and seeing the different states of a problem's solution. When learning core concepts, students need to write, think, speak, and formulate questions.
- Minilectures using video can be useful for demonstrating certain processes, either in a software application or in a lab. They can also be useful for conveying some of the soft skills of interacting with people, including observing and responding to body language.
- Think drama; think theatre. Make the online lecture a scene in the acquisition of a concept – ideas plus practice, application, and managing data.

Tools for Lecturing Online

Here are descriptions of a few of the tools useful for lecturing or presenting online. The category name for these tools is still in flux. Some of them are called *screen capture* or *screen recording* tools; others are called *help authoring systems* or *training software*. The events using these conferencing tools are called *webcasts* and *webinars*. This early terminology reflects their origin as utilities to support product demonstrations, presentations, and tutorials. The category may settle into *content creation*, *e-learning development tools*, or *simulation tools*.

Camtasia Studio 2 (www.techsmith.com)

Camtasia Studio 2 is a suite of tools designed for capturing and manipulating screen recordings, images, voice, and video from Windows desktops. In addition to Camtasia Studio, TechSmith also offers SnagIt. These tools are used by businesses and increasingly by e-learning companies to create content for teaching, training, websites, documentation, and business presentations.

RoboDemo 5.0 (www.ehelp.com/products/robodemo/)

RoboDemo is one of a suite of products from eHelp corporation designed to support publishing, training, and content management. The company is now part of Macromedia (www.macromedia.com). RoboDemo is designed to create content for online user support, product demonstrations, and interactive simulations.

HorizonLive (www.horizonlive.com)

HorizonLive provides web-based conferencing capabilities that can be used for synchronous learning sessions. It enables the use of audio or video without a software download. Tools include a live full screen, cross-platform application sharing and follow-me web browsing. All the tools are plug-in free and work in both IE and Netscape across a broad spectrum of platforms.

Additional Tools to Explore

Here are three additional products worth exploring:

- Viewlet Builder 3/4 from Qarbon (www.qarbon.com)
- Firefly from KnowledgeImpact (www.kimpact.com)
- SoftSim from Outstart (www.outstart.com)

Many of these products are designed and run primarily on Windows, so it is important to check their system requirements before you buy. The good news is that most outputs, such as tutorials, simulations, and demonstrations, are designed to be available through web browsers. Some campus faculty centers provide access to these tools.

Video With a Human Touch

Over the last few years, the tools and services for supporting video delivery and audio and video webcasts have improved greatly and become much more accessible. The first step in choosing audio and video online tools is determining just what you want to do. Many tools for asynchronous and synchronous collaboration are built into the CMS systems, so it is good to examine what you might already have.

An excellent resource on videoconferencing is the Video Development Initiative (www.vide.net). This very active site features a *Videoconferencing Cookbook*, in its 3.0 edition as of April 2002 (www.videnet.gatech.edu/cookbook). Ten organizations support this project, including the University of Alabama at Birmingham, Australian National University, Georgia Institute of Technology, Penn State University, and Southeastern Universities Research Association. The vidnet project is closely associated with the Internet2 initiative.

Assessment Tools

While most of the CMS provide built-in assessment tools, new devices are emerging that enhance the capabilities of the leading CMS tools. One example is Respondus (www.respondus.com), which has features such as the ability to create exams offline, move assessments from one CMS to another, and print and archive exams. It also has the ability to retrieve reports and databases from the CMS, and includes a mathematical Equation Editor and spelling checker.

Other online assessment tools you might wish to explore include

- Hot Potatoes (web.uvic.ca/hrd/halfbaked);
- Markin (www.cict.co.uk/software/markin/index.htm); and
- Questionmark (www.questionmark.com/us/home.htm).

Plagiarism Tools

Now that online assessment has become more prevalent, so has online cheating. Fortunately, with the rise of cheatsites for students, there is a parallel set of new sites to assist educators in combating this problem by providing tips and detection software. Many institutions have developed their own internal sites with suggestions. A web search on the topic will produce a wealth of helpful addresses. Here are a few to serve as a starting point:

- Plagiarism.org (www.plagiarism.org/)
- Plagiarism and the Web (www.wiu.edu/users/mfbhl/wiu/plagiarism.htm)
- "Anti-Plagiarism Strategies for Research Papers," by Robert Harris; version date: March 7, 2002 (www.virtualsalt.com/antiplag.htm)
- The Plagiarism Resource Site (www.plagiarism.phys.virginia.edu/)

The primary value of an educational experience, in addition to certification, is the learning best facilitated by well-designed educational experiences. We know that content resources that are well structured support teaching and learning in pleasurable, efficient, and effective ways. Faculty, content publishers, and content-creation software vendors will be defining new roles and relationships as we figure out how to best use all the new tools and resources that we now have.

Stories From the Field

The following story by the Dean of Distance and Mediated Learning at Foothill College (CA) describes an ongoing institute designed to provide support and community for faculty teaching in online environments. The Cyber Teachers' Institute Series is an online training program "dedicated to promoting excellence in online teaching and learning." The institute is "designed to bring teachers together to learn from each other, explore teaching innovations, and search for solutions to the unique challenges of the online learning environment. The tremendous dialogue on sound teaching strategies is the highlight of our program." The Cyber Teachers' Institute Series consists of three courses, one each for faculty thinking about teaching online, for faculty just starting to teach online, and for faculty experienced at teaching online. The Cyber Teachers' Institute website address is http://foothillglobalaccess.org/cyber-cti/.

It Takes a Community to Develop A Peer

Contributed by Vivian Sinou

"I laughed, I cried, I had a good time and I learned something new every day," wrote Suzanne Floyd from West Los Angeles College in her evaluation of the Cyber Teachers' Institute (CTI), summer 2003.

Like most early adopters, CTI founder and designer Vivian Sinou figured out what it takes to establish a successful online learning environment through experimentation, imagination, and motivation to venture into uncharted territory with students willing to sign up for her courses. By spring of 1999, Sinou had taught online for several terms, yet she was still the only one who was teaching online on her campus. She felt isolated from colleagues on other campuses who were exploring teaching with web-based technologies. She had no one to share student success stories or her excitement about the gains she was making, and she had nowhere to go to learn how other faculty dealt with the challenges she faced.

In May of 1999, Sinou attended an online learning seminar that had promised to provide an opportunity for meaningful exchange with online teaching professionals. The format and content of the seminar proved of no value to her, as the participants were new to online teaching. However, at about the same time, Sinou attended a workshop on the Great Teachers' Seminar, a program designed to bring great teachers together to learn from each other's teaching successes and challenges. Vivian met David Gottshall, founder of the National Great Teachers Seminar, and was inspired by his and Cindra Smith's exemplary work, *The Great Teachers' Format: Why Does It Work?* Cindra Smith is Director of Education Services for the Community College League of California.

Reflecting on the principles of the Great Teachers' Seminar, Vivian found herself wishing she could get online teachers together to share successes and failures and learn from one another. She wondered whether a cyber version of the Great Teachers' Seminar would work. If online instruction allows for personal interaction, as she and many other advocates of e-learning argued, then bringing teachers together in a focused virtual classroom should be effective. And that is how Cyber Teachers' Institute (CTI) was born.

The Classic Cyber Teachers' Institute (EDUC 101) was first offered in the summer of 2001 at Foothill College. Three years later CTI had evolved to include two more courses: EDUC 100, a course for wannabe's in the field of e-learning and EDUC 102, an advanced course for faculty who want more.

The CTI series is now offered online every summer through Foothill College. The program enables participants to share success stories, celebrate teaching excellence in the online or traditional classroom, and address principal online teaching and learning challenges. Participants are expected to construct reasonable solutions to the challenges by reflecting, analyzing, and learning from what they know works.

As reflected in the feedback from the participants and the completion rate (95 percent), the program is a valuable and rewarding learning experience:

> "I was told that if one enjoys Kindergarten, they would enjoy and take a positive approach for the remainder of their educational career. I guess that is why I am receiving such a positive experience with this trilogy of courses." —Peter

> "I am going on my third year of teaching online and ON-SITE so I am considered new to academia. However, I have learned more in these short weeks than my three years." *—Mark*

CTI has confirmed the belief that "all knowledge is created socially" (National Learning Infrastructure Initiative), whether online or face-to-face. It is open to online and traditional faculty, recognizing that a passion for teaching others what we know is the best way to learn.

Nearly 80 instructors from several California Community Colleges complete the program every summer; it serves as a meeting place for faculty to learn, unlearn, and relearn how to be effective teachers in an evolving digital era.

The program is facilitated by Don Megill, Vivian Sinou, and Dave Megill, who guide, support, reinforce, and challenge participants to rethink the teaching of their disciplines. The trio is constantly present but strives to leave the center stage for learners. They believe that it is the participants, novices and veteran online teachers, who bring to the learning process their expertise, passion for teaching, and genuine desire to grow.

What links the facilitators is their desire to keep the participants at the center of the courses and establish different levels of freedom for them based on their individual circumstances and experience with online learning. They attempt to coordinate the participants' goals with the goals for the program, always ready to change the game plan to make things work.

A successful part of CTI is the warm-up vignettes, designed to highlight online teaching challenges and to allow faculty to see how differently each participant would handle them. CTI participants are encouraged to explore new ways of teaching and to be unafraid to abandon traditional practices that may no longer meet changing needs. The program invites faculty to place the learner at the center of the learning process and to embrace opportunities for growth.

Participants find the pace of CTI very intense and have suggested that we warn faculty about the time commitment required. The courses require two to three hours of work per day and are offered back to back for six weeks every summer. Each course earns participants two quarter units and can be taken for credit or pass/no pass option. Participants have requested that we explore offering graduate credit for CTI so that the units can be counted toward advanced degree programs in online teaching and learning. They have also asked that we offer the program throughout the year instead of just in the summer.

CTI is delivered in ETUDES (Easy to Use Distance Education Software), a learning management system developed at Foothill College. The ETUDES environment handles the structure, pace, organization, and management of the courses.

Chapter 9
Stories About Online Teaching and Learning

s teaching an art or a science? How much can be directly designed and how much comes together spontaneously with the gathering of students, faculty, knowledge, and contexts?

The stories written by faculty and faculty support personnel in this chapter provide insights into the life and times of faculty as they design, develop, and deliver courses online. While much of what faculty are doing might be anticipated, the creativity and adaptivity of faculty and students within the online environment continues to be a source of revelation. The first edition of this book featured eight stories; this edition features updates from some of the original stories that started back in the earliest days of web technology, 1994-1996, plus many new stories. Each is a joyful testimony to teaching and learning.

These stories illustrate the three basic types of courses: web-enhanced, webcentric (hybrid, blended), and fully online courses. In addition to examples from these three types, there are also stories that describe complete degree programs or describe a resource that might be used by faculty and students in any of the models.

A brief introduction to each story comments on issues that might be of greatest interest pedagogically and administratively. Common to all are the changes the online environment is making in three aspects of higher education:

- Changes in the amount of *time* faculty and students spend collaborating with each other
- Changes in the *expectations* of faculty and students
- Changes in the types of *resources* that are being used in teaching and learning environments

The first section provides stories about full degree programs online. Other sections provide stories about individual courses being redesigned to update content, integrate new tools, meet the needs of students, and integrate new research into teaching and learning.

Online Degree Programs

These narratives describe degree programs now available fully online, which means that all courses can be taken anywhere, anytime. They have minimal or no requirements for location-based gatherings. An important point is that students often are attracted to programs offering a full sequence of courses leading to a certificate, degree, or specialization. This is the area that promises the greatest growth for the future.

This story is an update from one of the stories published in the first edition. Robert Schihl has been shepherding the design and development of online programs for over 10 years, working closely with accreditation agencies to assure quality in online professional degree programs. These programs are models of how to achieve effective learning and community online.

Computer-Mediated Distance Education 1994-2004: Ten Years Later

Robert J. Schihl

In fall 1994, Regent University's School of Communication and the Arts, one of eight graduate-only schools in the university, launched its online Ph.D. degree track, the university's first all-computer-mediated degree program. The tools available to us at that time seem quite primitive in comparison to what we have today. We delivered the program via the Netscape internet browser and the Eudora email software package. Permanent documents for the program, such as the catalog, forms, and syllabi, were simple HTML web pages. The day-to-day pedagogical operations of individual courses were conducted via email transactions. A website was developed for every course in the curriculum that was not performance or laboratory based. It worked.

The school then adapted its master's degrees in communication and in journalism to online programs. When members of the Southern Association of Colleges and Schools came to campus for their substantive change visit, and later for an institution re-evaluation visit, they remarked that they came as much to learn how we were doing distance education as they came to evaluate us. We were pioneers in the area.

Meanwhile, other schools on the Regent campus began experimenting with early web-based course delivery software such as Forums, WebCT, and Web-Course-in-a-Box. A few years later, Regent formed a universitywide committee to review 33 different web-based course delivery software tools. This review included tools that we could purchase and then host the developed course materials ourselves (*e.g.*, Blackboard) as well as tools that required the software developer to receive and maintain course resources (*e.g.*, eCollege). Blackboard won overwhelming approval and was introduced across the university almost immediately. We are now using version 6.0.

The immediate success of Blackboard opened new horizons even for on-campus degree programs. Schools now create Blackboard courses for on-campus classes as well as for online classes to distribute learning resources to students. Today, it is the exception if a course taught on-campus does *not* have an online companion site in Blackboard. Faculty have come to appreciate the opportunity to provide course content resources to on-campus students by uploading learning resources, such as PowerPoint slides initially shown in a class setting, for access by students during out-of-class study times.

Given the success of distance education at the university, Regent developed an all-distance school in 1997, the School of Leadership Studies. This school introduced its Ph.D. and M.A. as exclusively online programs, with no campus component except a minimal residency for the doctoral degree as required by the accrediting agency. Today, Regent recognizes 52 percent of its total student population of 3,109 as a distance population.

In 2000, Regent took the bold step of developing a degree completion program to meet the projected needs of countless community college graduates and dropouts from traditional four-year colleges or university programs. That school is the Center for Professional Studies. Two of the current degrees offered by the center are totally online, the B.S. in Organizational Leadership and Management and the B.A. in Communication. Each course is five weeks long, and these two degrees can each be completed in 18 months.

Faculty have learned many things about web-based distance education in the past 10 years.

- We learned that we had to standardize the distance learners' software. We now require the Microsoft Office package available in PC and Mac formats. The package gives us Microsoft Word for word-processing, Excel for statistical analyses, and PowerPoint for creating and reading faculty or student presentations.
- The fact that a course taught on campus and online is identical in title and content does not necessarily mean that it is the same course. Adaptation to the distance learner is required. Using a course delivery system creates a challenge and makes a difference.
- Web-based distance courses are more labor-intensive for faculty and learner.
- Anecdotally, more learning appears to occur online than on campus. The fact that student interactions are defined, and hence required, for distance learners increases participation, and one suspects that more learning occurs.
- Faculty learned never to say something couldn't be taught online. All things are possible in distance learning. Faculty have accepted the challenge to create Blackboard course sites for classes at one time not even considered for delivery online, *e.g.*, public speaking, video editing, and so forth.
- Faculty had to define expected distance learner contact in the syllabi of online classes. Student expectations of online faculty can border on the unreasonable: Some students expect faculty to respond immediately to emails or telephone calls. Faculty now set virtual office hours for responding to correspondence.

- Distance learners often appear to have a one-to-one interaction ratio with their faculty. Faculty learned to work with virtual groups and lessen the one-to-one interactions. Students, too, learned many things as they undertook the experience of distance learning.
- Not all students adapt to the rigor of the degree of self-motivation and the discipline of independent learning. Attrition rates are generally high in distance education. Students need the personalization and immediacy of faculty communication at all levels of course delivery.
- Students adapt well to using online resources (*e.g.*, in Blackboard) as a component to on-campus classes. They are served well if on-campus learning resources are made available to them out of class, online, for review and study at their own choosing.

And administrators learned many things about distance education as well.

- Most faculty never took a pedagogy course in distance learning; yet this is the generation *developing* distance pedagogy. One cannot rely on faculty learning about distance education intuitively. Most would just take on-campus resources and transplant them online.
- Faculty need course-development lead time. Online teaching is not just another copy of an on-campus syllabus. Continuing updated training for faculty is a necessity. Regent University profited much from the establishment of an ongoing center for development for distance faculty that includes online course development instruction as well as the production of multimedia resources.
- Faculty welcomed training in audio and video streaming, CD burning, and multimedia possibilities, as well as to additional resources available to distance faculty, such as the online grade book and online testing.
- Experience sharing for faculty is a must. Faculty themselves can and do learn a lot about distance learning and have things to share with each other.
- Distance courses are separate courses and therefore need to be considered separate faculty loads. This was not always true in practice.
- Administrators learned that there is a specific culture in distance learning that differs greatly from the on-campus culture.

What remains to be done in the next decade? It behooves distance educators to begin to develop distance pedagogical theory and the production of resources specific to distance learning.

Robert J. Schihl is Associate Dean and Director of Distance Education, School of Communication and the Arts, at Regent University in Virginia Beach, Virginia.

Ian Tebbett's story is an excellent illustration of developing online programs by leveraging existing programs and specialties. He tells of a program that met an obvious but unarticulated need and is now growing rapidly within the United States and beyond.

Online Programs in the Forensic Sciences

Ian Tebbett

The University of Florida has designed its online distance education programs in forensic science to meet the needs of today's working professionals. Each online program is open to appropriately qualified local, national, and international students, and is structured to provide students with a strong working background in their forensic discipline of interest.

The programs are novel in that they feature modules in forensic pharmacology, doping control, postmortem toxicology, blood-spatter interpretation, DNA analytical techniques, expert testimony, and quality assurance and control procedures. The program courses can be taken individually as well as in fulfillment of a certificate or M.S. qualification, and may be of particular interest to law enforcement agents, military personnel, pharmaceutical industrialists, clinical chemists, medical personnel, and students looking to enter the field of forensic science. The degrees offered are an M.S. degree with a specialization in forensic toxicology, drug chemistry, or serology and DNA.

Background to the Development of the Forensic Programs

The University of Florida assumed responsibility for the oversight of the state racing laboratory in Tallahassee in 1997, and I was appointed as its director. This laboratory is responsible for testing biological samples from all of Florida's racehorses and greyhounds for the presence of drugs. By 1999, the laboratory had been relocated to the university campus in Gainesville, and immediately several of the staff requested time off to take graduate-level classes in toxicology and drug analysis. While their enthusiasm was commendable, it was not practical to lose so many staff from the daily operation of the laboratory while they attended class. A compromise was reached: I would make my classes available on the internet, the laboratory would pay the employees' tuition, but they would study on their own time. The distance education program was thus born.

In fall 2000, after discussions with members of the Florida Department of Law Enforcement, we offered for the first time a graduate certificate program consisting of five three-credit courses. Thirty students enrolled in the program.

We subsequently received many inquiries asking if this certificate program was to be expanded into a master's degree. All 32 credits for the master's degree are now taught via the internet, with the exception of a final cumulative examination, held over a five-day period, in which the student is rigorously tested on the whole program. Students who are not successful are given the opportunity to retake the exam at a later date.

Current Programs

In 2003, two new master's programs were introduced following a similar format. Forensic drug chemistry and forensic serology and DNA are now available through the college of pharmacy, and the original M.S. in forensic toxicology is administered by the college of veterinary medicine. We currently have 300 enrollees in the programs. The majority are crime-laboratory personnel, although some attorneys, law enforcement personnel, pathologists, and pharmaceutical scientists also take the courses. These programs are primarily geared toward those already working in the field or related areas, and they include no hands-on or lab-based training.

All of the courses consist of 8 to 15 modules. Each module has its own set of learning objectives and an assignment that is emailed to the professor or teaching assistant for grading. WebCT is used and incorporates lecture material supported by digital photographs, case studies, animations, and links to sites offering further information. Interaction with the student is through email, bulletin boards, and real-time chat sessions. The level of interaction in these classes has been the most satisfying aspect of the program.

When a class includes detectives, crime scene investigators, medical examiners, attorneys, and crime-lab scientists, the discussions take on a life of their own and are far more interactive than typically occur in a classroom setting. We employ teaching assistants who have been through the courses and are employed in crime laboratories, so they also bring real-life experience to the class, and they understand well the need to provide timely feedback.

As for requirements regarding the sequence of courses, we don't have many. For example, students should take Forensic Tox1 before Forensic Tox2, but we have purposely kept sequence requirements fairly flexible, because we have such a diverse group of students. Attorneys, for example, may only want to take a couple of intro courses.

The demand for these courses has also been a pleasant surprise. This is attributed to the fact that there are very few universities in the United States and Europe that offer graduate-level instruction in forensic science, and no others offer distance learning programs. This is in part because of a lack of faculty with the necessary expertise. It is also extremely difficult for those who most need access to such courses to find the time and resources to attend one of the few institutions offering forensic programs. Consequently, demand for traditional education in this field is relatively low and is limited to students who hope to find future employment in a forensic laboratory. Distance learning programs make graduate-level education in this field available to a significant number of students without the need to relocate and take extended leave from work.

Future developments

Following the September 11 tragedy and other recent world events, interest in law enforcement and crime detection has escalated, and not only within the U.S. The University of Florida is working with a number of other countries to make its course material available in these regions.

The preferred approach is to partner with reputable institutions in foreign countries and work with them to regionalize the course material. In some cases, this may involve translation, but it also features case studies and other examples relevant to a particular region. The goal is to share information globally.

Edinburgh University in Scotland is a prime example of how this collaboration can work. Edinburgh has a world-renowned program in forensic medicine, a specialty that the University of Florida does not have. Edinburgh is therefore making its courses available to our students, and the University of Florida recognizes the credit from this foreign institution. The process will be reciprocated next year, when European students will register for University of Florida courses.

The advantage of distance education is that faculty and students can be anywhere in the world, and programs can be developed that take advantage of the strengths of different institutions, even though they are geographically separated.

Surprises and Lessons Learned

The greatest surprise was the speed with which the programs became popular even with very little advertising. We offer a preview in which students can take a one-week sample of the course for free. This is advertised by email or postcard mailings to members of relevant professional organizations, and it has been very successful. The use of a gearing-up module, in which students are told how to download free software needed throughout the course and gives them an exercise that shows whether they have successfully completed that download, has saved time in replying to emails from students who couldn't get various aspects of the course to work.

Feedback from students and faculty has been excellent overall. In many cases, the students indicate that without this program they would never have had the opportunity for graduate education. In most cases, the employer, who is typically federal or state government, is paying the student's tuition. There is usually a 10 percent drop rate of students who come to realize that online learning is more time consuming than they anticipated, and some faculty also discover that distance education, particularly the daily need to respond to emails, is more of a commitment than they expected.

Ian Tebbett is Director of Online Forensic Programs at the University of Florida in Gainesville.

This story describes how a collaborative, innovative effort led by a persistent, patient faculty leader enabled a rapid response to a critical workforce need. Note the institutions that are working together and the technologies and instructional strategies and design that made launching a 67-credit, six-semester program on multiple island locations possible within a relatively brief timeline. The total program is 89 credits, of which 22 are General Education credits. The students have clinical-lab components with preceptors and faculty in each of those semesters.

It's Our Community Too: Developing a Distance Radiologic Technology Program

Michael Tagawa

Harry Nakayama is a most unassuming gentleman. But in the past year, he has accomplished what most thought next to impossible.

Harry is the program director of the Radiologic Technology program at Kapi`olani Community College, the only campus within the 10-campus University of Hawaii system that offers the two-year associate degree. The program is of greatest need on the island of Oahu, with its large urban center. However, in terms of critical needs, the program is essential to the delivery of quality rural health care among the less populated islands across the state.

In 2002, Oahu's shortage of radiologic technologists had reached a critical point, and Harry assumed the challenge of increasing the size of his program with no additional resources. This was in response to hospital requests and a continued weak economy that provided no new funds for existing services. Expanding the program would stretch his program thin, but it was impossible for him to turn his back on the dual requests from his home island of Oahu and similar requests from the Big Island of Hawaii, where local hospitals were importing radiologic technologists from out of state at an extremely high cost.

Theoretically, the Big Island is served by another community college campus, Hawaii Community College. However, because demand for radiologic technologists is cyclic and the program has high start-up costs, that campus could not justify its own program. Harry's attitude was simple: "The Big Island is part of our community too, and we have an obligation to try."

Fortunately, the former program director had already initiated discussions with the hospitals and Hawaii Community College to deliver the program off the island. The initial plan was that the Big Island hospitals would pay for an additional instructor; Hawaii Community College would pay for equipment and supply needs through a rural health grant; and Kapiʻolani would provide the curriculum and program coordination.

The dean of health programs at Kapiʻolani gave Harry the go-ahead to begin planning, but requested that he consult with the accrediting agency on any special requirements. That marked the beginning of the first of many challenges in getting the program off the ground within a nine-month period. One interpretation of the accreditation requirements called for the delivery of the instruction from the Kapiʻolani campus by its own instructors. Without skipping a beat, Harry suggested that the program be delivered via distance technology rather than onsite. In that manner, the program delivered would be identical to the one available on the main campus.

Although the University of Hawaii had a point-to-point two-way interactive television system in place, a decision was made to go with videoconferencing via internet protocol, a form of technology already available among the Big Island hospitals. That decision would enable Kapiʻolani to deliver the program to any of the hospitals on the Big Island. Unfortunately, Kapiʻolani did not have such a system in place, and to make matters worse, the college was in the midst of a year-long upgrade of its entire campus network infrastructure.

Harry began to work closely with Kapiʻolani's technology services unit to ensure that the necessary equipment would be acquired and tested, and that the building in which his program was housed would be given the highest priority in the networking upgrades. The technology team promised to give the program a high priority, but stopped short of making any guarantee that everything would be in place in the time allotted.

While wrestling with the technology infrastructure, Harry and a counselor began working with the Hawaii Community College counselors to provide orientation, placement testing, advising, and admissions services to prospective candidates. This, too, turned out to be a problem area. Standard practice called for admitting the best-qualified students, but there was a need to ensure that the students were representative of each hospital's local community, since each hospital was contributing toward the cost of delivering the program and providing clinical training sites.

To make matters more challenging, the counselor had initiated a workforce skills development program for all incoming health students. The program assessed student skills and provided intervention training in such areas as applied math, teamwork, listening, and observation skills. While students at the Kapiʻolani campus were able to access the program on campus, off-campus students did not have access to the learning support software.

A few months into the planning process, it was clear the leadership from Kapi`olani Community College, Hawaii Community College, and the local hospitals were all on board with the distance learning strategy, but legal issues emerged that required resolution. Contractual relationships needed to be established to define the scope of responsibility and financial contributions from each partner. At the operational level, affiliation agreements needed to be established with each clinical training site to define the legal relationship between the hospital and the program. Although key leaders agreed with the concept of the plan, it was not unusual for the legal offices of the hospitals and the University of Hawaii to haggle over issues such as liability. At the same time, each clinical site also had to provide a preceptor for any student training at the site, and Harry began to identify and prepare the preceptors for the program.

At the beginning of summer 2003, three months before the start of the program, none of these issues had been fully resolved. Nevertheless, Harry politely kept on everyone to get their piece of the puzzle in place while he and the newly hired instructor began developing online course materials and tests to be delivered via WebCT. The decision to go with online testing made it necessary to arrange for exam proctors at each site. To enhance the online materials and lectures, Harry and the new instructor also began to develop a series of PowerPoint presentations to incorporate into the program. By mid-summer, Harry's hair seemed to have turned two lighter shades of gray as he planned the finishing touches by locating and hiring someone to provide laboratory supervision at the receiving sites on the Big Island.

In August 2003, the technology services unit had just finished networking the health sciences building and installing the videoconferencing unit. On the first day of instruction, minor bugs caused the loss of video, but by the second day the technology was fully operational.

The incoming class turned out to be a good representative mix of students from all over the island of Hawaii, resolving the issue of providing graduates for each hospital. The college received funding, and monies were used to purchase a web-based version of the workforce skills development program. Not all instructional materials have been completely developed, but the pressure to develop a considerable amount of online materials has been alleviated due to the decision to employ videoconferencing.

An instructor and preceptors were identified and provided the requisite supervision for labs and clinical sites. At this point, the legal documents appeared to be moving toward final signing, even though the program had already started.

Students enrolled in the program are very happy with it, although they are still adjusting to learning in front of a camera. They have adapted well to WebCT and use its bulletin board for online interactions among themselves and with the instructors. Each student possesses a computer and completes much of the supplemental coursework at home.

The hospitals are also happy with the program. Although the cost of each two-year cohort is well over a quarter of a million dollars, the alternative of hiring out-of-state technicians was costing even more – up to several million dollars per year. The two colleges are happy they have been able to meet a critical workforce need during a time when college budgets were being cut.

Harry Nakayama's positive attitude managed the challenges of resolving technical infrastructure, instructional support, student services, instructional development, clinical support, and legal issues, and brought them to resolution within nine months. He effectively brought together many partners and players and made each of the pieces fit together into a functioning whole.

It was never a matter of *if* Kapi`olani Community College was going to do this; it was always a matter of *how*. And that is what makes the program so successful. It was inspired by the college's responsibility to ensure the quality of health care for its island communities, and driven by a truly exceptional individual who had little understanding of why things could not be done.

Michael Tagawa is Dean of Health and Legal Education, Library, and Technology Services at Kapi`olani Community College in Hawaii.

Courses Using the Online Environment: Content Focus

After some thought about the stories written by faculty for this chapter, it became apparent that another mode of secondary classification of these course experiences might prove useful. The basic categorization we have been examining is whether a course is fully online, a webcentric course, or a web-enhanced course. The second categorization considers another dimension, that of *why* a course is being changed.

Generally, there are four catalysts for curricular change: (1) need or desire to update or change much of the course content, (2) desire to change based on new research, (3) need to change due to the characteristics of the students, and (4) desire to change a course due to the new teaching and learning environments (Kolb, 2001). Of course, many institutions and faculty choose to update a course or change its format for two or more of these reasons.

Two of the following stories are great examples of faculty recognizing a need for designing and developing new courses because of the obvious content development that had occurred in a particular discipline. In these two cases, the content developments in graphic design and the development of a whole set of global positioning systems (GPS) in agriculture were the primary catalysts. While updating the courses, it seemed an excellent time to also make them more accessible by offering them in one of the three types of online modes. The third piece, about a course on music in multicultural America, is a story of curricular transformation dually inspired by the interests of students and the waves of new musical approaches.

In this story, notice Patrick Grigsby's careful consideration of students with regard to the basic set of internet skills that might be the best fit as they started using the course management system. This is an example of a web-enhanced course that may be evolving to a webcentric course with a reduction in on-campus class time.

Graphic Design Visualization Courses Taught in the Web-Enhanced Classroom

Patrick Grigsby

I said it wouldn't work, and I was wrong. I teach graphic design courses at Santa Fe Community College (FL). Courses on our campus were moving to totally online scenarios as well as blended or hybrid models of meetings online and on campus. Clearly, an initiative to move or enhance online classroom delivery was here to stay and growing in popularity.

In the last 15 years, the graphic design industry has seen sweeping technology changes, many of which have overwhelmed traditional-minded professionals and processes. I saw designers, printers, and press operators who lamented digital design and criticized its shortcomings. That wasn't so long ago, but their obduracy now resembles the inflexibility of those who resisted the horseless carriage or the electric light. I, too, was falling prey to inflexibility as a graphic design educator, and I didn't even realize it.

Perhaps fear of change or comfort in the ways we know prevent us from embracing new methods and models. Regarding an online classroom, I didn't see what I wanted, so I wasn't paying attention to what was there. When campus administrators continued to sing the praises of the online classroom, I decided that it might be worth a second look. Maybe I even wanted to prove to them that not everything was right for online teaching and learning.

Only eight months later, I am convinced that the online classroom models provide for quantum leaps in education, and that as an instructor, I have never been better. Similar to the graphics industry in its evolution, educators should move quickly to grab hold of the benefits of web-enhanced classroom environments.

My initial distaste for online formats centered on communication. The field of graphic design requires designers to communicate ideas and concepts convincingly and confidently. Email can be efficient and succinct and even mask difficult communication, but I had always thought of it as a second-best method for presentation. How would young designers learn to respond, react, and improvise client solutions without the immediacy of the classroom meeting? For visual design presentation, what kind of internet skill set must these students have to succeed? What is the most basic, lowest-common-denominator skill set so that *all* students can experience online classroom teaching and learning?

These questions helped me prepare for the delivery of online instruction. Santa Fe Community College had selected WebCT as its course management system for other online courses, and had held workshops to familiarize faculty with this tool's options. Santa Fe's commitment to teaching teachers is at the foundation of my success. I learned about the tool; then I used the tool to do things it wasn't necessarily designed for, but that I felt were essential for online delivery of a graphic design course.

The online course I prepared, ADV2211 – Advanced Advertising Design and Graphics, is an intermediate class combining the graphic design software tools and conceptual thinking. The course description in the college catalog reads: "Advanced design projects in visual communications. Concentration will be on analysis and application of design principles for logos and trademarks, brochures and flyers, and newsletters. Other topics include psychology of color, typography, color, and black-and-white visuals."

Students taking ADV2211 have not generally completed web design courses and are not prepared to create web pages. My first question at the outset of the class was how well students could embrace and participate in an internet classroom without having previously experienced web design. Many students leap right into technology courses, but others have considerable fear factors. The least technology-savvy student needed to be comfortable before we could have any success as a cohesive class.

The advice I received from online-instruction veterans was to proceed simply and reveal only the essential tools needed from within the WebCT course design. This guidance made wading into teaching with the tools an almost immediate success. The students sensed my confidence and quickly shared my vision of feedback on graphic solutions throughout the week, rather than only at class time. Feedback from classmates and the instructor flourished between class meetings, and designs were better and problems resolved faster than ever before.

My concerns were phantom fears that quickly vanished. The student who was quiet in the physical classroom was effusive in the online classroom. The confidence gained online resulted in more communication success in the physical gatherings we did have for the course.

Student Newsletter Example

This experience was a steep learning curve for me as an instructor, but it has opened up positive enrichment opportunities for all of my classes. My participation in the online classroom involved checking postings throughout the day; adding new resources, links, and helpful tips; responding to students with email after email; and sharing answers to all students at the same time. Students working at 11 p.m. at night were receiving answers to questions from other students by 1 a.m. – before I ever had the chance to respond the next day. This was learning exponentially expressed. It was the most excitement I have ever had in teaching.

My full-time faculty colleagues have adopted similar formats, and adjunct instructors are taking to the format as well. It is my goal to see all of our graphic design courses in the Associate of Science degree program with online components in two years. The nontraditional students working or raising families never had such an opportunity to take courses and maintain stability and confidence in all aspects of their lives as they seek to improve their quality of life.

It is fantastic to consider how an open-door policy can have such a significant meaning regarding online delivery methods. Educational opportunities have never been more open. Instructor awareness and teaching skill, coupled with a college's online teaching strategies, can take interactive classrooms to new heights of student success.

Patrick Grigsby is Graphic Design Technology Coordinator at Santa Fe Community College in Gainesville, Florida.

This story details the experiences of a faculty member in the later phase of his teaching career. Rather than just riding out the last years to retirement, Jim Hynek learned the tools of the new online world along with his students and went on to design and develop a set of six courses in agricultural education. We see in this story that the design and development of online courses has a positive feedback loop to campus courses. This faculty member embraced the new technologies and refreshed his own teaching career with significant contributions for students, the college, and himself.

Teaching Online Courses in Agricultural Education

Jim Hynek

In 1965, I attended Iowa State University to earn a B.S. and M.S. in Agricultural Education. Technology was at a very low level. I did not have access to a computer, and even a hand-held calculator cost $500 – hardly within this college student's price range. So, I am one of the few surviving souls who know how to use a slide rule.

I have been teaching crop and soil production at Kirkwood Community College for the past 31 years. It is astounding what changes have occurred during my lifetime of teaching. I avoided turning on a computer until nearly 10 years ago, when I took the same computer class our students take as a requirement for Ag Science. I did get an A in the class, with some help from my teacher, and was teaching the class a year later. That is when I really started learning how to use the computer for my classes and for myself.

Use it or lose it seems to be the main theme for retaining what we know about anything, but especially in regard to computer skills. I very quickly required students in my agronomy classes to use spreadsheets and to write papers using the computer. These requirements provided reinforcement of their computer skills and also made reading their assignments much easier for me.

In 1998, I made the decision to add a new course in Applications of Global Positioning Systems (GPS) for our students in Ag Science. This technology had become available to consumers in 1995, and many agricultural applications quickly developed. Previously, this technology had been a military secret used to give our forces an advantage over enemies in battle; it is still used for that purpose today.

I attended several workshops and tutored myself to get up to speed with this new technology. Our college was very interested in getting online classes started, and I thought this would be a good course to put online as well as offer face to face. I struggled with how I would deliver the labs over the internet, and decided to make a series of videotapes on how to use these systems. I also selected a text and developed a study guide for each chapter. For exams, I drew 90 percent of the questions from material covered in the study guides.

It seemed logical to make the study guides and exams mirror one another, as the study guides focused on what I thought was most important. Students appreciate this consistency any time, but it is especially helpful in an online course. I also created a list of web assignments for the students to research to see the range of applications companies are making from GPS technology. These websites give students the tools they need to find equipment, identify job possibilities, and provide links to use after the course.

I developed my class around WebCT, which has been the course management system for our college. I enrolled in a set of staff development courses on WebCT, FrontPage, and Respondus (JVB) from our college. This all takes time, but I have found it to be very rewarding as I enter the twilight years of my teaching career. I enjoy setting high goals and then striving to achieve them, and this has caused me to work harder the last five years than I have at any time during my teaching career.

I have developed six three-credit online courses over these years: Applications of Global Positioning, Crop Production, Ag Fertilizers and Chemicals, Introduction to Arc View, Row Crop Production, and Integrated Pest Management. These classes are part of our Ag Science Curriculum. I also teach these courses face to face, to first- and second-year community college students. Many of them come from farm backgrounds and are preparing for a future in agriculture sales or production.

One of the biggest decisions I wrestled with while developing the online courses was how to do the testing. I decided that I would move from closed-book to open-book exams; it seemed complicated and impractical to try to bring students to testing facilities for exams. I set up all of the testing for the online classes on timed, multiple-choice, open-book exams, reasoning that most of us make our decisions in life based on data we have gathered, and then determine the best way to solve a problem. Why, then, in education, do we rely on giving exams to students that make them memorize facts they will forget soon after the exam is over?

After five years, I have found that students do about the same with this kind of test as they did with the closed-book exam. I tell my students to study for these just as they would for a closed-book test, because during the hour of testing, they will have time to look up only 5 to 10 questions.

I have started to use my WebCT exams for all my classes. The students have liked the format. I give them class time to take their tests online for a limited number of hours on a certain day. I do not have to print, administer, or correct exams; most important, I do not have to administer makeup exams. That saves me a lot of time and saves my college a lot of materials. The exams are presented randomly for each student from a pool of questions.

I cannot say that there is not a possibility of cheating, but it has not been much of a problem to date. For 25 years, I had to deal with every form of cheating. I used to give students days to take the online exam, but had to go to restricting the time to a specific hour or two; otherwise, copies of the test would be available to students taking the exam later. The test can be printed when the student is finished. Using this process, I found a student taking a 50-question multiple-choice exam in seven minutes and scoring 80 percent. This led me to have a heart-to-heart talk with that group of students and eventually personally monitor the exams. That was the end of the seven-minute exam.

Online classes are not for every student or for every faculty member. Students and teachers both must have self-discipline. Online students need to make a schedule for themselves and keep to it, or faculty will be signing drop slips. As for faculty: I was quite the procrastinator before I started teaching online courses; I always convinced myself to do things at the last minute because I worked best under pressure. But with online courses, you need to check on students daily and keep them informed. Every time a student turns in an assignment, I strive to give that student assessment within 24 hours.

Online faculty also need to be extremely organized, be excellent communicators, and have everything planned and ready online at the *beginning* of an online class. My organizational skills have improved as I have developed the online classes, and my face-to-face classes have benefited from these changes as well.

I take some pride in the fact that I have developed six online courses for Kirkwood Community College. I am far from being a computer guru. I have used the resources provided by my college and the help of people who *are* computer gurus at my college to develop and put these courses online. It seems a long stretch from using a slide rule to offering six classes online using WebCT, but that is my story.

There have been a lot of bumps in the road, but you find out what you need to do to fix that bump, and go on. When I retire, I plan to continue teaching some of these online classes; after all, I can be in Australia and check on a student's assignment, or give a final exam while I am on vacation in Montana.

I only have to log on, and class is in session.

Jim Hynek is Professor of Agricultural Science at Kirkwood Community College in Cedar Rapids, Iowa.

Elizabeth Barkley redesigned a campus music course, updating the content, the strategies for teaching the core musical concepts, and choices students have for learning these concepts. Note the course design elements, providing students with choices of content and format. Note also the size of the course and how it is organized administratively.

Music to My Ears: Turning a Curricular Catastrophe Into a Cause for Celebration

Elizabeth F. Barkley

"Sometimes I feel like a partner in an unholy alliance," commented a colleague. "I pretend to teach, and my students pretend to learn."

As I recalled my feelings teaching a traditional on-campus music course several years ago, I decided that in my case, he was only half right: In that class, the students weren't even pretending to learn. They stared at me with blank, apathetic faces as I struggled to engage them in a lively discussion on the structural nuances of a Beethoven symphony. Beethoven? Excuse me? Their musical heroes were rapper Tupac and the rock group Nine Inch Nails.

This crisis was the catalyst for a transformation in which I created an entirely new course. My efforts paid off. Enrollment increased from 45 to over 1,000 students annually, and students are generally enthusiastic and apparently learning. To share the story of this curricular transformation, I must go back almost a decade.

In 1994, I returned full time to the classroom after a nine-year hiatus as academic dean. I was stunned when I greeted my first class: The students sitting in front of me represented an almost unbelievable array of ethnicities, races, ages, and backgrounds. Although as an administrator, I was aware of demographic changes, I was not prepared for the pedagogical implications of those changes. Several of the students had limited English language abilities. Many seemed to be struggling with a variety of issues – job demands, caring for children or aging parents, physical and learning disabilities – that tended to disrupt their class attendance. Finally, there was a wide gulf between student interests and the curriculum I was supposed to teach. Distressed and alarmed, I started making changes.

To address the content issue, I created Musics of Multicultural America, a course that traces music genres such as the blues, jazz, gospel, folk, Tejano, rap, and various Asian fusions from their roots in the ethnic traditions of a specific immigrant group to their development into a distinctly American music.

To address ability and attendance issues, I created what I called safety nets, ways for students to access materials outside of the classroom either for review, if they couldn't quite follow in class, or because they were absent due to work or home demands. At first, this simply entailed leaving materials at the library's reserve desk. Then one day at a staff development workshop, a colleague demonstrated an online course delivery program he had designed called ETUDES. As he described the program, it became evident that even I, who had not even once gotten onto the internet, could do the kind of copy-and-paste text from word-processing documents that his program required. Using ETUDES, I was able within weeks to set up an initial bare-bones online site to house these documents and to facilitate messaging and threaded discussions.

Enrollment increased steadily. At first, students came from the regular on-campus population because the course had been recommended to them by friends. Soon, students from nearby universities, especially Berkeley and Stanford, were enrolling because they found the course a great way to meet their ethnic studies requirement. Eventually, students were enrolling from all over the world. Each quarter, I changed, added, and enhanced the site. Building incrementally, I have now a fairly comprehensive site, and as I assess it at this point, I can share the good and the bad.

What is Working Well

- The course is taught in a blended manner in which students select on an on-going basis where they want to be on a continuum from traditional face-to-face learning activities to entirely web-based activities. This flexibility allows students on a day-by-day basis the opportunity to determine how they want to move through the course.
- Students are given a variety of activities organized into a series of topical modules (*e.g.*, blues, jazz, Cajun). Each module includes required assignments (reading, worksheets, quizzes) and optional activities (written essays that describe what students learned from attending lectures, going to concerts, viewing films, visiting museums and historical sites, conducting interviews). Attendance of on-campus lectures is documented through an in-class portfolio that contains lecture notes, handouts, and student summaries of classroom discussions. This format of a menu of activities allows students to select assignments based on their personal preferences, physical abilities, and learning styles.
- Each assignment is given a number of points, generally 0-50, based on quality indicators such as content, thoroughness, and grammar. Final course grades are determined by the total points at the end of the quarter (*e.g.*, 1,750+ earns an A, 1,500-1,749 earns a B, and so forth). Students can therefore target a grade based on the quantity and quality of work they

choose to do. If they are very interested in a particular module, they can invest more time and effort doing assignments in that module. Alternatively, students can omit some modules or assignments that do not fit well into their schedules or areas of interest.

- The large enrollment now justifies an instructional team, which consists of multiple lecturers and graders. In this way, no single lecturer is responsible for the entire course. This allows me, for example, to have African-American specialists present on jazz, gospel, blues, and other African-American music genres. Furthermore, some teachers are particularly effective in the performance aspect of working with an face-to-face class; others are particularly good communicating with students online. The flexible instructional model allows all faculty members to play to their strengths.

- Over the years, I took content off the site completely and eventually had it published as a textbook (*Crossroads: Popular Music in America*, Prentice Hall, 2003). I did this primarily because I found that when I had the text lectures on the site, students were tending to copy and paste and then simply edit their answers to worksheet questions. My belief was that if they had to keyboard in their own answers, they learned the content better. Also, having a separate textbook allowed them to move away from the computer and study in different locations more easily. Finally, having the content in a copyrighted textbook protected all of my hard work in generating the information and provided me with royalty payments as well.

- The class sounds complex, but it is managed very efficiently in a single online course shell. Regardless of whether students take the course totally online or completely on site, or, as most students do, customize the delivery such that it lies somewhere in the middle of the continuum, the online shell is Course Central. I still make announcements in my lecture class, hold office hours, and maintain a folder of documents at the reserve desk of the library, but these are now the safety nets for the few on-site students who cannot or will not log on to the computer. In the online course shell, I maintain and manage student enrollment, communication, tests, assignments, and grading.

Ongoing Instructional Issues

- Some students are overwhelmed initially by the flexibility and choice. They are accustomed to being told what to do, and become anxious because the course is so learner-centered.
- The large and fluid attendance of the on-site classes along with multiple instructors results in extensive reliance on a lecture format in which students are passive. The instructional team is looking at strategies for improving the on-site delivery by incorporating more collaborative and active learning work.

- High course enrollment in general makes it difficult for the instructional team to get to know students by name and as individual learners, and that undermines the quality of individual student experience in the class. We are looking for ways to increase community and interaction within both the on-site and online environments.

- There are certain concepts, such as music structural characteristics, that are difficult for students to learn. Although in the on-site course, these concepts can be explained and demonstrated, this is more difficult in the online environment. Many of these concepts are ideal candidates for the creation of Learning Objects that could be shared across environments and in several other courses.

- Students who attend on-site classes experience guest musicians and speakers from the cultures represented in the course. We would like to incorporate video files of these musicians to provide a more comparable learning experience for students who take this course in a totally online format.

- The course requires students to do a large amount of work that in turn needs to be assessed, commented upon, and graded. Although the high productivity of the course allows for several instructors to participate in the grading, it is not always easy to find enough faculty members who are willing to read student work closely enough to preserve assessment integrity and a high level of teacher-student interaction.

- While students consistently report that they have learned much in the course, they are not always able to articulate clearly what they have learned. We would like to make the intended learning outcomes for the course more explicit, and ensure that assessment is directly connected to learning outcomes.

Nine years ago I found myself wondering if trying to teach today's students had become my worst nightmare. Most of them were not only different from me, but they were also different from each other, in race and ethnicity, in the music they listened to, in their preparation for college education, in their worldview. At the time, creating a course that bridged the gaps while not compromising academic integrity seemed an impossible dream. Today, that dream has mostly come true. Although there is still much to do, teaching no longer feels like an unholy alliance. Rather, it feels like a healthy and invigorating partnership in which my students, colleagues, and I work together to achieve more powerful learning.

The fall 2003 Music of Multicultural America Instructional Team is Robert Hartwell, Milissa Carey, and Olga Sheykhet. The course website can be accessed by going to www.foothill.edu to online classes to Music 8: Music of Multicultural America. ID: "guest," Password: "guest."

Elizabeth F. Barkley is Professor of Music at Foothill College in Los Altos Hills, California.

Multimedia Tools Within Interactive Environments

The first three stories in this section are examples of how faculty and institutions are transforming courses because of the power and availability of multimedia tools within interactive environments for teaching dense and complex disciplines, such as chemistry at the University of Wisconsin, statistics at DeAnza College, and economics at the University of Minnesota.

The second set of three stories illustrates how the development of rich, complex multimedia course content can assist in student learning, particularly when combined with the flexibility of the online environment. These are stories of a course in Consumer Law at Sinclair Community College, a course on Dante at The University of Texas at Austin, and a children's literature course at Foothill College.

This story, written in November of 2003, is about a web-enhanced course in chemistry that illustrates how a campus course has evolved over time with the use of the internet and related technologies. John Moore teaches a large number of students each semester with the help of graduate students and a variety of information technologies. It is easy to see how technology made a difference in this web-enhanced course.

First-Year Chemistry Students Take to Technology

John W. Moore, Colleen McCabe, and Kathleen Christoph

John Moore has been a chemistry professor at the University of Wisconsin-Madison for 15 years. During that time, he has continually faced the challenges of teaching beginning chemistry, including labs, to large numbers of students. In January of 1989, he anticipated some of our now common online web tools by writing these prophetic words in the Journal of Chemical Education: "Computer-simulated experiments, interactive videodisc lessons, instrument simulators, and computer-based data collection and analysis provide a golden opportunity to greatly broaden the horizons of laboratory instruction." More than a decade later, Moore integrated these computer-based tools and internet applications into two different general chemistry courses. One course enrolled 250 to 350 students each semester and the other enrolled 600 to 800 students. Each course consisted of lectures, discussion sections, and laboratory work.

The smaller course was a two-semester sequence; the other was an accelerated one-semester course that taught the same material and assumed the incoming students had learned a significant amount of chemistry in high school. The use of email, the web, CDs, and video technology enhanced learning and improved safety for these students.

A course-management system was used to offer online quizzes and online assignments that have replaced homework and prelab assignments. Students now had easy access to multimedia-rich tutorials that supplemented lecture material, and to descriptions of procedures, equipment, and techniques that they used each week in the chemistry lab. The online quizzes tested their understanding of each week's course content.

There were three kinds of online quizzes each week: one that replaced a pencil-and-paper quiz, a prelab quiz, and homework. Students had two opportunities to take each prelab quiz and to do each homework assignment. They received immediate feedback on the quiz as soon as it was submitted. For any wrong answer, students were given resources for exploring the answers on their own before retaking the quiz.

"This really helped results," said Renée Cole, then a postdoctoral fellow, who created the quiz questions and tutorial references. "Students may have learned the proper procedures and vocabulary in high school, or they may not have. They may also have some significant gaps in their backgrounds. This method of pretesting provided a review for some students and an important introduction for others." Online review was especially important in the one-semester course, because it assumed students had a strong chemistry background from their high school courses.

Using a course-management system lightened the workload for the teaching assistants. Quizzes and homework were scored, feedback delivered, and grades recorded electronically. The course-management system also maintained a database of questions and answers that were valuable as study materials for exams.

Weekly quizzes were given in a special online testing room that provided a controlled environment designed to minimize cheating. Online weekly quizzes were only deliverable by computers in the testing room, and there was a proctor who checked students' photo IDs as they entered the room. A chemistry proctor was present to respond to student queries about quiz content and to observe students so that copying would not occur. The course-management system was used to generate a complete class roster each week that included a quiz deadline time for each student. The deadline time prevented crowding of the 34-seat quizzing room by the more than 800 students in three lecture sections of the fall semester. Quizzes became available at noon each Thursday and had to be completed by 5 p.m. on Friday.

Both the course-management system and the chemistry department web server hosted the online syllabus, previous exams, lecture notes, teaching assistants' home pages, and website references. The interactive lecture, which used multimedia presentations and live demonstrations of chemical reactions, prohibited the web from substituting for class or lab attendance. According to Moore, "Although some redundancy was inevitable, and even desirable, students know there is unique information in the various methods of delivery. Technology has allowed us to expose students to material in different ways and thus touch a variety of learning styles."

At the beginning of the semester, students were provided with two CDs that contained video clips, computer-generated animations, and software programs to supplement the traditional textbook. Moore stated, "Our main objective was to have students develop a conceptual understanding through problem solving rather than memorize some facts they might expect to know for an exam."

Students with their own computers were best situated. However, the chemistry department had its own computer lab, and the campus had 15 computer labs at locations around campus. Some of these computer labs were open 24 hours a day and some are n the dorms, so no student was at a significant disadvantage. During the 2002-2003 academic year, more than 95 percent of students reported that they typically did their prelab quiz and online homework each week on a computer in the dorm.

Students were encouraged to use email to ask questions of faculty and teaching assistants. Moore reported that "students are quick to send email if they feel something is wrong with a quiz question or answer." Cole noticed that "some students are not comfortable with face-to-face interactions and can ask their questions at a convenient distance by using email."

The chemistry department was fortunate to have a professional videographer who could quickly provide a multimedia clip specific to lectures or labs. This videographer has also served as a resource to more than a dozen visiting faculty who have come to Madison to create video and multimedia materials. Moore estimated that more than 10 person-years were wrapped up in video production for the chemistry department – not an insignificant cost. Much of the funding for these efforts was provided by two NSF grants.

The technology that Moore envisioned more than 10 years ago was not just a pipe dream. The chemistry department at the University of Wisconsin-Madison worked toward making his vision a reality, to the advantage of faculty and students alike. Students who were comfortable with computers could use the tools of email, a course-management system, CDs, and the internet practically anytime, anywhere to participate in the learning process. For those who are interested in creating a similar learning environment, the questions are available from the Journal of Chemical Education Digital Library (http://www.jce.divched.org/JCEDLib/QBank/index.html) and the online tutorials will soon be available from the same source.

Even more critical to Moore than the improved access to learning that technology offers was the way technology changed the student role in the learning process: "I believe that the most important criterion, and the most important improvement technology can bring, is to place students in an active rather than a passive role. People learn best by doing, observing, thinking, making choices, and discovering the consequences of those choices – by being active."

John W. Moore is Professor of Chemistry and Colleen McCabe is Secretary of Academic Staff at the University of Wisconsin-Madison. Kathleen Christoph is Director of DoIt Academic Technology.

This story focuses on the design and development of an online course in elementary statistics and probability. It illustrates the power of collaboration to search out and use effective and efficient learning resources, as well as a feedback loop for continued improvement. The course described here won the 2002 California Virtual College Online Teaching Award.

Elementary Statistics and Probability

Barbara Illowsky and Susan Dean

Each year, approximately 2,500 students at De Anza College in Cupertino, California, take Elementary Statistics and Probability, an undergraduate, lower-division course. The target audience is any person who needs to learn non-calculus-based statistics. This course fulfills the math requirement needed for University of California, California State University, and many private college and university general education requirements for graduation when no specific math course is listed. Most social science, biology, and business majors also require the course. College graduates returning to school for a master's degree often take it as a brush-up or for a requirement for their area of study.

In the early 1990s, we taught our first distance learning Elementary Statistics and Probability course. In those pre-widespread-internet days, the pedagogy consisted of live lectures taught over television. Lectures were broadcast over a local cable television channel. Video recordings of the broadcasts were then made available for checkout for students out of range of the cable broadcasts. These lectures included an opportunity for students to call in during the broadcast, with the instructor answering questions live.

Over the years, with the improvement of technology along with its increased accessibility, the distance learning component of this course evolved to an almost completely online course. With 2,500 students, we feel obligated to offer the course in a variety of delivery modes to accommodate our diverse student population needs. Some of the specific reasons for moving the course online are

- More access for students outside the cable viewing area;
- More access for students who cannot regularly come to campus;
- More flexibility for students' schedules and learning styles; and
- More resources, which generally results in improved instruction.

Currently, we use the WebCT course management system, as well as chat rooms and whiteboard applications for tutoring services and for group work.

We also use asynchronous discussions and mail, Student Management, Open-Up Calendar, Course Lectures, and Introductory QuickTime Videos. The digital tools we use include MediaPlayer, Tegrity, QuickTime, Flash Player, Shockwave Player, and the Virtual TI-83 Graphing Calculator. These resources can be downloaded free from the internet. We integrate TI-83 demonstrations in our video and internet course demonstrations. Students may use a TI-86 or TI-89, if they already have one. Access to the internet is required. Optional closed-caption video programs that we record in De Anza's television studio are available on local cable TV and on videotape for overnight checkout from the De Anza Media Center.

Elementary Statistics and Probability serves approximately 100 to 120 students per quarter, four quarters per year, and fills up every term. Before starting the course, the students are required to complete an online orientation managed by the Distance Learning Office. They are welcome to attend the instructors' lectures on campus; each term, 5 to 10 students will take advantage of that option on an occasional basis.

Students are also welcome to do labs in on-campus sections. They take exams in Instructional Testing with proctors, at a scheduled exam time with faculty administering the tests, or, in special cases, off site as administered by a trusted individual. Labs and projects can be done individually or in groups. Groups can meet physically or virtually in the chat rooms or with the whiteboard. Students email, mail, fax, or drop off assignments to the Distance Learning Office. All lectures are available online with audio- and videostreaming using Tegrity WebLearner, which supports an instructor at a whiteboard doing examples. For each chapter, there are online quizzes with immediate grading and feedback.

Development of the online course took approximately one year. This included the time to learn the WebCT system and to design, develop, and test the course, and to produce the videos. Both instructors received course release time for one term plus a summer stipend. We received assistance from our Educational Technology Assistance colleagues in graphics, animation, and design.

We've had a few surprises along the way. Many students who are enrolled on our campus classes used the resources for the online section. We found that both the stand-alone video programs and the online integrated videos were especially useful for physically and learning disabled students, English as a Second Language students, students who had been ill and missed classes, and students from other sections who wanted a second hearing of the material. We were probably most surprised about how popular the course is. Students who do not succeed the first time they attempt the course will re-enroll in the online course instead of a traditional on-campus section.

This course has been a success for many students. Our retention rate has remained high. Motivated students like the online course for the independence and flexibility it offers, and it has been ideal for working, organized students and for students attending other colleges or universities. However, students with weak mathematics or organizational skills often are surprised that this delivery format is harder for them than taking the course on campus. They are the ones who withdraw from the course, get far behind, or earn poor grades. Overall, this delivery method has enabled De Anza to extend the offering of this course to more students. We have also brought in other instructors to teach for a term, and we have found that it is easy for a faculty member who did not develop the course to come in and teach it.

As much as we wish to be finished with development, we are always looking at what we can do next. Except on rare occasions, we have not had our exams proctored outside our locality. We plan on developing more online assignments. We also plan to stream audio into the chat rooms and whiteboard. In addition, we want to incorporate the use of spreadsheet software into the online component. Many of our planned developments are results of student suggestions, which we welcome and incorporate.

And the improvement continues.

Barbara Illowsky is Professor of Mathematics and Statistics and Vice President of the Academic Senate, and Susan Dean is Instructor of Math and Science at DeAnza College in Cupertino, California.

Brian Buhr is an associate professor from the Department of Applied Economics at the University of Minnesota who teaches an intermediate undergraduate course, Livestock and Meat Marketing Economics. Students learn about the structure of the livestock and meat industry, the economic principles of price behavior in the industry, and related marketing procedures, tools, and issues. Buhr has developed a successful WebCT-delivered trading commodities simulation for his students that mimics conditions in the real market.

Chris Scruton interviewed Buhr about this web-delivered simulation trading game, which was first used by 27 students in 2002, and is now a permanent module in the course. An extended summary of the interview is available at http://dmc.umn.edu/projects/trading-sim/.

Futures Trading at the University of Minnesota: An Interview With Brian Buhr

Chris Scruton

Brian Buhr's students often found understanding futures and futures trading difficult, because, unlike cars and houses, futures and future trading exist only in the abstract. Additionally, about half of his students had only minimal exposure to the principles of micro- and macroeconomics. Buhr needed a module that, in his words, would help students learn how it is possible "with no ownership, no prior investment, [and] no actual physical commodity or asset" to "execute trades and to hedge risk on the future market."

In 1995, Buhr designed a virtual trading project for his students so they could experience the futures market without any real risk. His students analyzed market conditions, observed trading behavior in both the classroom and the real-world markets, developed buying and selling strategies, communicated the rationale for these strategies to Buhr and their peers, and submitted trades and market analyses to him on paper. He then recorded the trades, calculated the results, and graded the analyses. At first, the system worked well for a couple of reasons. The students bought and sold futures just as they would in the real marketplace and learned skills such as data analysis and research methods that they would likely use in their future professions. And they used real-world factors in their market analyses to make decisions about their trades.

However, the project also had a couple of drawbacks. It became a paper blizzard for Buhr and an isolating experience for the students, who interacted almost exclusively with the instructor and consequently weren't exposed to and affected by other trader-students' strategies, as are their real-world counterparts.

To solve these problems, Buhr considered developing software that would present, record, and act upon user input in real time. In late 2001, he met with Brad Cohen, another instructional technology consultant at the Digital Media Center, and then decided to adopt a simpler strategy using readily available tools. He started in early January, and less than three weeks later, he had created the basic information pages and had the interactive tools for the trading simulation ready. He used a variety of software applications:

- MS Word to create website content and Netscape Composer to modify the website
- MS PowerPoint to support and deliver lectures and tutorials
- MS Excel to manage trades for the whole class
- WebCT to deliver course content and the trading project assignments

How did Buhr prepare his students for doing the trading simulation with these tools? He used one class period to describe the project, its goals, and the general structure of the technologies used. He also met informally and individually with the students early in the term to introduce them to the technologies.

The students also used a variety of basic software for the trading game:

- WebCT to review HTML course content and other outside trading sites
- WebCT's quiz tool to test their knowledge of economic principles and trading practices
- WebCT's discussion tool to post trades
- Adobe Acrobat, Microsoft Word, or Netscape Composer to create market analyses
- WebCT's student presentation tool to access the Excel trade management spreadsheet and share the market analyses

Later in the game, Buhr assigned alternating teams of student moderators to administer class trade accounting summaries of the simulation. This process meant that students experienced trading as something like a series of data snapshots, rather than a continuous activity. Although less intense than real-life trading, the experience still provided students insights into their peers' and their own trading strategies.

At first, the students had some problems accessing PDF files and converting Microsoft Word documents into usable HTML files. Buhr and his students eventually decided to use Netscape Composer as their primary web development tool since it was available for free, which significantly diminished these problems. According to Buhr, the web-delivered simulation trading game was a success. Some of the positive instructional outcomes he observed are described in the following sections.

Students Learned from Each Other

The students engaged in more realistic trading behaviors. They engaged in much greater volumes of trading, used more of the strategies employed by professionals in the field, and based more of their trades on others' successful strategies. "You could see students talking to each other on the [WebCT] discussion board [and gravitating] toward winning positions, which is exactly what happens in the [real] market," Buhr reported.

The students produced more realistic, professional analyses. "You very distinctly saw that students [were looking] at other students' presentations," Buhr noted, which soon led to "a sort of arms race as students rapidly began to assimilate those features into their own reports. [As a result,] the quality of the analyses rose rapidly over the course of the entire semester."

This realistic behavior was perhaps the best and most exciting outcome because it was serendipitous: "You'd like to say that that was your objective to start with, but...the only real goal [was] to take this analytical piece outside of the class and get the market analyses to run alongside [class discussions of economic principles]."

However, the effects were much broader. For example, a student who performed technical analyses as part of his job with a trading firm in Minneapolis began to do so while trading in the simulated market as well, and this began to pay dividends. A number of other students also adopted these methods, something Buhr didn't see happening during the six or seven iterations of the paper simulation. "The possibilities for interaction piqued [students'] interest more than I though it would," Buhr said. "I really didn't expect to see [the improvements in analytical techniques and presentation skills] so quickly."

Instructor and Students Interacted More

The instructor was free to spend more time on instructional activities. Since students occasionally took on the role of moderators, he had more opportunities to stand back, observe, and comment on the students' performances. The student moderators also gained additional valuable learning experiences, in particular because they were able to view the aggregate market activities and observe how important trader interaction is to markets.

Buhr and his students became collaborators. Buhr's early individual meetings with the students were especially successful. "We were having to work out together how to get these market analyses posted and accessible to the participants. It took us out of the normal teacher-student relationship and made us a collaborative problem-solving unit," he said.

Students Responded Positively

Buhr incorporated questions into an end-of-term student evaluation questionnaire that asked students to rate the use of technology in the course on a one (very poor) to seven (exceptional) Likert scale. The web-based lecture notes were rated most highly (6.2/7.0 mean score). The mean scores of answers to questions about the use of the internet (5.3/7.0), the computer-assisted simulation (5.5/7.0), and the market analyses (5.6/7.0) were above average, which Buhr described as a "B or so." The two questions with the lowest mean scores asked students to rate the use of WebCT in general (4.2/7.0), and specifically its use to facilitate the trading simulation (4.6/7.0). Buhr attributed these lower scores to the slow response of WebCT when students accessed it over a modem and sometimes when they accessed it over the campus network during critical periods, and to students' unfamiliarity with HTML file structures, linking techniques, Microsoft Word's HTML conversion feature, and WebCT's file-transfer protocol.

Future Uses of the Web-Based Simulation

In the next iterations of the WebCT trading project, Buhr intends to encourage students to create their HTML documents with Netscape Composer rather than Microsoft Word. He expects that connections to WebCT course sites will become faster and more reliable and that students' opinions of the project will improve as a result of increased response time.
Buhr identified several issues that instructors who teach with technology may want to consider:

- Consult with teaching and technical support personnel and clearly identify the instructional goals.
- Learn to teach with technology by jumping in and being flexible.
- Expect to spend the same amount of time supporting students' use of technology as it usually takes to administer paper-based activities.
- Expect students' technology skills to vary widely.

Chris Scruton is an Instructional Technology Consultant at the Digital Media Center of the University of Minnesota.

This story of a course that was transformed using the familiar soap-opera medium is a soap opera in itself. It has a large cast of characters skilled in varying disciplines working together over time to create a series of learning resources that students can use online and on campus to achieve the course objectives, including developing a frame of mind as an intelligent consumer. The department head even serves as the lead motivator who gradually wins over the faculty member, who in turn pitches ideas to the technical department to gather a team to do the makeover of this course. One of the messages to take away from this story is that content development of complex and sophisticated learning objects, which these video modules are, takes time and generally an array of talented folks. The outcomes, however, can be worth it, as the learning objects are flexible, always available, and generally engage students in real thinking.

That's Edutainment: Consumer Law 103

Nadine Ballard

Like a car with 150,000 miles on it, our Gen-Ed Consumer Law course was old, tired, and worn out. It was time for an extreme makeover. As we thought of all the possible changes for the course, our ideas evolved from considering a talk-show format to a fast-paced, slapstick soap-opera series that would engage students in the real-life problems of the video characters. Instead of a boring lecture and written story problems, we brought to life a continuing story by creating an eight-episode soap opera full of conflict, betrayal, intrigue, and plot twists to allow the students to laugh while learning.

This makeover took the collaborative efforts of the department head, the instructor, a number of technical staff from the distance learning department, the theater department, and many volunteers outside of the university including families, friends, and cooperative merchants. How did we pull this all together and get all these people to volunteer their time? We were all motivated by the *fun* of it, and by the excitement of producing something new, innovative, and creative. In fact, the common attribute of all those who worked on this project was their ability to be creative.

After trying for several years to convince me to update this class with current material, the department head was finally successful by promising me that it was going to be fun. We brainstormed ideas and agreed that using real-life, high-quality video vignettes would be a creative way to teach consumer law in the context of real-life applications. We wrote an outline of the issues that had to be addressed to cover the hot topics in consumer law, and brainstormed again about how the topics could be combined and what type of video presentations could be arranged.

As lawyers, we were trained to learn and teach law issues through the use of hypothetical situations, where the student must learn to apply the law to a given situation. We agreed that a story using the same characters facing a new consumer issue week after week could be both fun and effective. I began to outline a story that followed a couple from their engagement through their wedding, running into problems with everything from layaways to leases to lending issues.

When I pitched the idea to the creative tech from the web-course development team assigned to write the script, produce, and film the vignettes, he gladly jumped on the bandwagon. He immediately saw the opportunity to create *The Young and the Litigious*, a soap-opera type story, full of stereotypical soap-opera characters, including the meddling mother-in-law, the father in a coma, the pretty ex-girlfriend, and the dim-witted brother who vies for the mother's attention and approval. To create a classic conflict, he chose the rich-versus-poor class struggle, so the mother could manipulate the financial transactions to convince her son that his poor fiancée was just a gold digger seeking the family fortune.

The first script set the stage for a format that allowed the characters, in a 6- to 12-minute drama, to experience a consumer transaction such as a ring purchase, car lease, car repair, internet transaction, or telemarketing scam, and to incorporate the refrain, "Remember what Dad said" on legal or common-sense advice before experiencing the accident that put him in the coma. Each episode ends with a cliffhanger in which a cast member directly addresses the students and asks, "What should I do?" This open-ended question dovetails into that week's homework assignment, which requires the students to help resolve the character's consumer problems. I worked with the video producer on each of the scripts to make sure that all the legal issues were raised, and that "Dad's advice" was a correct statement of the law.

While the graphic artists were working on documents, the video producer was writing the script, finding costumes and props, and auditioning theater students for the soap-opera roles. We considered Sinclair Community College to be a big movie studio with its video production department, personnel, and theater department. Because of the incredible creativity of the video producer, the script called for costumes to support scenes of the characters dressed as rock stars, mimes, civil war buffs, country-western folks, sci-fi fans, and Renaissance characters. The many crazy props included a wristwatch-style GPS device complete with a satellite dish that actually rotates.

Shooting the eight-episode series was fun, exhausting, and very rewarding. It was also a significant logistical challenge. For instance, almost every episode features a flashback scene that takes place in a car. We needed a car with no windshield in a big, quiet space so that we could set up lights, costumes, and so forth. Predictably, no one offered us the use of a car without a windshield until the City of Dayton volunteered a municipal vehicle that had been in a nasty accident. Since the damage was not visible on camera, the car performed beautifully. An hour after we finished shooting in it, the car was towed away to be sold for scrap.

The college also provided several locations and scenic backdrops that the stories required. When we did have to shoot elsewhere, we discovered that the college has such a good reputation in the community that it was easy to get permission to shoot just about anywhere. During filming, we had the foresight to take digital photos of the characters in costume on location for use in the website materials. These photos were distributed throughout the course materials, with informational or funny statements inside dialogue bubbles to keep the soap opera theme visible throughout the course.

The video theme was also carried out in a consumer law quiz that the students take in Week One to test their knowledge of consumer law as they enter the course. The quiz was created as a Flash animation, with the characters from the video asking the questions. After the students responded True or False, they were given the correct answer along with the legal basis for that answer. Each answer ended with, "What would Dad have said?" – wisdom from the father in the video.

Throughout the course, students were provided a consistent format with a weekly list of activities to be completed:

* View an episode of the video, *The Young and the Litigious*.
* Read the instructor's overview of the topic.
* Look at internet resources with links to the full text of the consumer law, as well as resources from federal, state, and private sites.
* Check out the wording on legal documents.
* Answer critical thinking questions.
* Participate in group discussions of application questions in the discussion forum.

To further connect the video story to the work the students would do in class, we set a goal to create all the written documents used in the story with the characters' names and the featured consumer product or transaction detailed. For example, the store advertisement that led the characters to the jewelry store was reproduced, and the students were required to analyze it for its compliance with advertising law. Similarly, the estimate for a car repair was reproduced, and the students were required to analyze it for its compliance with the law pertaining to the repair and service of motor vehicles.

The video connection was even carried through into the student assessment component. Several of the homework assignments required letter writing on behalf of one of the video characters. One example was a letter to correct an error in the credit report that was reproduced for the video character, listing the unauthorized debts, which the video depicts debt collectors trying to collect by very unorthodox but humorous methods.

Each week, the students demonstrated their level of understanding of the law and related issues by individually responding to critical thinking questions. Many of the application questions, assigned to small groups for discussion, asked the students to explain what the character should have done based on the law or what consequences the characters would suffer if they took a certain course of action. The final exam gave the students six scenarios that featured the characters from the video and asked them to pick three to prepare a small-claims complaint. For each scenario, they also answered a series of questions in which they had to identify specific violations of any consumer law presented in the course.

The successful development of this class took the cooperative effort of experts in the law and in videography, and drew from those with acting, filming, and editing skills as well as those with internet research, website creation, word processing, and graphic arts abilities. Everyone agrees that the process was as much fun as the outcome, and that the highly entertaining and engaging materials are now a primary ingredient in successfully educating students.

Nadine Ballard is Part-Time Instructor at Sinclair Community College and a Full-Time Magistrate in Dayton, Ohio.

This story describes the inspirations and processes for the development of a multimedia web resource on Dante. It illustrates the type of talent and the amount of time and resources that are generally behind rich, engaging, and comprehensive content resources. This story is based primarily on an interview with Guy Raffa, a Dante scholar who was the lead faculty on a prize-winning resource for students used in a web-enhanced instructional environment. For faculty, this ongoing project demonstrates the power of scholarly teaching. For students, a difficult and complex literary work becomes engaging and accessible.

Developing Danteworlds: A Conversation with Guy Raffa

By the Staff at the Center for Instructional Technologies

"Using technology is not a shortcut to good teaching," says Guy Raffa, associate professor of Italian at The University of Texas at Austin. "The good technology that we have now must go hand in hand with good pedagogy. Faculty members need to think long and hard about how they're teaching their classes, and then how technology can help them to maybe do it a little differently."

Raffa developed *Danteworlds* (danteworlds.lamc.utexas.edu) to use with his course on Dante taught in the Departments of French and Italian. Students in several other courses have also benefited from this beautiful and informative way to present Dante's *Inferno*. A humanities lecture class of 300 students at Stanford University has already included use of the website in the course, and Raffa has received inquiries and comments from many other universities as well.

Although there are other web resources available about Dante, most are text based. These are good for scholars, but Raffa wanted a resource he could use to engage undergraduate students. The *Danteworlds* site is distinctive, with its original artwork depicting scenes from the text and audio recordings of passages in the original Italian.

"In teaching *The Divine Comedy,* you learn quickly that students need to visualize what's happening. The user of *Danteworlds* needs to be able to see what Dante sees as he journeys through Hell, up the mountain of Purgatory, and through the spheres of Paradise," Raffa said. As he developed concepts for the project over a number of years, Raffa reflected, "I was already thinking about how I was teaching the class and how this project would complement and enrich aspects of the teaching." His goal was to use images of Dante's *Inferno* to help his students better understand and interpret the text.

This was Raffa's first instructional multimedia project. He emphasized that a team approach was necessary for the project's success, drawing on programming and technical assistance as well as support from his department, college, and university resources such as UT Austin's Center for Instructional Technologies. As he developed the site, student feedback was also important. Raffa asked his students in class and on questionnaires what would help them the most and what they would like to see in the project.

Student comments from course evaluations show that they appreciate the multimedia approach the *Danteworlds* site offers. "The website was invaluable to my understanding of the *Inferno*," remarked one student. "The pictures, both old and new, added a new dimension to the reading, as did the audio recordings." Raffa found that students do better by several measures: They come better prepared for class because the supplementary material is available on the web, it is engaging, and it helps them see and hear the text in new ways.

Quiz scores are better as well, Raffa has noticed. Students use the site to prepare for class or to review and enhance what they've learned from class discussions. In class, discussion can reach a higher level more quickly. He can spend less time on some of the basic information in class and talk about other elements of the course related to the poem. That is one of the pedagogical advantages of this project, he believes: changing the way the classroom teaching occurs and enriching the students' experiences.

Raffa is currently working on the next phase of development. Dante's *Divine Comedy* has three parts. "We've been in Hell so far; now it's time to move on to Purgatory, and then Heaven." Experience from the processes used in the *Inferno* project has helped. Raffa is writing the commentary, notes, and study questions for the next parts, and collaboration with the artist and technology specialists at UT Austin is under way. Raffa advises other faculty who are interested in developing instructional technology projects to start thinking early about how they are teaching their class and how the technology will help, and then to talk to as many people as possible who have technological expertise.

Another area that needs careful consideration is copyright and permissions. "Having an artist actually create the images means that we have the copyright to these images. Other images we were able to get and use, because they're in the public domain, since they were produced so long ago. So we're able to use them without infringing on others' copyrights or paying costly fees," he said. Because he is a Dante scholar, Raffa was able to write his own commentary and notes, so those can be used and posted on the web. He cautions others to avoid the temptation of taking information, images, or other material that may be available and putting these together for a project. Some materials may be copyright free if just used in the classroom, but if they are to be freely accessible on the web, without strict password protection, permissions may be needed.

For Raffa, the project has been a serendipitous combination of factors, and he warmly acknowledges the assistance he has received. He is fortunate, he says, because of the variety of support at The University of Texas at Austin for faculty using instructional technology in their courses. Raffa believes that instructional technology is a good way to bring together the different components of a faculty member's teaching, research, and other work. The process has helped him to develop new ideas for his research, which in turn becomes part of his scholarship. His teaching and scholarship have been energized through working on this project, and he is eager to continue the journey through the next phases of development.

Rosemary Arca has been teaching children's literature for four years. She has an M.A. in English Composition and has been an avid reader of children's literature after taking a survey course in children's lit for her Reading Specialist's credential. The website for this course was developed by a team. It uses an internally developed Etudes courseware tool for its communication and management and content resources structures. For more on Etudes, including Etudes II, see foothillglobalaccess.org/etudes/.

Roots and Wings: Capturing the Exuberance of Children's Literature Online

Rosemary Arca

English 8 – An Introduction to Children's Literature, is a survey of children's literature from many periods and cultures, including classics, picture books, folktales, biography, poetry, fantasy, and contemporary fiction. Emphasis is on the didactic and sociological ideas included in books usually read by children and young adults. The URL for the course is fh.etudes.fhda.edu/etudes.cgi?request,logframe!cs_id,1642663198!.

Course Development Process

The design and development of the content and resources for this course website was a team effort. The team consisted of the faculty member, an instructional designer, a graphic designer, and a programmer. The team brought invaluable advice and expertise in course design, graphics, and learning-object design. For example, instructional designer Robert Griffiths created the template for the lessons (Learn, Apply, Explore, Evaluate) and verified the Bobby Approval elements for disabled students. Graphic designer Ana Gamaza found the Luna theme and created the Flash animations and the Lesson themes and color palette. Programmer Drake Lewis designed coding for the virtual pop-up book, the Build a Folktale machine, and the databases.

The website was created in Dreamweaver using the Foothill College Etudes courseware shell; it uses Flash and QuickTime objects. The team worked over six months, meeting each Monday for two hours, with phone consultations in between. After the Monday meeting, where we set the to-do list for the week, we each spent three to four hours a week working on our own assigned tasks.

English 8 migrated online in response to two events: (1) the English Department re-organized to offer each of its literature offerings once a year on campus, but offered additional times in online or evening format; and (2) the instructor desired to preserve the legacy of student research, using a searchable archive and her belief – and design challenge – that the energy and charm of the on-campus class could be reproduced in an online environment. In the exit surveys given to all students at the end of the course, we ask if this whimsy is in fact achieved. Most students comment on the energy and delightful interface of the course, coupled with the depth of information and learning that takes place in it. In other words, they work hard but they have a great time doing it!

The Design Process

At the first Design Team meeting, all agreed that this course should echo the imagination, wonder, and fun of children's literature as well as providing tools and resources to enhance learning. We created two lists of design elements to achieve this combination of fantasy and pedagogically relevant environment. Here are the lists of the Shoot for the Moon/Just for Fun elements and the pedagogically relevant elements:

Shoot for the Moon/Just for Fun Elements

- Virtual pop-up book
- A Folktale Machine that showcases student-written tales
- Animations highlighting illustration techniques
- Videos of former students sharing their favorite books
- A virtual storyteller who models good storytelling techniques
- Virtual poetry readings to emphasis the power of the spoken word
- The Unmasking of Luna at the end of the course, morphing Luna into the instructor

Pedagogically Relevant Elements

- Luna the Storyteller, who stands in as guide and teacher persona throughout the course
- Animated Landscape of Children's Literature with descriptive rollovers
- Archive database that allows students to input and access a variety of resources
- Annotated bibliography database that allows students to suggest good books in a variety of focus areas and allows students to search for books in those focus areas
- Authors and literary agents who visit the forums to answer students' specific questions about their work and about publishing
- Forums of principal concepts and tasks that encourage student discussion
- ADA approved access to course

The design phase was full of creative energy; anything seemed possible, and as a result, each team member grew professionally as we created a website that included all the Shoot the Moon/Just for Fun elements we'd envisioned and all the pedagogically relevant elements we needed. We learned new software. We imagined innovative solutions to design problems. We shared a commitment to make sure this popular course was equally as engaging and entertaining as the on-campus version. We were intent on giving the course good roots in content and technology while gifting it with wings of imagination and wonder.

Students responded with enthusiasm to the course and actually produced more work more willingly than in the on-campus class. And this work was archived so that other students could share its legacy where appropriate. In exit interviews, students noted that they had a deep understanding of the course material, because the multimedia explanations were clear.

My students say they're online about the same amount of time they'd be in class, five or six hours a week, not counting research and writing time. I'm online about three or four hours a week, commenting on their work and answering questions. The website is very efficient from a teacher's point of view. The course is fully online. The on-campus class accesses the website to submit work, and thus the on-campus class becomes a sort of hybrid. The average class size is the maximum – 50 students – for a literature course. The retention rate is about 80 percent, evidence of the fact that they enjoy the work.

I reveled in the streamlined annotation of student work, since the databases allowed me to quickly access student bibliographies, and the forum search function enabled quick searches for student participation. Additionally, I was able to include many more teachable moments in the class, because I could hear an author interview on the radio or read a review of a book and immediately attach the relevant URL in a message to my students. The course improved in breadth and depth as a result of its online form. It also became a living document that grew as people added resources.

The course is evolving as it enters its third year. Some streamlining of processes in the course design is taking place. Some course tasks have proved nonproductive, and they are being revised. Overall, the course seems to give students both the roots and wings needed for their exploration of children's literature.

Rosemary Arca teaches children's literature in the Language Arts Division at Foothill College in Los Altos Hills, California.

Courses Based on New Research

This section features two stories that have much in common with the previous stories illustrating new tools and new environments. Additionally, these courses were redesigned with an explicit desire to build on research related to teaching and learning. This is not to say that the other courses did not also do this, but it was a more explicit design variable in these two cases.

Lisa Gerrard's technology story has its beginnings in the early 1980s, when she started her students using primitive word processing software that ran on an IBM 3033 mainframe. Gerrard noted that the pedagogical catalyst for using technology was the research in composition showing that instilling an attitude toward writing as a "malleable rather than a one-time event" encouraged better writing. The new technologies make revision, editing, and writing much more accessible, and thus the focus can be on the writing rather than struggling through the media.

Rhetoric in Cyberspace: A Campus-Online Hybrid Class

Lisa Gerrard

The students in English 132D, Discourses in Cyberspace, are primarily upper-division students satisfying requirements for a writing assignment course. The catalog description for English 132D states that it "defines and explores special topics that relate matters of rhetoric/writing to social, political, or cultural concerns," *i.e.*, each instructor chooses a different theme for this course. This course is taught in a computer lab on campus with significant use of a course website and a variety of other software. The class has an enrollment limit of 20, because of the number of available computers.

Every writing course at UCLA has a theme, and the theme for this one is "The Rhetoric of Cyberspace." I have two parallel goals for students: (1) Analyze and write about different virtual spaces, and (2) participate in and create virtual spaces themselves. I see it as an outside-inside cyberspace perspective. For the outside perspective experience, students follow weblogs, review websites, and observe and analyze online forums, discussions, and boards. Their purpose is to analyze the overall personality, audience, and effectiveness of the virtual space for the particular community, from what goes on in these spaces. For the inside perspective, students build websites and participate in cyberspace discussions, forums, and lists. Their purpose is to "experience the virtual space to know what it is like," and to talk and write to people about the experiences.

Pedagogical Strategies

Here is a summary of the pedagogical and technological tools I use to teach this class, from an interview in May 2003. More examples of faculty stories at UCLA are at: www.college.ucla.edu/edtech/interviews.

I use the online discussion boards and chat rooms on our website to create a community. I have students work in small face-to-face groups first, so that they can get to know each other offline. Then the groups make informal presentations in the chat room, or initiate a discussion with the class. Students are very comfortable talking in the chat rooms; they are much more willing to participate there than in face-to-face discussions among 20 people. The chat room makes it easier for everyone to join the conversation.

I also use a MOO, a virtual reality environment where students can take on characters and give them descriptions. They can also interact by typing commands that show their characters performing actions, *e.g.*, "Joe waves at Carole." The MOO is also used by people outside of the class, so students interact with complete strangers as well as with their classmates.

This feature gives students practice writing for audiences other than the teacher and their peers. Students can also see how effective their rhetorical skills are because their writing usually elicits an immediate reaction from others. Writing in a MOO also gives students practice writing descriptively; they can create places – *e.g.*, rooms or gardens – and furnish them with items such as benches that visitors can sit on, books they can read, and people and animals they can interact with. That is, they can program the objects they create, using only words, to respond to commands a visitor to their room might type in.

I also use a piece of software called Network Assistant in the computer lab, which allows me to project images from students' computers. For example, I may give them a passage from one of their papers to revise. Afterward, I can project what they wrote onto a large screen at the front of the room, so that the class can discuss it and make suggestions for revision.

I use the class website in several ways. In addition to the chat room, I include links to sources they can use for their papers. In some of my classes, we do a rhetorical analysis of websites, talking about who the audience is and what the different rhetorical elements of the site are. Also, students email each other through the website and meet in small groups in the chat room to work on collaborative projects.

Technology makes it much easier for a writer to revise; and it also helps break students of the notion that they have to write a paper in a single block. They can begin anywhere they want. They can experiment; computers give them flexibility as stylists. I don't know if students are learning more than they did without computers, but much of the writing process is easier and a lot more fun for them.

One of the newest tools for writing instruction is weblogs. Students can keep online journals in which other students comment on their writing and link to sources that might be relevant to their topic. What's happening now with weblogs is a good example of the kind of experimenting that goes on routinely in computers and writing: Whenever a new technology comes along, instructors try to see how it might work in the classroom.

Student Response

The students seem comfortable with the technology. When I first started teaching my classes with computers in 1980, I had to teach my students everything from scratch. Now I show them what to do, and most of them have no problems. The students who are most comfortable with the computer help me assist the ones with less experience, so that we spend little class time on the technology itself and can focus on writing.

One of the first things I noticed is that the technology serves to socialize the class very quickly. Students look at each other's writing without being asked or encouraged to do so. Also, the students get very excited about building a website. Websites appear to be something mysterious and difficult, and when they can do it themselves after a few days, they feel very empowered. Their response to the MOO virtual reality cyberspace is different. This appears to be a space that encourages playfulness and experimentation with language and objects.

How do I see the course evolving? I really see that the class will be making more use of weblogs in the future. I haven't decided whether or not to introduce the keeping of a class log. A recent addition to the reading list is from Michael Lewis' book, *Next*. This reading encourages thinking about how the internet is changing our basic ideas about culture, such as who has the authority to be an expert when a 15-year-old can be an expert dispensing legal advice. This reading also encourages discussion about the types of rhetoric that are emerging and maturing on the internet.

Building Community in the Classroom

I teach writing, and one of my goals is to teach students to shape their work in a lot of different ways. I also try to create a community in the classroom with lots of personal interaction. I like students to feel comfortable and relaxed where they can make friends and not be afraid to express themselves. They should not feel as if they will be judged every time they open their mouths. I also think it's important that the class is hands on and that I don't do a lot of lecturing.

With these tools and strategies, the atmosphere of the class is fairly noncompetitive, and the students take responsibility for their own learning.

Even in a chat room with 20 students, it is very unusual for any student to be silent. They are actively involved and socializing with each other. They relax in a way that doesn't come easily in a face-to-face setting. Also, while some of them may not be strong writers, most of them have wonderful language skills. Best of all, the focus in the cyberspace environment is on the students and their writing, not on the teacher.

Lisa Gerrard is a Lecturer in the writing program at the University of California at Los Angeles.

This story is for you if you have difficulty backing off from online involvement in everything your students do. William Allen learned it accidentally by going away for a week! The particular context is a course in the history of photography, an upper-division course focusing on the history, aesthetics, and appreciation of photography. The students are generally full-time students, and the primary appeal of the online course is its convenience. The students purchase a textbook, and digital resources are protected behind a password system. Students have access to a large and growing online database of articles.

Web-Enhanced History of Photography Course

William Allen

Here's the story of my experience in learning to back away a bit from teacher participation.

I had taught art history in the classroom for abut 20 years when I accepted my first online teaching assignment. I liked the classroom, the give and take of discussion and interaction with students. Most of my students liked the classes I taught. They were lively, I did my best to intuit the chemistry of each group and modify my approach to teaching material accordingly. As I looked over the Blackboard CMS, I said to myself, "The discussion board is where an online course will become a community, if it is to happen."

I decided to make the discussion board an important part of the class, including the grade I would assign to students. I told the students that each week, I would post one or more discussion topics. Each student would receive three grades for participation. The first grade could be automatic. I set a day for students to show up on the discussion board and say something. If they satisfied the time limit, they got five points for doing so.

The second grade would be 1-5, depending on the substance of their participation, especially on their first response to the topic. I expected the first response to indicate that they had read the textbook assignment for the week and that they had thought about the topic for the week, organized it, and posted a short essay-like contribution.

The third grade, again 1-5, would be determined by their weeklong participation on the discussion board. I expected each student to read the contributions of all students and to respond critically to what they read. I did not expect each student to respond to every post, but to respond to several and to respond to the subsequent posts by students. I made it clear that "I agree" or "I like what you said" would not count as responses.

During the first two weeks of class, I was disappointed. The students were posting and responding, but the board had a "meet the requirements" quality. I visited the board several times a day and always responded to each new post. I wanted my students to see that I was interested in what they said. I was determined to encourage them by showing my continuous surveillance of the discussion board and prompting them to expand on something or investigate a different aspect of what they had written. The requirements were being met mechanically, but the students were not becoming engaged with the topic or with one another.

The third week of the semester I had to be out of town. I told my students that I would try to check in with them as I could, but that I would not be there as regularly as I had been. I did check in and made a comment or two, but that was all.

When I returned, I went to the discussion board to assess the week. I was astounded and humbled. What I had been hoping for had begun to develop. Without my constant presence on the discussion board, the students had begun to talk to each other about the topic, and the board had taken on the traits of conversation: genuine give and take among the students, expansion beyond the confines of the assigned topic, a bit of teasing and socializing.

I suddenly realized that I had been in the way. My obsessive effort to be involved constantly on the discussion board had been an obstacle. Students were responding to me, not to the topic and not to each other, at least not as I had intended. I realized that I needed to create some distance between the teacher and students for the discussion board to take on a life of its own.

Once I realized this, I made an effort to intrude myself into the discussion board only to offer an occasional summary or to correct an error, although I gave students a chance to do this before I did. By the end of the course, and within the evaluations handled by the chair of my department, students were saying that they had never worked so hard on a course, rarely had enjoyed a class as much as this one, and had come to know their classmates better than in a traditional classroom setting. Part of the success of a distance education course depends on there remaining some distance between teacher and class. It was a lesson I am glad I learned early in the semester's progress.

William Allen is Professor of Art History and Director of the Center for Learning Technologies at Arkansas State University.

Programs Evolving Over Time, From Online to On-Campus

The next two stories are characterized by their redesign to meet the flexibility needs of the students, and to accommodate the learning curve of faculty members as well. The first story is of a program that has evolved from web-enhanced to fully online, while the second concerns a program offering students their choice of delivery formats.

Lisa Young describes how some of the characteristics of her students proved to be key motivators for her experimenting with different types of online courses, and shares how she learned some of the subtleties of ensuring good interaction on a discussion board.

Online Courses in Water Resources Technology

Lisa C. Young

I have been using online components in my classes for over five years and have found the practice to be very useful for myself as an instructor and for my students. I have dabbled with web-enhanced, hybrid, and fully online course delivery methods.

To understand why I am now using the web to aid in providing essential knowledge to my students, it is important to know what subjects I teach and who my students are. I am responsible for teaching Water Resources Technology, specifically, the core classes for degrees in Hydrologic Studies and Water, Wastewater, and Industrial Treatment Technologies at GateWay Community College in Phoenix.

You may think, "Those subjects are substantially ingrained in scientific principles and field-based hands-on experiences," and you are correct. However, I have used an online approach to teaching and learning because of the diversity of my students. The majority of my students are re-careering adult learners in their 40s who have existing career, family, and other life responsibilities. My student population ranges in age from 16 to 67; some are still in high school, while others have completed graduate degrees. Many of my students have not taken a class in over 20 years; many are already working in this field and are taking classes to enhance their knowledge base. These students are often working 12-hour shifts with a three-days-on and four-days-off schedule.

These characteristics of my student population encouraged me to try some special scheduling techniques. I have found that using the internet to deliver parts or all of the content of my classes has resolved a lot of scheduling issues and increased enrollment and retention. I started using online course components to provide students with additional opportunities to interact outside of the classroom and to provide additional resources such as lecture material to the students. The students were thrilled with the opportunity to explore and share their ideas at a time that was convenient for them.

I initially used the Web Course in a Box software, and later, Blackboard. Eventually, I decided to try to offer some courses completely online. This was met by a mixture of reactions from the students. Some of the students were horrified that they would not be meeting regularly with an instructor, while others were thrilled to have the pressure of dealing with scheduling and child-care challenges go away. When I met with students to advise them on the appropriate courses to take, I strongly encouraged them to schedule time for the class and to attend it just as if they were taking the class on campus. Students who did this had no problem completing the course; those who did not were often asking me for incompletes at the end of the semester. After a few semesters, I established due dates for the assignments, and students are now able to better plan their time and submit their assignments in a timely manner.

The biggest surprise I had in regard to online class delivery was in getting class participation. I knew students would submit their assignments, but I was concerned that the students would miss the class interaction. Making friends, networking, and the wonderful in-class discussions are often more valuable than reading the textbook, conducting research, viewing resources, and doing the assignments.

I knew discussion boards would be the key component to providing dynamic interaction in an online course. I formulated open-ended, somewhat controversial questions for each topic area and provided a framework of timeliness and respect within which the students were asked to participate. The initial results were incredible. Students were asking questions of each other and conducting research that was not included in the questions, yet was applicable to the subject matter; they were conversing about key water issues.

The discussion board was a huge success in the first class in which I used it. The second class was a different story. Students answered the questions, but they did not go any further; it was a stagnant discussion board. What I found is that when there are one or two students who set the bar for the discussion board, the rest of the students follow suit. Without these champions, the instructor must ask additional open-ended questions to stimulate the curiosity of the students and to light a fire in them.

I have thoroughly enjoyed teaching online. Developing the online courses is a never-ending task. The materials must continuously be reviewed and improved. I am currently in the process of updating my courses with 3-D visualizations of processes and video of machinery in use, as well as developing virtual field trips. As technology changes, I try to adapt, learn, and incorporate it into my instruction.

Lisa C. Young is Program Director of the Water Resources Technology Program at GateWay Community College in Phoenix.

This story is about the evolution of a Foundations of Nursing course based on ongoing evaluation and student comments. The course is offered in three formats simultaneously: as a campus course, as a hybrid course, and as a fully online asynchronous course. For courses with higher enrollment needs, this strategy can be effective and efficient for faculty and students.

Increasing Access: Multiple Course Delivery Systems for Nursing

Jay Keith

Pamela Korte is a veteran online educator, having taught a fully online version of Nursing 110 – Foundations of Nursing since 2001. This one-credit nonclinical course at Monroe Community College (MCC) introduces students to the nursing profession, exploring the history of nursing, the health care delivery system, the roles nurses play in this system, and the legal and ethical bases for the practice of nursing.

Most of the students in the program are adult students, balancing their education with the demands of family life and a job. In 2001, for example, the average age of students in this program was approximately 32 years. The college recognizes that most students must attend the program on a part-time basis and allows nursing students up to five years to complete its program.

The clinical portion of MCC's nursing program adds to the time pressures on students by requiring their presence at health care facilities off campus for large blocks of time every week. When Professor Korte began teaching Foundations of Nursing online, her course was part of the program's response to the changing needs of its students. Offering Foundations of Nursing online provided increased flexibility for program access, helping to decrease the time students need to graduate. In addition, this online version of the course has taken full advantage of the web, using a great variety of online resources to enhance existing course material.

Over time, student course evaluations of the online version of Foundations of Nursing expressed a renewed interest in synchronous discussions to delve more deeply into some of the assignments. Other students wanted synchronous discussions to help them become familiar with the course management system use – the SUNY Learning Network – and the professor. This interest demonstrates students' engagement with and interest in the course material. The course is designed to confront ethical and legal issues in the nursing profession, and beginning nursing students easily see themselves as stakeholders in the debates and discussions in which the course engages them.

Moreover, students' desire for more synchronous contact with their professor during the early stages of their education is quite natural in a program designed to educate health care professionals.

Despite students' desires for synchronous discussion, however, the time demands on these students have, if anything, increased. Therefore, any changes made to the online format had to balance the personal touch of a traditional classroom with the reality of shrinking schedules and looming workloads in students' personal lives.

To meet these seemingly contradictory demands, Professor Korte created a fully synchronous version of Foundations of Nursing as an alternative to her existing online version of the course. The synchronous version used the same course content and the same evaluation methods as the online course, but offered students the security and immediacy of the traditional classroom. With two delivery methods offered simultaneously, students could choose to take Foundations of Nursing either online or in fully synchronous mode. Response to the synchronous version of the course was overwhelmingly positive, but it soon became evident that many nursing students needed simultaneously the flexibility of online education and the human contact that only synchronous discussion can provide.

In response to these needs, the Foundations of Nursing course is being offered in three formats: a hybrid version, a fully synchronous classroom version, and fully asynchronous online version. The hybrid version of this course will combine the benefits of both online and traditional classes; it will give students the opportunity to meet and interact with their professor and fellow students periodically to discuss difficult concepts, engaging issues, and progress in the course. At the same time, the course's asynchronous component will allow students the flexibility to complete assignments at times that are convenient to their busy schedules. Professor Korte believes that providing this course using all three delivery systems simultaneously is the optimal way to maximize student access while accommodating a variety of learning styles.

Jay Keith is an Instructor at Monroe Community College in Rochester, New York.

Stories and More Stories

The stories in this chapter are only a sample of the innovative course redesigns by creative faculty and faculty support personnel. Many institutions are now creating faculty galleries of innovative courses and projects. Here are a few additional links to get started:

- The Faculty Gallery at UCLA
  (www.college.ucla.edu/edtech/interviews/)
- Faculty Projects at the University of Minnesota
  (http://dmc.umn.edu/projects/index.shtml)
- Conversations With Faculty at The University of Texas
  (www.utexas.edu/academic/cit/gallery/utprofiles/conversations/index.html)

The idea of moving to a new teaching and learning space, a space that is really not a well-defined space at all, is exciting, stimulating, and intimidating. As we have seen from the faculty stories in this book, however, we are discovering, as a community, ways of making the most of this new space, creating transactions and teaching and learning strategies that were hard to imagine with the earlier generations of tools. We are already almost at the point where we find it hard to imagine how we ever taught without the web. The holodeck described in Chapter 11 is one scenario of the future and where all this might take us!

Chapter 10
Issues in the Online Environment

Over the course of this book, we have addressed many issues that faculty and administrators face in the online environment; however, we have not addressed them all. Strategies for dealing with these issues are still evolving, but the issues are complex and often challenge strong cultural traditions. Answers are few and far between; what we have now are temporary strategies to use while technologies and practices evolve.

Five recurring issues are a source of ongoing frustration for developers and managers of online courses:

- Class size in online courses
- Managing interactions with students and between students remotely
- Copyright issues and intellectual property policies
- Assessment and evaluation
- Balancing life and learning

The quick pace of the online environment provides little time for exploration and resolution of these issues. Our discussion is a snapshot of where we are now.

Issue One: Class Size in Online Courses

The question about size for online classes has been persistent. It is difficult to collect research data on this question, given the speed of adoption of online learning and the infinite number of course models being implemented. We now have enough experiences with teaching and learning online that we are gradually evolving to the same answer as we have for campus teaching and learning: It all depends.

The usual variables apply in answering what it depends on. These variables include the institutional image and mission, the instructional goals and objectives of the course, the capabilities of the students, the amount of interaction required based on the content level and difficulty, and so forth. Useful information also comes from our best practices for campus class sizes. For example, an overall average of 30 is often used, with higher numbers for undergraduate classes, decreasing numbers for upper-division classes, and class sizes of 10 to 15 for graduate seminars.

Additional variables apply to online learning. These variables include the experience of the faculty member in online teaching, the amount of campus infrastructure and support, the availability of the tools for online teaching and learning, the efficiency and design of these tools, student access, and experience with the tools.

As researchers, however, we still want to know what the available data actually support for the recommended size for online classes. There are other closely related questions having to do with faculty time. How much time do faculty spend in teaching an online class, and are there any data on the amount of time required for online courses? What is the impact of each additional student? Is there always enough time and room enough for one more student?

The search for answers to these questions took us to three different types of information sources:

- Research studies, analyses, and articles
- Consortium and association guidelines such as American University of University Professors, State Higher Education Executive Officers and Western Cooperative for Educational Telecommunications (WCET), Southern Regional Educational Board , Colorado Online , and policies from online universities
- Postings in online discussions such as the Distance Education Online Symposium List (DEOS-L@lists.psu.edu), the Professional and Organization Development Network in Higher Education (POD@LISTSERV.ND.EDU), and the Teaching and Learning with Technology Group (TLT-SWG@LISTSERV.ND.EDU)

Some of these resources include input on the expectations of students for interaction with faculty traditional distance learning professionals. A project by the Western Cooperative for Educational Telecommunication (www.wiche.edu) resulted in the development of a set of Principles of Good Practice for Electronically Offered Academic Degree and Certificate Programs. These principles were also adopted and enhanced by the board setting up the new Southern Regional Electronic Campus (SREC) (www.sreb.org). The following statement appears under the section on curriculum and instruction: "The course provides for appropriate interaction between faculty and students and among students" (p. 24). The faculty support section of the principles from the SREC follows with, "The program or course provides adequate equipment, software, and communications to faculty for interaction with students, institutions, and other faculty."

Research, Analyses, Articles

A few resources address the size of online classes most directly, and there are rich resources on topics closely related to this question. For example, there is literature on the size of *campus* classes and also on strategies for teaching large campus classes. A bibliography located at a Canadian university (www.wlu.ca/~wwwidev/IDlarge.html) is useful. Another general online web source that provides regular scholarly reports and analyses on online learning is the Asynchronous Learning Networks site (www.aln.org) sponsored by the Alfred P. Sloan Foundation.

Short List of Annotated Articles

Boettcher, J. V. (1998). How Many Students Are Just Right in a Web Course? *Syllabus, 12*: 45 – 49 (www.designingforlearning.info/services/writing/number.htm).

This article is from 1998, when teaching online was an adventure undertaken only by innovative faculty willing to create most of the infrastructure themselves. During this time, the first generation of faculty teaching online provided anecdotes about the size of online classes. The earliest recommendations for the size of online classes were 18 to 20 students, plus or minus 5, with the probability of larger classes becoming more feasible as the communication tools and access to technology improved. Some of the anecdotes included recommendations for a very small class, such as 10-12, for a faculty's first online teaching experience. This article is interesting now for its historical perspective about faculty moving into the new online experience.

Hiltz, S. R., & Turoff, M. (2002). What Makes Learning Effective? *Communications of the ACM, 45*(4): 56 – 59 (doi.acm.org/10.1145/505248.505273).

Hiltz and Turoff describe the characteristics of effective learning networks and how the roles of faculty and students function in the online environment. The characteristics of cognitive, affective, and managing strategies are described, as are the design characteristics of the communication tools.

Lazarus, B. D. (2003). Teaching Courses Online: How Much Time Does It Take? *Journal of Asynchronous Learning Networks (JALN), 7*(3), pp. 47-54 (www.aln.org/publications/jaln/v7n3/v7n3_lazarus.asp).

This article focuses on the time teaching online requires. It is often assumed that one can derive a recommendation for the size of online classes from this data. This case study from The University of Michigan-Dearborn examined the amount of time faculty from three courses of 25 students in 1999-2000 spent in each of three activities: (1) reading and responding to email; (2) reading, participating in, and grading 10 online discussions; and (3) grading 15 assignments. Quoting directly from the abstract, "The data showed that teaching each online course required three to seven hours per week, with the greatest number of emails and amount of time required during the first and last two weeks of the semesters. Participation in and grading of the discussions took the greatest amount of time and remained steady across the semester."

Turoff, M. (2000). Managing a Large Distance Course Using Webboard. Accessed October 3, 2003 (eies.njit.edu/%7Eturoff/Papers/manageDL.html).

In this 2000 article, Turoff identifies two significant factors affecting a faculty's ability "to deliver distance education and to augment face-to-face classes" in online environments. Those two factors are (1) the nature of the software that provides the group communication process, and (2) the facilitation and leadership role of the instructor. This paper describes Turoff's experience at using Webboard to manage 40 to 50 active students in a single course, Management of Information Systems CIS 679, which has "high pragmatic content and encourages a collaborative approach to education."

Policies and Guidelines

Guidelines and policies from various organizations and consortia can also inform the issue of class size. The question of class size is usually addressed implicitly by providing guidelines as to the frequency and immediacy of feedback that should be provided to students and the amount of recommended interactions between the faculty and the students.

Class size restrictions on campus have traditionally been a way of addressing a spectrum of classroom management issues. Class size is often viewed as a way of estimating the amount of time for teacher-student interaction, for tracking and monitoring student learning, for review of tests and projects, and for assessment and grading responsibilities. Faculty need to complete these same functional responsibilities in an online setting. Whether online or on campus, one recommended strategy for effective, efficient teaching and management is to place students into different size groups and teams for various teaching and learning functions. This strategy can serve to facilitate interaction via discussion boards, group assignments, and other exercises.

Another approach to the question of class size is to identify a different metric to assess time commitments and responsibilities. The Colorado Online (COL) briefing, for example, asked whether an appropriate metric might be faculty workload; for example, a teaching institution might ask how many students faculty should be responsible for during any one academic term.

Table 10.1 provides a list of resources that address some of the issues in class management, class size, and faculty responsibilities in different contexts.

Table 10.1 Class Management, Class Size, and Faculty Responsibilities

Association of University Professors (1999). Statement on Distance Education. 1999 AAUP Committee report on Distance Education (www.aaup.org/statements/Redbook/StDistEd.HTM).

Bourne, J., & Moore, J., Eds. (2003). *Elements of Quality Online Education: Practice and Direction.* Sloan-C Series, The Sloan Consortium (www.aln.org/publications/books/volume4.asp).

Colorado Online Education Programs Study Committee (2002). Key Issues Briefing: Quality, Class Size, and Student-Teacher Ratio. Accessed October 3, 2003 (www.cde.state.co.us/edtech/download/osc-classsize.pdf).

Epper, R., & Garn, M. (2003). *Virtual College and University Consortia: A National Study.* State Higher Education Executive Officers and Western Cooperative for Educational Telecommunications (WCET), p. 80 (wcet.info).

Western Cooperative for Educational Telecommunications (2003). *Principles of Good Practice for Electronically Offered Academic Degree and Certificate Programs* (www.wcet.info/projects/balancing/principles.asp).

Twigg, C. (1999). *Improving Learning and Reducing Costs: Redesigning Large-Enrollment Courses* (www.center.rpi.edu/PewSym/mono1.html).

Assumptions Underlying Guidelines for Online Learning

Policies and guidelines for online teaching and learning are often based on a number of assumptions; further research will determine whether or not these assumptions are warranted. Here are some of the assumptions that have been used in the development of current policies and guidelines.

- All online learning is asynchronous.
- All students are seldom brought together as a group.
- Faculty ought to monitor and track all student interactions.
- Students who take online classes do not learn as much as students in face-to-face courses.
- It is more difficult to assess student learning in online classes.

What are the assumptions on your campus or in your department about online learning?

Obviously, these assumptions developed prior to the development of the tools and applications now commonly available. As tools change, and as the number of models for online learning increases, new assumptions are emerging. What are the assumptions on your campus or in your department about online learning? False assumptions can create many divisions and frustrations.

Online Boards and Discussions

Collecting anecdotes about faculty's thoughts about the right class size provides important data points; online discussions are one source of these anecdotes. Following is a series of relevant postings from a discussion hosted by the International Forum of Educational Technology and Society (ifets.ieee.org) that took place in October 1999. *Question*: What is the norm for online class size per instructor? As a member of a distance education committee, I am looking for a resource, a case study, research, or just experience on training via the net. What is the optimum class size, or rule of thumb?

The postings to the query reflect the state of the tools and practice at that time. Many of the comments, however, are timeless. Some postings have been edited for succinctness and anonymity.

- We have just started an online MBA program, and our current class size is 19. All the students go through the classes in a cohort. We have set a limit of 25 for each cohort.

- We also have a few internet-delivered courses taught by members of our faculty. The overwhelming opinion is that the workload seems to go up exponentially with class size. The folks who do internet classes seem to find 20 to 25 is about tops, but it depends on the subject.

- I haven't done a formal study of optimal class size, but from teaching a number of courses, I believe the optimal size to be around 15. My current graduate course in human-computer interaction (HCI) has 23 students, and I find it difficult to keep up with all the discussion postings and homework assignments. On the other hand, I'm managing. [When asked for more context, this faculty member responded that the 23 grad students were almost all working software engineers with five or more years of experience, and that the class was part of a master's degree program. Students were required to participate in weekly asynchronous discussions; five bi-weekly nontrivial homework assignments, such as cognitive task analysis, HCI design, and evaluations; and two small-group projects – one website assessment, one real-time system HCI design and evaluation.]

- As with all other modes of communication, it depends on what you wish to achieve. If the materials are designed to be either self-instructional with automated objective testing or a surrogate lecture – one big presentation with a small time for question and answers that are later covered by FAQs – try thinking about a class size of 50,000 to one. If it is convening a community of reflective practitioners, it will depend on the level of support and mentoring you feel is appropriate in different stages of the coalescence of the group. If a faculty member is using the online environment to replace seminar and tutorial work, the numbers are about the same as for that current model. There is no economy in teaching time. The economy comes in other ways.

- Ideal class size depends on whether you are running synchronous or asynchronous courses, the age and experience of the group, the skills of the moderator, and the nature of the course.

  If you are web posting or emailing courses with follow-up discussion or chat, without assignments to assess within a tight deadline, larger groups of 25 and even more can be managed.

- If you are running a literature or study project whose goal is to foster the exchange of ideas on one or more topics, then the group sizes should be smaller, such as 15 or so, especially if you are working with younger students, such as precollege.

- If your online course is a development professional course, where members submit weighty papers or research for assessment or joint development, a small seminar format probably makes the most sense.

We all probably wish we could talk at more length with these respondents about these ideas, but the basic theme is that there is no one ideal class size, whether online or face to face. The right size depends on the goals and objectives of the learning, and on the environments and the expectations. It comes back to a question of design.

In summary, the variables in determining the ideal class size for online classes depend on

- Goals and objectives of a course
- Infrastructure and tools
- Features and design of the tools
- Experience of faculty
- Age and experience of students
- Assessment strategies
- Overall faculty workload

Table 10.2 provides a step-by-step process that might be helpful in arriving at a recommendation for the ideal size of any particular online class.

Table 10.2 Class Size Determination Process

- Start with what the class size would be on campus, including the instructional team and support for the class.

- Evaluate the goals and objectives of the course, including teaching, learning, and assessment strategies.

- Evaluate the infrastructure and tools for the delivery and support of the class.

- Evaluate the readiness and experience of the faculty member or team.

- Increase or decrease class size or instructional team based on this analysis.

A final note on this question has to do with the evolution of the teaching and learning environments and of the tools. A posting by Ania Lian of the University of Canberra/AU noted, "Computers may bring a change about in education in spite of the educators themselves: *i.e.*, they remove more and more teacher control over the sources of education and their possible applications." This statement seems prescient, and suggests further that the question of class size is one we need to continue to monitor. Class size is an important factor in the cost of educational events and programs. And the cost of the faculty and the personnel involved are major considerations. If educational programs and experiences can be designed that reduce the time commitment of the faculty member but respect the function of the personal interaction cycle between the instructor and the student, the numbers of students served by institutions might be increased, along with quality and satisfaction.

What About Faculty Time in Student Interaction?

As faculty teach online, they discover that they are spending more and more time interacting with their students. Suddenly, 30 students, a common on-campus class size, can overwhelm faculty online. One reason for class size concerns online is rooted in our traditional communication patterns in the classroom. In the classroom, the most accepted pattern of communication is primarily from the faculty to the students, and from the students back to the faculty.

Marie A. Cini from Duquesne University agrees with this, and feels that the challenge of managing many students online is that "we are still hung up on some form of contact with the instructor as the model of instruction." Marie goes on to say that one of her biggest goals when teaching online is to wean students from dependence on her and to "point them toward one another." She believes that the accepted number of students in a web course will grow, because the expectations of instructor contact will decrease.

The faculty-to-student communication is a very efficient model of communication for some purposes. The teacher is speaking to 25 or 30 students at the same time, and their eyes and body language communicate the extent of student attention and understanding. In this environment, the faculty member is often assumed to be the one and only expert. We are still strongly influenced by this concept of the faculty member as the lecturer dispensing information to the students. ITV classrooms, telecourses, and talking-head presentations on the web reinforce this model of knowledge flowing primarily in one direction with a feedback loop back to the faculty or instructor.

In the online environment, the lines of communication are more divergent. We have a fully linked network of communication lines, including threads among all members of a web course community and among multiple groups of students as well. This network pattern of communications between faculty and students and between and among students creates a powerful tool for inviting and supporting student involvement and thinking. Students are more likely to contribute their experiences, share their insights, and frame thoughtful, reflective questions with this network model of communication.
Therefore, the course process of creating a knowledge community among the student group and a knowledge base within each individual springs from many sources. Expertise can come from many directions; however, confusion may also be more prevalent. This confusion can become a step in developing knowledge and can highlight needs for more content development. Given a network model of communication, it is possible that faculty members will spend course time listening and reflecting on thoughtful questions and analytic comments.

At the same time, we are aware of the reality that responding to students' queries via email is more time consuming than the responding face to face. In a 1996 web posting, L. Estabrook, Dean of the Graduate School of Library and Information Sciences at the University of Illinois, noted that a faculty-student conversation during a class break can take 30 seconds, while that same information may take two to three minutes to exchange in an email message. The next wave of technology, including networking and camera imaging, will likely alleviate some of the time being required for faculty-to-student

> The good news coming out of all these changes is that as faculty become more experienced in teaching online and adapting to more divergent lines of communication, they will be able to reduce the amount of time managing online classes, and students will become more active learners.

interactions. Small cameras attached to computers may encourage faculty to return to the mode of synchronous office hours so they can talk rather than write to students. The good news coming out of all these changes is that as faculty become more experienced in teaching online and adapting to more divergent lines of communication, they will be able to reduce the amount of time managing online classes, and students will become more active learners.

Another useful approach to measuring the amount of time faculty are spending on student and course communication is to estimate the amount of time that a faculty member spends with each student over the course of a semester. Estimates of about two hours per student, including student testing and evaluations but not lectures or preparations, have been rejected by some faculty.

In a presentation on this topic in March 1998, Frank Jewett of the California State University System Office noted that, although the two-hour-per-student figure has been rejected, sometimes vigorously, if one calculates the number of hours per week in a semester, divides by the number of hours available for student interaction, and then by the number of students, it becomes apparent that two hours is about right. It is simply not possible to spend much more time than that. We may feel that we should spend more than two hours per student, but there are simply not enough hours in a semester to do so. It is no wonder faculty often feel stressed by the demands of online teaching, student communications, and student evaluations.

Faculty Workload and Faculty Working Conditions

Analyzing the question of student enrollment in a web course leads inevitably to questions about faculty pay and workload. As early as 1990, Murray Turoff, in a foreword to a book about online communication, noted that "the workload for faculty is linearly dependent on the number of students" (Harasim, et al., 1997, p. xii). Some distance learning programs in the mid to late 1990s began implementing new salary policies to acknowledge the extent to which larger numbers of students affect faculty workload.

A 1995 posting to the American Association for Higher Education listserv, Bill O'Neill of Southern Utah mentioned two examples worthy of note. In one university engineering program, an additional $150 per student was added to a faculty member's salary for every distance learning student, and an additional $50 per student was sent to the department's budget. At one state university, faculty teaching distance learning courses received a $100 bonus for each student, once the enrollment exceeded 25. In another example, in a library information program on the East Coast, faculty received an additional $50 per out-of-state student enrolled in the course.

In the classroom models of learning, faculty workloads in many institutions are based on formulas yielding 10 to 12 hours a week for every class or section taught. In some institutions, however, the number of hours per week per section can be as low as four hours. The baseline number of students is generally 25 to 30 students. If class enrollment reaches 40 to 50 students, faculty are sometimes able to negotiate for additional support for the class.

These classroom models and their associated workload estimates are built on the bundled model of course production in which faculty do everything related to their own course.

Fundamental Questions

So where does that leave us in answering the question of student numbers in a web course? The ability to put courses on the internet caused many of us to speculate in the early 1990s that master teachers from the top research universities would be able to reach thousands of students. The early recommendations of no more than 15 to 20 students for online classes have now given way to recommendations and requirements closer to the regular on-campus level of 30 students. This probably reflects a body of more experienced faculty and students, plus much-improved online environments with simpler tools and advanced sophistication of systems overall. However, these numbers are far from the much larger numbers originally dreamed of by administrators and legislators.
Other technology-based models of distance learning have supported very large numbers of students by using mass delivery methods. Telecourses are beamed to thousands of students. Closed-circuit television and interactive video classes often support numbers ranging from 40 to over 200 students. We are now wiser about when large numbers of students in online classes are appropriate.

The issue of class size in online courses is causing us to look at basic issues we have not discussed for some time in higher education.

- Expectations of students: How much access and interaction with the faculty member is appropriate for the class content and goals?
- Expectations of faculty: How much time should a course take under our current model and under the new model? Is it time to look seriously for strategies that will help us deliver online learning more efficiently while reducing the faculty burden?

- Expectations of administrators: What size classes and what types of courses do we offer our students while maintaining and developing our desired institutional image?
- Expectations of society: How can we change the model to achieve quality, low cost, and high satisfaction for all?

We might also consider that we haven't come very far in the science of learning if a teacher is always required to be involved in the process. In what alternative form might the teaching function be constituted? In what other forms might learning be offered?

While it may not be something we want to consider, we may have to put some creative thought into how we can use technology to structure and deliver really great learning experiences with less effort on the part of a teacher. If we continually design and redevelop the same course every semester, are we not still a cottage industry in how we design and deliver learning? Must we always do it this way?

Issue Two: Managing Interaction With and Among Students

The debate over the issue of class size is ongoing but in the meantime, faculty must manage online communication that is different in pattern and in amount required from the usual classroom-based communication. When we wrote the first edition of this faculty guide, our primary focus on this issue was how to manage the mountain of email usually delivered to a new online instructor; this is still a challenge today. Judith relates the following story concerning her initial experiences:

> "Because I was teaching a campus course about distance learning, I thought it was important that the students and I practiced what I preached. So in the middle of a Sunday afternoon, I found myself staring moodily at the contents of my Eudora Inbox, wondering why I had ever decided to handle all communication with my students myself.

> "The latest assignment for my students was a project description. After two hours of trying to sort my email into some semblance of order, I still had not found the project description from 5 of my 29 graduate students. Every one of my students, it seemed, had managed to create a different name for the subject heading of their mail files. Later in the semester, these same students sent their completed projects to me in every imaginable file format. They also sent files, I later learned, with obscure viruses that were difficult to eradicate. Seven students were

quite inexperienced in the use of technology at the beginning of the course, which added additional spice to this mix.

"To my surprise, I soon added myself to the inexperienced list. I learned that I really knew very little about managing course delivery over the web or communicating with students using this new teaching and learning environment. I learned that actually doing this type of teaching is definitely more challenging than just talking about doing it."

Based on our experiences teaching hybrid and online courses, we formulated the following list of what *not* to do when communicating with your students over the web. Fortunately, online courses now feature tools and applications that dramatically increase the efficiency of managing online communications.

1. Do not let all communications from students come to you via email. Consider designating an online discussion area as your online office, in which students can pose content and assignment-related questions. This way, the question is asked and answered once; it allows learners to provide answers that they know to questions such as, "When is Assignment 1 due?" If an online office is used, email can be reserved for the discussion of individual and personal issues.

If you have team assignments, set up group discussion areas in the course site for each group and, if you wish to monitor the teams, go to their discussion areas. Do not require them to email every team communication to you. If students email a question about content and assignments, instruct them to post it in the online office and tell them you will answer it there, *or* email the answer to them and then ask them to post both the question and answer in your Online Office. Responses to these questions can become the basis for additional course guidelines and frequently asked question (FAQ) lists.

2. Do not assume all students will read and participate successfully in your class discussion during the first week of the semester. The processes for providing learners with online course access and textbook purchasing capability are still not smooth or adequately automated in many higher education institutions. For institutions using some of the new tools, this situation is improving and may become automatic. For other institutions, and especially for students at a distance, a lag of one or two weeks for all students to be up and running with the technology is not unusual. In planning online courses, then, some backup strategies may need to be identified.

Access to course content must be assured and reliable. With distance learning students, a good strategy is to have them support each other in gaining access to the content information. Technology support is another critical piece that must be in place. For solving technology access problems, a lag of two weeks is usually sufficient. Students can be directed to an institution's help desk and the local internet service provider, if an external one is being used. Students can also successfully team up with each other to resolve technology problems.

Because the logistics of an online course may take a week or two to be sorted out, it is advisable to plan assignments that are more reading based, with less group discussion until Week Two or Three. This rule can be adapted for experienced groups of students.

3. *Do not be vague about the names of assignments.* If you want your students to turn in assignments via electronic means, be very specific about what should go in the subject line of an email or discussion board message or Drop Box/In Box title. In fact, you may want to develop a simple algorithm for naming these files. The algorithm might have three parts, such as "Assignment 1: Theoretical Principles, Student Full Name." For a project sequence, you might want to develop a subject, such as "Project Prospectus," "Project Summary," or "Course Summary Paper."

To ensure that the assignment name that students use is always accessible, this information can be directly available from the course calendar on the web. The first part of the subject heading eases the use of the filter feature of many email programs, automatically filing the assignment emails into the special assignment mailbox. The second part of the algorithm, the content name, makes it easy to sort by subject once the messages are in the appropriate mailbox, and it may help keep the learning objective evident.

You may wonder why we suggest that students include their full names in the subject heading. The email names they use may not even remotely resemble their real names, and students may not use the signature block feature available on many email packages, and will occasionally submit assignments from another students' mail folders. Requiring that students include their names in the subject heading is actually an updated version of the now ancient plea to for them to put their names on their papers. With paper assignments, we often had a student's handwriting to clue to his or her identity. Now faculty detectives have to search through email logs or other lists for matching email.

4. *Do not be available to your students all the time.* Many dedicated and committed faculty truly enjoy all the student interactions involved with teaching and want to be easily available to their students in this new online space. Additionally, as we move teaching and learning interactions to the online environment, we are constantly reminded that the power of technology enables us to be available anytime, anywhere. Consequently, many students expect faculty members to provide answers and responses to email questions immediately. We are becoming increasingly aware of how rapidly technology is moving and how slowly our bodies and minds are adjusting to the use of technology. Just because it is possible to be available 24 hours a day, 7 days a week does not mean we have to or should be available anytime, anywhere. You can manage response expectations from the very beginning of the course by using one or more of these suggestions:

> **Just because it is possible to be available 24 hours a day, 7 days a week does not mean we have to or should be available anytime, anywhere.**

- Set up a standard turnaround time for response to email or questions in your online office. Usually, saying that you will attempt to respond within
- 24 hours is considered reasonable. It can be useful to specify the hours that you will definitely not be responding as well.
- Announce that there will be times when the 24-hour response time will be suspended. This includes weekends, announced vacations, conferences, and unexpected emergencies. You also agree to announce to the students when this response time will be suspended. It is not always easy to access the network from anywhere, anytime. Rita tells students she has one recharge day a week during which she tries to stay totally offline. Her students have her cell phone number to call in the event of an emergency on the day she is offline.
- If you choose, you can set times at which the 24-hour response time will be even shorter, particularly just prior to deadlines or exams. Some faculty set email office hours when they will be actively monitoring and responding to student messages.
- You might want to remind your students that your faculty role includes more than teaching responsibilities.

5. Do not assume that communications are received or read in any specific time frame. Internet communication is not as fast or as immediate as a telephone conversation or a fax, and it is not as slow as the postal service. When we send electronic mail, it moves in discrete packets over a local network and through numerous gateways and other networks before it is received by the addressee. We have all heard of letters being mislaid in post offices or warehouses and finally being delivered after many years; email can be similarly delayed or totally destroyed. The increasing sophistication of spammers and viruses can also dramatically slow email delivery by hours. Therefore, do not assume that your mail will move rapidly or at all, or that it has been successfully received and read by the addressee. Because the possibility of lost or delayed email exists, asking for a confirmation on time-sensitive or critical messages is wise. Setting up an automatic confirming reply when an email is received is another option.

Also, do not assume that students access the course site within 24 hours of your posting. You may wish to require them to post an acknowledgement that they have read critical announcements in the course site.

6. Do not structure the communication flow so that you are the hub of all communications. This will save you time and create a better learning environment. Part of the power of internet communication technologies is that students and faculty can craft a true learning community in which dialogue and communication flows in all directions. Some faculty members set up online problems, dilemmas, and seminars in which students launch, manage, and summarize a discussion or solve a problem. The faculty role in some parts of a course is not to lecture, but to monitor and mentor student discussions or problem solving. In these cases, faculty may choose to compose a response, analyze the content, and provide feedback on a weekly basis to ensure that students stay on track with the development of content and ideas. In this way, students interact with each other and test and hone their ideas with their peers.

7. Do not forget to provide feedback and evaluation of student progress and learning. Although we all want to believe that students are taking courses because they are intensely interested in learning the content, in fact, they are also there to earn grades and meet program requirements. Consequently, students want timely and personal feedback on the work they do.

As with most things in the online environment, faculty need to state what students can expect as far as turnaround for assignment feedback. Some institutions mandate 48-hour turnaround to their faculty, but this is not possible with every type of assignment, particularly research papers and projects. In this case, a one-week turnaround, as is normal in the classroom-based environment, is more reasonable. This turnaround timeframe affects the design of the course as well. Assignments that build on one another, such as sequential submittals of sections of a paper, demand a faster turnaround. During the grading, faculty have less time to monitor or facilitate learning activities on the course site. Therefore, activities that require substantial faculty-student interaction should not be planned during the expected assignment turnaround period.

Grading and providing feedback to students is an area of opportunity for web course management tool vendors and other software developers. One topic that generated much discussion at a distance learning seminar was techniques on reading, evaluating, and correcting electronic documents. Some faculty are experimenting with the use of audio files for feedback on papers, finding that spoken comments can be completed more quickly than can written ones.

8. Do not put anything in your student correspondence that you would not want to see on the front page of a local or national newspaper. Legal battles are still brewing about ownership and privacy of messages in the workplace.

There are also many perspectives about the wisdom and difficulty of deleting computer files. So it is best to assume that at any time, course content, including email messages and other materials, could become public in a broader sense of the term. To borrow a quote from the Newseum in Washington, D.C., "If you don't want to read about it in the newspaper, don't do it." A better option would be to pick up the phone and discuss it.

9. Do not go unprotected from viruses. Update your virus protection software regularly and often. If you choose to run your machine unprotected from viruses, be vigilant about the attachments you receive from students and others. Do not open any suspicious or unexpected files.

10. Make sure all communications can be accessed by all learners. This is last in the list but certainly not least. It is imperative that we remember that students with various challenges are members of the learning community. This is particularly important as we move into using new communication tools such as audio and video. Include presentation notes and transcripts on audio and video communications and presentations. For further information, see the Bobby site (bobby.watchfire.com/bobby/html/en/index.jsp).

Issue Three: Copyright Issues and Intellectual Property Policies

Copyright has always been an important issue in distance learning and is now assuming even more importance as the use of the online environment affects both campus and distance courses. Questions surrounding the ownership of academic courses and faculty retention of copyright of their publications are being discussed with increasing frequency. The topic of intellectual property is very alive in the world of educational technology. New approaches such as Creative Commons (creativecommons.org) are also being explored. Our discussion provides general information regarding copyright issues. We encourage any faculty member who has copyright questions to consult the institution's policies and guidelines or to seek legal advice from appropriate professionals.

Looking at Copyright: User or Owner?

It is good for faculty to be knowledgeable about copyright law from two different perspectives: (1) using materials copyrighted by others for teaching, learning, and research; and (2) developing materials that are then copyrighted by themselves, their institutions, or publishers.

All the rights and privileges of copyright owners in the U.S. are based on copyright law that has origins in the U.S. Copyright Act of 1790. The document that has been the basis of the current laws dates from October 19, 1976, modified by a number of succeeding legislative acts. The Digital

Millennium Copyright Act was passed in 1998 to address the new digital copying and delivery capabilities. This was followed in 2002 by the Technology, Education, and Copyright Harmonization (TEACH) Act, which clarified sections 110(2) and 112 of the Copyright Act.

The TEACH act in particular sought to clarify what use of copyright materials is legitimate and non-copyright infringing for distant or remote classrooms. The types of materials identified in the law include but are not limited to print, still images, audio and video recordings, diagrams, charts, and graphs. Articles and toolkits for interpreting the implications of the TEACH act are included in the list of copyright resources provided later in this chapter.

Harper (2002) summarizes the act: "The TEACH act expands the scope of educators' rights to perform and display works and to make the copies integral to such performances and displays for digital distance education, making the rights closer to those we have in face-to-face teaching." Harper goes on to note that there is "still a considerable gap between what the statute authorizes for face-to-face teaching and for distance education." Bruwelheide (2003) sums up the gap as follows: For distance learning situations, think "clips and snips" which represent "reasonable and limited portions" for audiovisual works and dramatic or musical works.

The Law on Copyright

The sections of the copyright law most pertinent to teaching and learning from the 1976 act are Sections 106 to 118. Copies of the Copyright Law are available from the Copyright Office in Washington, D.C. (www.copyright.gov). Circular 92, *"Copyright Law of the United States of America and Related Laws Contained in Title 17 of the United States Code,"* incorporates the provisions from the 2002 TEACH act (June 2003).

Section 106 of the copyright law quite clearly states that copyright owners have certain exclusive rights:

1. Reproduction of the copyrighted work in copies or phonorecords
2. Preparation of derivative works from the copyrighted work
3. Distribution of copies or phonorecords of the copyrighted work to the public by sale or other transfer of ownership, or by rental, lease, or lending
4. Performance of the copyrighted work publicly
5. In the case of literary, musical, dramatic, and choreographic works, pantomimes, and pictorial, graphic, or sculptural works, including the individual images of a motion picture or other audiovisual work, to display the copyrighted work publicly
6. In the case of sound recordings, performance of the copyrighted work publicly by means of a digital audio transmission

These rights, as specified in Section 106, clearly reserve the right for visual and sound images to the copyright owners. Hence, websites with visual and sound images that belong to various movie and television studios are restricted in their use. For example, commercial websites with images of "Star Trek" characters and sound clips may be in violation of the copyright owners' rights if they are used without permission.

In practice, copyright owners do not sue for every violation. Most copyright suits are brought when significant amounts of money are involved, or when it is perceived that the use of copyrighted material damages the image or reputation of either a copyright owner or the copyrighted work. Higher education institutions can still be very vulnerable. Therefore, faculty need to be aware of the real possibility of lawsuits from the illegal use of copyrighted materials.

Fair Use for Educational Purposes

What about the fair use doctrine? Every academic is somewhat familiar with the concept of fair use, but generally not familiar enough. Often, fair use is interpreted much too broadly, as if any use of copyrighted materials is all right, so long as the material is being used for teaching and learning purposes.

Section 107 defines the Doctrine of Fair Use, a legal principle that sets limitations on the exclusive rights of copyright holders. This section says the following:

> Fair use of a copyrighted work . . .including reproduction . . .
> for purposes such as criticism, comment, news reporting,
> teaching (including multiple copies for classroom use),
> scholarship, or research, is NOT an infringement of copyright.

However, we must note that "fair use is not free use." Section 107 provides some criteria to give guidance in interpreting this right of fair use. There are four criteria that can be used to evaluate whether a user of copyrighted materials can claim fair use. These criteria are based on how the copyrighted work is to be used, the characteristics of the copyrighted work, the amount or substantiality of the portion to the whole, and the effect on potential market value of the work.

The first of these criteria is that of purpose. If the purpose for using the copyrighted work is for commercial use, then generally, permission for use must be obtained. This criterion must be applied in the following example: If faculty incorporate copyrighted material into educational materials and then sell those educational materials commercially for profit, this is not fair use, as the faculty will benefit from the copyrighted material with no compensation back to the original copyright holder. If the purpose for using copyrighted work is nonprofit use, as educational or research use is generally considered, then fair use can usually be applied.

The second criterion focuses on the nature of the work. If the work is nonfiction or simple factual material, then it is easier to use the copyrighted work without explicit permission. It is more difficult to claim copyright violation for a diagram showing the process of osmosis, for example, than for a diagram of a fictional invention or a work of art. It is difficult to prove that some factual material is unique, belonging solely to one individual.

The third test is that of the amount of copyrighted work being used. This criterion involves the percentage of the work being used in relation to the entire work. An easy way to remember this test is to think of a 10-line poem. Generally, use of a small portion of a copyrighted work is permissible provided other tests are met, but use of a large portion is not allowed. Thus, use of the complete 10-line poem would need permission, but 10 lines from a much longer work might not.

The fourth test is that of market value. Does the use of the copyrighted work without permission damage or restrict the copyright owner from appropriate compensation for the intellectual work? This is the argument often used in the area of software piracy, for example. Software publishers claim that their revenues are significantly lowered if their software is shared among groups. Publishers of academic journals often make this same claim when their works are placed on reserve and students make photocopies for themselves.

Additional Guidelines on Fair Use

Additional help in interpreting Section 107 appeared in a discussion of fair use in a House of Representatives report from September 1976. That report noted that "despite the fact that the courts have ruled on this 'fair use' doctrine many times over the years, no real definition of the concept has ever emerged," and "as the doctrine is an equitable rule of reason, no generally applicable definition is possible, and each case raising the question must be decided on its own facts."

However, this House report provided three additional tests or guidelines to be used in interpreting the doctrine of fair use. To apply under the fair use doctrine, use of copyrighted material must also meet the three tests of brevity, spontaneity, and cumulative effect.

Brevity refers to the percentage-to-the-whole criterion previously mentioned. This reaffirms that short segments are more acceptable than longer segments.

The next criterion is that of spontaneity. If a faculty member decides to use material for educational use, and there is, reasonably, not enough time to seek and receive permission, then fair use generally allows use of the material for that one time. However, faculty may be at risk if they use the same material over a number of semesters for significant parts of their instruction without asking permission. This guideline suggests that sustained use over a number of semesters is not fair use. Finally, the guideline of cumulative effect suggests that multiple copying by faculty over the course of a semester needs to be restrained. Cumulative effect also refers to the number of items that can be used from the same author or collection.

Ownership of Academic Materials

Ownership of academic courses is a complex issue. In the traditional model of campus courses, the question has rarely been asked. In the traditional distance learning model, however, in which a team of faculty has developed the course, the answer would likely be that the institution that provided funding for the course owns it. In fact, a course is difficult to own or even to copyright, because intellectual work is only subject to copyright when "the work is created and fixed in a tangible medium of expression." Much of what constitutes a course is not "fixed in a tangible medium of expression." Perhaps only components of a course, such as a book, website, or set of exercises, can be copyrighted.

Some institutions follow the policy traditionally called "work for hire." This means that any work done by a faculty member while under contract belongs to the institution. Other institutions have a policy about joint ownership and revenue sharing similar to patent agreements. Other times, the faculty can negotiate to retain all copyright, including that for instructional materials. This is most often the case with textbooks. In any event, the time to discuss the ownership of any instructional material is before any project gets under way. Some distance learning projects involve a negotiated agreement between the faculty, the institution, and the publisher.

What abut the related question, "Should faculty retain copyright ownership of research publications?" We all have become accustomed to a model in which faculty write research articles and submit them for publication, and then an institution purchases the research journals that publish the articles. In this model, the faculty turn over the copyright of the articles to the publisher in return for the publishers' work in reviewing, editing, publishing, and distributing the work.

Two trends are causing higher education administrators to question this model. One trend is the steadily increasing cost of academic journals. The cost of many journals has become prohibitive, and institutions find it difficult to purchase the journals in which their own faculty have published. Another closely related factor is that subscriptions for digital archives are usually purchased on an annual basis, and the articles available one year might not be available in the future.

A second trend is the increasing time it takes to ensure that faculty are staying within the copyright rules regarding their own materials. The provost of the California Institute of Technology, Steven E. Koonin, made headlines on September 18, 1998 (*Chronicle of Higher Education*, p. A29) when he proposed that faculty no longer hand over the copyright for journal articles to publishers. Subsequent discussions noted that this idea had been suggested in March of the same year by a group that published their views in an article available at the Association of Research Libraries (ARL) site. A letter to the editor from a senior vice president at Elsevier, a well-known academic publisher, suggested that the publisher added value through managing the review and editing process and that a distinction exists between the submitted manuscript and the final edited paper. Faculty retained the right, apparently, to putting the submitted manuscript on their own website.

In practical terms, what does all this suggest? As they become knowledge entrepreneurs, faculty should consider negotiating with publishers for a new set of rights concerning faculty work, including the following:

- Copyright ownership for their own teaching, learning, research, and speaking engagements. This would include the right to copy, distribute, and perform their own work without needing to ask permission.
- The right to include their material on personal and course websites.
- The right, on behalf of the institution, for other faculty at the institution to use the work in similar ways.

Joint copyright ownership of teaching and learning materials may or may not be reasonable. But it is important that we find ways to acknowledge the right of a faculty member to personal work, and an institution's right to reasonable access to the work of faculty members.

Resources on Copyright

Multiple websites address copyright laws, starting with the Copyright Office itself, (www.copyright.gov). The following websites also provide information about copyright laws, including tutorials and FAQs.

- www.utsystem.edu/OGC/Intellectualproperty/cprtindx.htm. This site at The University of Texas system features a Crash Course in Copyright, ranging from topics such as fair use, ownership, and TEACH act Updates. It also includes The University of Texas System copyright policy.

- www.utsystem.edu/ogc/intellectualproperty/teachact.htm. This is a direct link to an article by Georgia Harper, "The TEACH Act Finally Becomes Law," an excellent summary of what the TEACH act means in the context of online and distance learning programs.
www.nea.org/he/abouthe/intelprop.html. This list of intellectual property and copyright resources from the National Education Association (NEA) is another good starting point, linking to some of the other resources in this list.
- www.copyright.gov/legislation/pl107-273.html#13301. This url links to the text of the legislation of the TEACH act. Be sure to search on the number and exact name of the section in which this is located: SEC. 13301. EDUCATIONAL USE COPYRIGHT EXEMPTION. A better way to search actual wording of the provisions is to use Circular 92, available on the copyright site (www.copyright.gov), which integrates the legislation into the copyright code.
- www.lib.ncsu.edu/scc/legislative/teachkit/overview.html. This is a site at the University of North Carolina providing a TEACH Toolkit, with basic and expanded checklists to help faculty determine if their use of copyrighted materials meets requirements for avoiding copyright infringement uses in online and distance classes.
- www.educause.edu/asp/doclib/abstract.asp?ID=ERM01610. "Balancing Copyright Concerns: The TEACH Act 2001," by Laura Gasaway, a professor of law at the University of North Carolina, provides a concise review of TEACH act provisions (Gasaway, 2001)
- www.indiana.edu/~ccumc/. This site provides a related set of links on copyright and intellectual property issues. It is part of the site for the Consortium of College and University Media Centers (CCUMC), a group of instructional technology and media professionals in higher education

Issue Four: Assessment and Evaluation

Assessment and evaluation in online and distance learning are additional areas that often must be redesigned for online and distance learning. Faculty and students both are quite dependent on the characteristics of campus environments for getting to know each other and for strategies for assessing student learning. The probability and ease of fraud and deception in online environments can often be a major concern. Some of the faculty stories include some creative strategies for addressing this area. We will focus first on assessment of student learning outcomes and then provide a few thoughts on program evaluation. These are two areas that are often lumped together, but require quite different analyses.

Assessment of Student Learning

A good starting point on assessing student learning is the AAHE site (www.aahe.org) and its Assessment Forum resources. The AAHE Assessment Forum is a national networking group that promotes thoughtful, effective approaches to assessment that involve faculty, benefit students, and improve the quality of teaching and learning. Some of the distinguished people involved in this forum include K. Patricia Cross and Theodore J. Marchese.

One particularly relevant resource from the Assessment Forum group is the set of "Nine Principles of Good Practice for Assessing Student Learning (www.aahe.org/assessment/principl.htm). (See Table 10.3.) It is worth noting that these principles are consistent with Vygotsky's theories as well as the other cognitive and constructivist theories of students developing their own knowledge structures and concepts over time. These principles also reinforce the role of environment, which implicitly involves technology, in supporting learning. The principles also reinforce the responsibilities of educators to the larger societal context. Don't miss the detailed explanations of these principles, available at the online site and in other cited resources.

Another useful starting point for assessment of student learning is The Center for Instructional Innovation at Western Washington University. This site includes a set of resources on student learning outcomes, and includes a useful bibliography (pandora.cii.wwu.edu/cii/resources/outcomes/how_assessment_works.asp).

One of our challenges in dealing with technology is achieving a common vocabulary. The Evaluation Center at Western Michigan University provides a rich glossary of terms dealing with both assessment and evaluation. (www.wmich.edu/evalctr/ess/glossary/htm).

Assessing Student Outcomes and Technologies

Questions about which technology is most effective in supporting learning have been with us a long time. When the book came on the scene, faculty lecturers worried that their students would no longer have to come to class. When the public library became a presence in small communities across the country, it was thought that the knowledge of the world was freely available to all. Now, faculty and administrators are concerned that if the content for a given course is on the web, students will not come to class. We have discovered that students come to campus and to class for something other than content. They come for the experience, for the networking, and for the speed, support, and structure that a faculty member and a class provide.

Table 10.3 Nine Principles of Good Practice for Assessing Student Learning

1. The assessment of student learning begins with educational values.

2. Assessment is most effective when it reflects an understanding of learning as multidimensional, integrated, and revealed in performance over time.

3. Assessment works best when the programs it seeks to improve have clear, explicitly stated purposes.

4. Assessment requires attention to outcomes but also and equally to the experiences that lead to those outcomes.

5. Assessment works best when it is ongoing, not episodic.

6. Assessment fosters wider improvement when representatives from across the educational community are involved.

7. Assessment makes a difference when it begins with issues of use and illuminates questions that people really care about.

8. Assessment is most likely to lead to improvement when it is part of a larger set of conditions that promote change.

9. Through assessment, educators meet responsibilities to students and to the public.

Source: Assessment Forum at AAHE

During the next decade, we need to decide what to measure and how to measure it. To bridge the gap in assessing student learning in online courses, consider the following options:

- Instruction can be designed so that students' knowledge and skills are gradually developed and revealed over time. Some faculty members do this by using strategies we discussed in the section on collaboration. Other common strategies include multiphasing project requirements so that the steps in the development of the project are evaluated along the way rather than solely at the end.
- For students who must meet internship and mentoring requirements, some programs set up tutors and mentors who are located geographically closer to the student. The mentors are often graduates of the same program.

- Some of the web course management tools come with modules that make designing short quizzes easy. Faculty use these types of tests to build competencies and provide practice; other graded tests are often delivered at proctored local sites. Students within commuting distance can be required to come to campus one to three times a semester for testing and evaluation. Other assessment is based on practice, participation and projects.
- As the infrastructure for electronic commerce develops, it will be able to provide security for completing tests and evaluations at a distance. Videoconferencing also supports security in testing. The development of technology for easy and effective assessment is lagging behind other software technology, but that may pose serious problems. As we in higher education move to more customized learning and to an emphasis on collaborative and constructive teaching and learning, the type of online evaluation that we will want will probably change. The tools that we will need then are not the tools we think we need now.

Another initiative on the use of technology for improving teaching and learning is the Teaching, Learning, and Technology (TLT) Group's Flashlight project, (www.tltgroup.org). The goal of this project is the development of training and evaluation tools that guide effective uses of information technology. The Flashlight program seeks to assess and improve educational uses of technology. It offers surveys and tools for assessing the effectiveness of technology tools. This program is described at www.tltgroup.org/programs/flashlight.htm.

Program Evaluation

The Principles of Good Practice adopted by the Southern Regional Education Board, which are being widely adopted by electronic campuses, recommend the following good practices in the area of evaluation and assessment. Note the emphasis on the evaluation of the program itself, in addition to the student evaluation. Student and faculty satisfaction are also being measured.

- The institutions evaluate program and course effectiveness, including assessments of student learning, student retention, and student and faculty satisfaction.
- At the completion of the program or course, the institution provides for assessment and documentation of student achievement in each course.
- Program or course announcements and electronic catalog entries provide appropriate information.

The fact that program and course announcements are being evaluated is worth noting. If students sign up for a course or a program expecting one set of outcomes and experiences, and later learn that the program and experiences are very different from what they expected, the level of satisfaction may be very low. The student may perceive the program to be of low quality because it did not meet the particular set of expectations created by the announcement. It may become higher education's version of truth in advertising.

Issue Five: Balancing Life and Learning

Online learners have varying lifestyles, but most of them have one thing in common: Their lives are too busy for them to come to campus. While online classes erased the on-campus requirement as well as the set class-time boundary, this has proven to be both an advantage and a detriment to students. Just as learners often expect faculty to be online 24/7, so too do some faculty expect learners to be involved in the course 24/7. And it is just as impossible for learners to do this as it is for faculty.

Therefore, as faculty, we must carefully examine just *how much* work we are requiring from online learners and *why* we are requiring it. Every activity should be mapped to objectives and competencies, and the activity time should be estimated. Faculty should periodically ask learners to evaluate time spent on various activities to ensure that estimates are accurate and that there is an appropriate value-time learning benefit.

We should also be flexible in our expectations of how online learners will fulfill our requirements. Often, it is necessary to give incompletes when life happens to an online learner, who is usually an adult with family and professional responsibilities. Boundaries are still needed for how much learner time is needed for a course. If we are requiring workloads that are significantly higher for online learners, we need to examine why that is the case and find ways to design a more efficient use of learning time so that students can balance life and learning.

Concluding Thoughts

This chapter has addressed just a few of the issues of great concern to faculty and administrators. As we adapt to, design, and transform the online teaching and learning paradigm, we will be depending on mutual understandings of institutional priorities to develop reasonable strategies for addressing these issues.

Examining these issues, we may begin to ask the question, "Is this all worth it?" It's important to remember that not only does online learning have the potential to increase access for working professionals, but it also enables lifelong learners to access programs that can enrich both their personal and professional lives.

Chapter 11

Perspectives on the Future

Where will we be in teaching and learning in higher education in the year 2010? Will we have come to terms with the role of technology in learning? Will we have sorted out and accepted the many roles of faculty? Will we be comfortable with the role of the for-profit education companies? Will an entirely new type of institution, focused on updating the professional needs of adults, be solidly in place? No doubt, we will inch our way closer to these answers over the next few years. After all, the future is always clearer once we are there.

This chapter has two very different sections. In the first section, data points are used to predict, suggest, and anticipate what higher education might look like in 2010. This first section looks at the higher education enterprise from six different perspectives. It is comparable to taking a walk and watching the world as it subtly changes with each step. The shifts in perspective are small but significant. As with a kaleidoscope, virtually all the elements of teaching and learning will be there, but they will group, regroup, and assume unfamiliar shapes. This section was first written in 1999 and has been only slightly updated.

The six different institutional elements of higher education addressed are (1) the higher education enterprise as a whole; (2) degree and continuing education programs; (3) the institutional infrastructure; (4) faculty and student tools and roles; (5) content resources; and (6) research in learning. Because we looked at each of these in some detail earlier in the book, these predictions are broad-brush views.

The second part of the chapter is a fantasy about what learning might be beyond the year 2010. Having been an aficionado of science fiction since her youth, Judith is continually drawn to thinking about how technology might be changing the education profession in the future. In fact, the turning point of her interest in the future of education came while she was in the doctoral program at the University of Minnesota in the late 1970s. At that time, students were required to take a class in either the history or the future of education. Judith figured that one could always go to the history books to see what had happened in the past – with an apology to historians for their very needed perspective! However, she wanted to explore, contemplate, and discuss the future of education. From that point on, the future of education, specifically the influence of technology on the teaching and learning processes, became her lifelong passion and interest.

The fantasy is called "Student-Centered Learning in the Lasting Experiences Ltd. Holodeck: As Good as It Gets!" This was first published in *Syllabus* in June of 1998. A holodeck, a creation of the "Star Trek" television series, is a three-dimensional simulated environment in which people can interact fully with computer-created special effects creating a real experience. The thoughts in this chapter are intended as both playful and serious. We hope that you will enjoy reading it as much as Judith enjoyed writing it.

Forecasting the Future of Teaching and Learning

Science fiction writer William Gibson captured well the process of our adoption of technology and the worlds we create with it when he said, "The future is here; it is just not evenly distributed." As we look at each of the six major components of the higher education enterprise, the prediction statements will all have some wiggle room to account for this uneven distribution of the future. For example, some institutions have been mandating that all courses have a web presence or a web course site of some type since the late 1990s. Those institutions are moving forward quickly by creating a campus environment that is aggressively embracing the new environments, new tools, and new processes, while other institutions are more conservative and move forward more slowly.

The Higher Education Enterprise and the Big Picture

- A new category of higher education institution, the career university, will evolve to meet the needs of working professionals.
- National and global partnerships will be common and will extend institutions' specialties around the world.
- The size of the higher education enterprise will grow dramatically, and the greatest growth will be in nondegree and learning professional areas.
- Certification services will expand considerably as the focus on skills, abilities, and accountability increases.

The higher education enterprise as a whole will continue to change radically over the next 10 years. The greatest changes will arise in response to the greatest needs: working adults who need to increase their knowledge base, upgrade their skills, and change careers multiple times during a lifetime. These working adults range in age from 24 to 74 and generally hold bachelor's degrees. To meet the needs of these individuals nationally and globally, universities and colleges are creating new online organizations and virtual campuses. This is already under way; we see organizations such as Penn State's World Campus (www.worldcampus.psu.edu), Western Governor's University (www.wgu.edu), and the Southern Regional Electronic Campus (www.srec.sreb.org).

Many of these universities and consortia are addressing local and national needs today and are also partnering with other universities around the world for global needs in the future. The Western Governor's University is already highlighting its particular offering of competency-based online degrees, and boasts of accreditation by four regional commissions. These mergers and partnerships will resemble the mergers and acquisitions in other industries, such as the current consolidations in the publishing industry and the new broadcast and media mergers. Well-established organizations are now are capitalizing on building brick-and-click operations, meaning their online and their physical operations complement each other, bringing the best features of each to their customers. This is not unlike what higher education is doing with its proliferation of webcentric, hybrid, and blended instructional programs.

Another major shift will be in the credibility of for-profit companies. Jones International University (www.jonesinternational.edu) and Capella University (www.capella.edu) are accredited by the North Central Association of Colleges and Schools. The University of Phoenix, (www.uophx.edu) is also well known for its wide range of accredited programs.

The higher education enterprise will expand its reach and in the process create a new category of higher education institutions or organizations that might be called career universities. These institutions will have expertise in teaching and reaching working professionals with programs that accommodate different sets of life-style and work needs. The necessity of keeping costs low will be reduced, as many of the companies that send their students to these programs will subsidize the time and cost of them. For professionals seeking to prepare for new careers, features such as access, flexible design, and relevant offerings will be the primary decision-making factors. Whereas most major universities have branches that reach out to working professionals, these may well become the foundation of entirely new learning organizations.

> **For professionals seeking to prepare for new careers, features such as access, flexible design, and relevant offerings will be the primary decision-making factors.**

One caveat: The best programs for working professionals will probably be offered by institutions with existing expertise in continuing and professional education and that are also supported by faculty research. We see examples of these in the executive and global MBA programs offered at Harvard, Wharton, Penn State, Duke, and Purdue, and the pharmacy programs at the University of Florida and The University of Texas.

Successful institutions may well expand into other high-priority, related programmatic areas. If very successful, these institutions may spin off entire portions of the university or college into nonprofit foundations or for-profit enterprises. Alternatively, highly integrated partnerships with leading industrial companies may become larger entities within institutions. Successful institutions may stay tightly integrated if they can solve the organizational and faculty challenges of diverse businesses.

Online Degrees and Continuing Education Programs

- Higher education program offerings will shift focus from degree programs to an almost infinite variety of certifications, modular degrees, and event programming.
- Many of the new programs will have significant components that are self-paced and self-tested and can be done anywhere, anytime. At the same time, synchronous events will grow in favor as learners value the interaction and dialogue with faculty and other students. Subscription alumni programs may proliferate. However, as learners need structure, successful programs will have well-defined experiences and requirements.
- Interaction with expert faculty, mentors, and peers will be integral to these programs. Access to expert faculty will continue to be expensive in both time and money. Scaling of quality interaction-intensive programs will continue to challenge us.

The design of most of the degree and continuing education programs will likely have a regional geographic focus that can support a mix of online and face-to-face meetings. We are already seeing tremendous growth in degree opportunities that are place and time independent. Now we will see an explosion of anywhere, anytime programs that meet a wide range of student needs, providing flexibility within courses as well as at the degree or program level. These programs may be complemented by highly concentrated residential experiences that can be completed with one or two weeks away from work.

Programs will reflect a design process that begins with a study of the lifestyles and needs of the target students followed by the creation of programs that fit the students' needs. This is part of the customization strategy of these programs. Many MBA programs are now available as intense, focused learning programs that use a supportive cohort of students to help address the problem of attrition among working professionals. Another strategy that institutions are using is the modularization of their degree programs. One expanding pharmacy program allows students to start a nine-semester program at the beginning of any semester. Other programs offer 8-week rather than 15-week semesters. Many of these programs have intensive conference-like orientation activities to help participants get to know each other, and then use frequent, asynchronous communications throughout the program to maintain a sense of community.

The focus of another category of professional programs already in place is on updating and upgrading knowledge in a specific field. This is most pronounced in the professional areas of engineering, business, medicine, law, nursing, dentistry, pharmacy, and education. Program content in the future will continue the focus on updating knowledge and skills, including areas such as perspectives, contextual problem solving, and networking. New professional tools and programs will likely incorporate the updated knowledge and skills into professional tools. Distinctions between working and learning will blur significantly. This may have interesting implications for continued annual certifications.

Other institutions with strong ethical and values traditions may offer continued growth in nonspecific professional programs and offerings. Institutions will likely design new ways of creating loyalty to their particular degree and nondegree programs. Institutions may choose to offer subscriptions to an integrated set of learning opportunities, which will include choices of learning programs, combined with access to large databases of content, special alerts, and networking opportunities with fellow students.

> **Institutions may choose to offer subscriptions to an integrated set of learning opportunities . . . .**

Another trend that may impact these predictions is the growth in the desire and need for an undergraduate degree. Some states will be facing significant enrollment pressures over the next 10 to 15 years. In these states, demands for alternative ways to provide undergraduate degrees may well encourage the development of new, focused models. One strategy being tested in Florida is the use of partnerships between community colleges and four-year institutions. In some of these programs, a number of upper-division courses will be offered on community college campuses.

Institutional Infrastructure

- The 1990s will be remembered as the decade of the web; the first decade of the 21st century will likely be known as the decade of mobile and ubiquitous computing. The two catalysts for this will be smaller, lighter, more portable computing appliances and the availability of wireless in more and more locations. This is a combination that supports teaching and learning anywhere, anytime.
- Organizations, tools, and applications that support teaching and learning anywhere at any time will become part of the critical infrastructure on higher education campuses.

The transition to the higher education institutional infrastructure of the future is well under way. Many institutions recruit, admit, and screen students from afar. Students can register, pay bills, check grades, update addresses and phone numbers, and receive consulting and tutoring online. Content resources are being accessed electronically from students' homes and other locations. Content resources are digital, dynamic, and distributed.

Standing in line on campus is being replaced by being online off campus.

The development of online campus services will continue to evolve rapidly. Standing in line on campus is being replaced by being online off campus. Student consulting and faculty office hours are being replaced by asynchronous email and synchronous chat, telephone calls, and videoconferences.

Future developments in information technology infrastructure will focus on enhanced security and reliable communication and collaboration tools. Information technology tools will also center on teaching and learning online. Web course management tools and collaboration tools will be rapidly enhanced with the fourth wave of innovation under way, reducing the amount of time and skill needed to teach and manage learning online. These tools will have templates for different types of courses, collaboration tools to assist faculty and students with different types of online dialogues, and testing and tracking applications for assessment and students' tracking of their own status.

It continues to be important to watch Internet2 developments, specifically what is being created in high-end collaboration tools for research and teaching, as well as innovations from the open-source initiatives such as the MIT projects and the Open CourseWare and Open Knowledge Initiatives. Sophisticated collaboration tools will have significant resource requirements initially, but these will decrease over time.

Barriers to effective, comfortable virtual learning are coming down, but are still significant for some faculty, students, and institutions. Access to mobile, portable teaching and learning tools will not be virtually universal for another 5 to 15 years. The cost of hardware is rapidly declining after a period of stability around the $1,000 to $1,200 point. Competition is heating up at the $500 to $700 level, and may be lower by the time you are reading this. Free options are also available, but with commitments for two to three years of subscription services, the cost still is close to $500 or $600.

The camera attached to the computer for one-on-one videoconferencing is becoming a standard accessory. Videoconferencing is the kind of tool that we want to use only if all partners in communication have access to it. This factor is slowing down greater use of this tool; however, there are also drawbacks to real-time video communication. Students in one distance-learning program complained that, when their one-way video system moved to two-way video, eating a pizza and putting their feet up were no longer good form!

If technology power keeps increasing at the rate of a generation of technology every 18 months, access will probably not be a problem. However, the cost of access to information may be an increasingly formidable challenge. Just as we have seen a shift from hardware costs to software costs, we are seeing a shift from the relatively low cost of internet access to the higher costs of accessing well-structured, easily searchable content. The digital library of today is not really free; the digital library of the future will not be free, either. Just as we subscribe to many sources of physical and virtual content today, including magazines, cable channels, and newspapers, we will be subscribing to many databases of content that are comparable to premium cable channels.

Over the next few years, we will see multiple generations of software agents come and go. Maybe by the year 2010 we will have become accustomed to personal robots, digital assistants who can help us remember our preferences and with whom we interact most frequently. These robots will write our summaries and to-do lists; anticipate the articles we want to read; help formulate the questions we might have; and provide guides, hints, and insights into answers. The new mapping systems available in some cars are one specific example of personal assistant.

Despite Peter Drucker's comment in 1996 that college campuses will no longer be needed, college campuses will still be needed to serve the core mission of educating 18- to 24-year-olds. Many portions of campuses will be redesigned to better serve 25- to 74-year-old learning professionals. Any institution undergoing construction should consider this population and its needs and the new type of occasional-event programming in the future. Small conference centers, as opposed to classroom buildings, may be the way to go.

If the primary classroom of the future is the web, designing and supporting the new teaching and learning environments will require some serious thinking and investment. The campus infrastructure must have digital-plant or IT organizations to design, plan, implement, and support teaching, learning, and research.

Faculty and Student Tools and Roles

- Faculty work and roles will become increasingly specialized.
- The approach to teaching and learning will become increasingly unbundled, with growing diversity and specialization of design and delivery responsibilities.
- Tools and resources to support teaching and learning online will evolve quickly.

Higher education teaching and learning today is in many respects a cottage industry. We have one person, the faculty member, doing a whole course. From design and development through delivery of the course, the one faculty member does it all. And this same process of creating and delivering the course is repeated every semester, because every time we teach a course, we revise it at least slightly. This is the model of the master craftsman.

In the last five years, The Pew Center for Academic Transformation (www.center.rpi.edu) has funded a number of projects focusing on large-enrollment general education courses to begin reducing the amount of work required by an expert faculty member. In the next 10 years, we may begin to address the challenge of customization with technology so that the expense of faculty can be more wisely invested. This is one aim of the MIT open-courseware initiative, in which faculty syllabi and course designs are made publicly available.

This prediction of effective investment of faculty resources may be the least reliable of all. Faculty work is already undergoing dramatic shifts. Faculty are now expected to learn the software tools that support teaching and learning on the web, often without any additional time. Yesterday's word processing is today's course management tool, and tomorrow will bring a new set of tools. In addition to learning how to teach in this online environment, faculty often must assist students in learning how to learn in a new place and with new processes. The active and collaborative modes of student learning are more demanding on the student; inevitably, time spent on the technology will divert some energies away from content learning.

> Yesterday's word processing is today's course management tool, and tomorrow will bring a new set of tools.

Teaching is becoming a technology-intensive part of the faculty member's responsibilities. The demands on the faculty will continue to increase unless specialization is acknowledged and supported. Not every faculty member can or should do everything. Some will focus on program design and development; others will focus on course delivery or overseeing tutors who manage the interaction with students.

Some faculty who delight in the combination of development and delivery may well become teaching and learning personalities, specializing in the creation of resources to be used by many others or the broadcast delivery of those resources. These faculty personalities may stay at colleges and universities, or they may become stars of the for-profit content publishers or for-profit institutions. Again, some faculty may keep doing what they are now doing for some time to come, but the new cadre of faculty will be expected to know how to teach online.

The shift to faculty specialization and online teaching is hindered by three major factors: time, resources, and habits. Time is precious, and change requires time. It also requires energy. Yet changing and rethinking our courses and programs on campus will require resources and skills that are not always available. Faculty need to ask fundamental instructional design questions about their courses. The good news is that many of the new faculty tools have some instructional design already built in. This will help the process. The change process will also go more smoothly if faculty have support in thinking through the questions about how to use these new tools in an online environment.

The question of habits is something we don't talk about often. Faculty and students have habitual ways of doing their work. Moving to these new tools is not automatic. These changes of habits will shift more smoothly and with much less stress if faculty are given time and tools to develop new habits.

While the majority of learning has always occurred outside the classroom, we will now see faculty doing much more teaching outside the campus classroom as well. This means not only online, but also off campus. Learning is moving to the home, to the workplace, to wherever the learner is.

Computers will not go away, even though sometimes we may wish they would. Time spent learning good new habits with computers will be time well spent. In our new world, a computer linked to a network will probably be our most important form of transportation.

Content Resources

- More materials, such as learning objects, simulations, labs, miniworlds and interactive tutorials supporting learning of core concepts and basic principles of fields of study will be more readily available and more easily integrated.
- More content resources will be structured for use by students for knowledge acquisition and skill development and competencies, and also for use by practitioners, especially in the scientific, legal, engineering, and medical professions.
- Access to well-structured content and databases will not necessarily be free. There will be free areas, subscription areas, and combinations of these, as has already happened with the *Wall Street Journal, The New York Times*, and *The Chronicle of Higher Education.*
- Rather than content being structured and designed to support a single course, it will be structured as discipline databases or feature knowledge clusters that can be easily selected for one or more courses.

Publishers are moving quickly to build large databases of content that complement and supplement textbooks. Their primary business model appears to continue to be focused on selling physical books. Their online content continues to be structured with the textbook as the center and focus of their relationship with faculty and students. Such databases of content linked with a textbook can be designed to constitute a large percentage of a course, as we have seen in the course design models. Rather than develop 40 to 60 percent of a course, a faculty member might only need to plan or redesign 30 percent of the course. In the area of lifelong learning, some publishers are offering free online courses as another way of selling books. As an example, see the Barnes & Noble University site, linked to the primary publisher sites (www.barnesandnobleuniversity.com).

These content databases have the potential to become attractive portals for discipline knowledge, but it appears that few publishers are experimenting with that as a model at this time. As we have discussed, the trend toward greater use of synchronous and asynchronous forums is growing. Each of these discipline portals could become a web channel for learning basic competencies in these fields. In some cases, publishers may spin off lifelong learning businesses using their rich sources of content. Faculty now work for publishers as writers and editors; some are now leading the publisher's free online courses, becoming discipline facilitators.

> **The need to acquire certifiable competencies is becoming as important as obtaining degrees.**

Some software training and publishing companies, such as SmartForce and NETg, are focusing on technical skill disciplines, offering self-paced, high-end, professional updating and certification tutorials, as well as courses that come packaged with a mentor. The need to acquire certifiable competencies is becoming as important as obtaining degrees.

Along with questions regarding curriculum changes in the new environment come concerns about cost. Although computer hardware costs are coming down dramatically, the cost of access to well-structured content databases is increasing. Many websites that used to be free are becoming subscription sites. We are learning that just as most books and newspapers are not free, much of the internet will not be free. We do have free broadcast television, supported by advertising dollars, and this model is being extended to the web. There will be free areas supported by advertisers and subscription areas financed by users.

Over the next decade, higher education will rethink the basic components and structure of its enterprise, including courses and degrees. It is possible that the course as the basic unit of structure for higher education will disappear, and criteria for competencies and assessment will move to center stage.

Research in Learning

- More research on learning, specifically research on the structuring of content for rapid acquisition of core concepts and principles of knowledge, will be funded. A number of initiatives are now under way, including work sponsored by the National Research Council that has resulted in what will likely be considered a landmark book, *How People Learn: Brain, Mind, Experience, and School*, published by the National Academies of Science. This work is free online at www.nap.edu/books.
- Technology, including tools, resources, and communication methods, will be used to provide flexibility and interactivity in meeting the learning needs of working professionals, and even throughout all levels of schooling.

Questions about the roles of computer technologies in teaching and learning, and about whether there is any possibility of technology ever replacing the teacher, have been asked for over 25 years. William Norris, CEO of Control Data in the 1980s, said that "if a teacher can be replaced by a machine, he or she ought to be."

That was a revolutionary statement at the time, but he meant what he said. With the benefit of an additional 25 years of development of technology and tools, we can now analyze more dispassionately about what portions of the learning process can efficiently be done without the intervention or interaction of a teacher. We now talk comfortably about teachers being mentors, coaches, and guides. We are now comfortable that the role of the teacher is to assist learners when they need help.

The question of how we can effectively use technology to help society meet its learning needs now and into the future is a fundamental question for the continued economic health of society. We have not been doing nearly enough research in this area. We are using information-age technology to support industrial-age learning experiences. We are rich in choices of tools today, but the wisdom of how, when, and where to use these tools is lagging seriously behind. Also lagging are serious efforts at building applications that might – with the aid of artificial intelligence – monitor, guide, and facilitate the learning process. More research on learning will show us how to improve the design of content materials and how to build resource materials with staying power.

Some work in this field is ongoing with institutions and publishers building simulations, miniworlds and interactive concept experiences. But much of this is being done without benefit of research into how these tools can be built more effectively and efficiently. Consider how the articles in *Scientific American* are written. Generally, anyone can read the first few paragraphs, but with each paragraph, the text and the concepts become more difficult, and a greater knowledge base of the discipline field is needed for full comprehension. When this happens, we often go back and reread. Sometimes this is enough to help us continue to broaden our own knowledge. Quite frequently, though, many of us give up and move to other content. That's OK when it is leisure reading. In learning situations, however, we need to persevere until we build and expand their conceptual framework with needed content and skills.

Educators know that learning needs to be rooted. Consider the tree of knowledge, which is still a good analogy. The core concepts, the essential understandings of a field of knowledge are the roots, the large lower tree trunks, and the large branches. Without that root system, many other concepts we might delight in – the smaller branches, leaves, and fruit – are not accessible. We need to have materials that can help students build knowledge structures effectively.

Moving On

We are only six short years from 2010. Where will we be at that time? Many of these predictions are extrapolations of current trends. We know that we will be surprised by the future; the web surprised us all. What other surprises are out there? As we come to a close of our journey to the online environment, here is an imaginary journey into a future where some of our visions for individualized instruction may actually come true.

Student-Centered Learning in the Lasting Experiences Ltd. Holodeck: As Good as It Gets!

A Minidream and Fantasy Voyage in Search of Lifelong Learning

Reprinted with permission from 101communications

Here I am at last . . . on an educational holodeck, modeled after the famous Holodeck of the Starship *Enterprise*. I have been thinking and dreaming about this ever since I watched "Star Trek" reruns with my children in the late 1980s. And I am very fortunate to have as my holographic tour guide my favorite educator and philosopher, Dr. John Dewey. John Dewey (let's call him Dr. Dewey from now on) is very animated as he leads me through a series of demonstrations in the newly dedicated educational holodeck called "Lasting Experiences Ltd." Dr. Dewey begins by taking a deep breath and saying that now, at last, we have a set of educational tools worthy of addressing his dreams of creating really effective and individualized student-centered learning experiences.

The Learning Continuum

Dr. Dewey says that one of the key concepts he wrote about early in the 20th century was the importance of *continuity* in learning, providing a continuum of learning experiences so that a student could build knowledge, brick by brick, layer by layer, synapse by synapse. Even back then, he continued, we knew that for effective learning, students needed an "orderly and ordered set of activities that could result in the completion of a learning process." Learning experiences, almost throughout the 20th century, were more a series of random events that may or may not fit the internal continuity of structure needed by students. We hoped that students would learn, and students did learn, but it was not very orderly, and many students missed a great deal. Most important, many students missed the orderly development of a rich and broad foundation of knowledge that would support them in becoming effective lifelong self-learners. The challenge back then was that dealing with even small groups of students made it difficult to provide the continuum of learning that could efficiently meet the needs of individual students.

Now, he says, look at what happens here in the Lasting Experiences Holodeck! Dewey stops before what looks like an old airport security checkpoint system. As students step through this arch, they pause and are recognized by the system. Then they hear their mentor's voice welcoming them and accompanying them to the section of the holodeck that is being individually and dynamically readied for them. Dr. Dewey explains that this is a security and identification point. As the students pause, the system recognizes them by their eyes, searches for their appropriate mentor, and recreates that mentor in holographic form. The student in front of us goes off with a holographic mentor of Gordon Moore, the famous CEO of Intel in the late 20th century.

Anticipating that I might object to such isolated and generated learning experiences, Dr. Dewey quickly explains more. He says that students must have a variety of learning experiences. The Lasting Experiences Holodeck is used for their conceptual development and some problem-solving experiences. The holodeck knows what aims or goals students have and creates, via artificial intelligence (AI), the types of experiences needed by the student to build the next layer of knowledge and relationships. The AI scenarios are integrated learning experiences, often combining two, three, or more disciplines – leveraging the interdisciplinary nature of most problem solving and creativity.

At this point, Dr. Dewey digresses. He says that it is important to know one other concept that really informs the AI scenarios here in the Lasting Experiences Holodeck.

At the Intersection: The Zone of Proximal Development

In the mid-20th century, he said, an educational theorist by the name of Lev Vygotsky developed the learning concept of the Zone of Proximal Development. Vygotsky's concept of the Zone of Proximal Development (ZPD) was that the act of learning occurred at the intersection of four components: the Learner, the Teacher, the Content, and a Problem that could be solved using the Content.

The ZPD represented the difference (or the gap) between what a learner could do individually and what could be done by the learner with the help of a more experienced person, usually a teacher or another expert. This zone might be thought of as the next layer of bricks, or the next sprout of new growth in the brain, or the development of a whole new area of knowledge. This concept also clarified the importance of the role of a teacher, in that the teacher was essential for more rapid and effective learning to take place than a learner could manage on his or her own. This concept helped teachers understand the importance of Dewey's own principle, the "continuity of learning experiences."

The ZPD also reinforces the concept of learning readiness with which it is closely associated. The readiness principle says that a learner needs to be at a point of readiness before learning certain material. Put another way, a learner cannot learn isolated facts easily, or integrate them usefully for the long-term and use them in any meaningful way. A learner can learn "facts" only if the knowledge can be related to knowledge or an experience the student already has. Vygotsky's principle of the Zone of Proximal Development suggests, that, in fact, the zone of learning possibilities for an individual learner might be a fairly narrow zone. On the other hand, it also suggests that the more we know, the more that we can come to know.

Dewey said that, for example, as they were experimenting with earlier versions of the mentoring and AI software, learners became frustrated either when the situation was too obvious or simple, or when the situation was too complex and the requirements too demanding. In the first case, learners would lose interest and search for more complexity, sometimes getting significantly off track, and sometimes misbehaving and causing trouble. In the second case, that of too much complexity, learners would make very basic mistakes due to a lack of understanding of core concepts and principles.

So the appropriate band or zone for learning needs to be carefully assessed. Over time, artificial intelligence software has been improved and can better assess just what zone of learning is possible for students, allowing students to optimize their time on task.

Out of the CAVE: Interaction

At this point, I was becoming anxious to move on. (Maybe we were getting out of my zone!) I saw learners going with their holographic mentors into special rooms called CAVEs. The students in these rooms were interacting with their mentors in what appeared to be live action scenarios. Dr. Dewey, sensing my impatience, said, "Oh yes, let's take a closer look at these CAVEs." This is where most students' interaction with their mentors and the content and problems actually occurs. The second core design principle underlying efficient learning is that of interaction. These CAVEs actualize that principle.

CAVEs were first developed in the late 20th century. They were early precursors of this more advanced holodeck. (I still remember some of my early experiences in similar environments: riding a pterodactyl over some ancient castles in Germany, and tending a 3D garden with some 3D friends.) The acronym CAVE was derived from Computer Automatic Virtual Environment. The first CAVEs were room-sized advanced visualization tools that created the illusion of complete immersion in a virtual environment using high-resolution, stereoscopic projection and 3D computer graphics. Inside these CAVEs, a user could experience the effect of being in a totally generated environment.

We have kept the name CAVE to indicate a specific category of holodecks for educational purposes. There is one CAVE, for example, designed for the learning of core concepts at the intersection of physics, math, and chemistry. As you can see, we have tried to move beyond the concept of a single discipline of study requiring students to solve real-life complex problems. As most problems have many possible effective solutions, students can play with scenarios of various solutions.

Over here is another CAVE focusing on the humanities, with interviews with famous artists such as Monet and Degas. Students here also experience the process of creating paintings similar to that artistic style, using all the new digital tools. We have another popular CAVE at the intersection of artificial intelligence, education, computer science, and media.

We need people in the 21st century to bring the perspective of multiple disciplines and create more CAVE experiences. You are aware, of course, that some of the most rapid innovation occurs at the intersection of the study of disparate disciplines. We hope to encourage that type of innovation by these interdisciplinary CAVE experiences.

Dewey continued, "I don't want you to miss one of the most exciting CAVEs for our study of the learning process. The software in this CAVE has the knowledge and experience of over 400 educational theorists, cognitive psychologists, and neurologists. This CAVE is being used to advance the design of the next generation of CAVEs for even more complex simulations. We still do not know nearly enough about just how to design and create learning scenarios for optimal efficient learning of concepts, and for the learning of problem-solving skills."

Some of the questions being researched include those suggested by Henry Kelly, from the Office of Science and Technology of the U.S. government in April of 1998 at a Net98 Conference. Dr. Kelly suggested that it was time, indeed past time, to elevate the importance of research on education and learning. Dr. Kelly argued passionately that our society needs to be able to respond more flexibly to the explosion of learning demands that have been brought on by the information age. He encouraged people at that conference to join together to more effectively formulate, articulate, and find funding for advanced and innovative research on learning processes, as well as on learning software and hardware and networking technology. "We are now benefiting from some of the studies funded back in the late 1990s!" Dr. Dewey assured me.

Let's go back to the concepts that Dr. Dewey felt were very important, and which we can now effectively do. One of his most impassioned messages was that the aim of education is the development of reflective, creative, responsible thought. To achieve this aim requires educational experiences that combine the two characteristics of continuity of learning and interaction with others in the learning experience. The *interaction* characteristic highlights the importance of the dialogue and communication underlying learning; the *continuity* characteristic emphasizes that the individual learner must be viewed as the key design element. In other words, we must design instruction so that each individual learner can effectively build on what he or she knows and has the resources and assistance to learn, or, in Vygotsky's words, "to navigate the Zone of Proximal Development."

Don't Lose Touch with the Mother Ship: The Role of the Teacher

The Educational Holodeck from Star Trek provides a more active and customized environment for student-focused learning than anything we have available to us. The environment accommodates itself to the readiness of the student, meets the student where he or she is, and takes the student to the next step of learning in an integrated experience guided by an individual mentor.

You might well ask, where is the teacher in this environment? Is it possible that the role and function of the teacher is to create the environment, to create the personality of the mentor, and to create the joining of time, place, the goal of the student, and the learning to be done?

During the tour, I did notice that many of the students were in fact quite young. When I remarked on this to Dr. Dewey, he said that yes, they were young. As the 21st century was beginning, he commented, it was obvious that our young people were staying in school until they were in their mid-20s, and even into their 30s for advanced degrees. As the concept of lifelong learning became accepted, we reinstituted the practices of apprenticeships and sabbaticals, encouraging students to begin work as young as15 in their chosen fields, and then taking sabbaticals of four to six months to upgrade their skills and advance to the next levels of their professions or to change or adapt their chosen professions.

Beam Me Up, Scotty

As we were finishing the tour of the holodeck, I asked Dr. Dewey about the costs involved in its development and operation, reminding him that one of the important goals in the late 20th century was for effective, efficient, and cost-effective education. Dr. Dewey shook his head a little sadly at that question. He shared that the costs for effective and efficient education were still increasing. He said that he hoped, however, with the next two to three cycles of hardware and software – over the next five years – we would at long last see some cost efficiencies. In the meantime, we have made learning more efficient and effective, even if not less costly. And we have addressed the priceless need for student-centered learning.

For a look at the current state of affairs of CAVEs and related virtual reality projects and tools, check out www.ncsa.uiuc.edu/VR/cavernus.

End Note

We have a busy and exciting time ahead. The pace of learning and teaching and the need to know have never been greater. As faculty and administrators, as educators, we have a chance to shape the future – again!

References

Barker, J. A. (1993). *Paradigms: The Business of Discovering the Future* (reprinted). New York: Harper.

Bates, A. W. T. (1995). *Technology, Open Learning, and Distance Education.* New York: Routledge.

Boettcher, J. V. (1995, October). Technology Classrooms, Teaching, and Tigers. *Syllabus*, 9, 10-12.

Boettcher, J. V. (1999, October). Another Look at the Tower of WWWebble. *Syllabus*, (*13*)50; 52.

Boettcher, J. V. (2000). How Much Does it Cost to Put a Course Online? It All Depends. In M. J. Finkelstein, C. Frances, F. Jewett, & B. W. Scholz, (Eds.), *Dollars, Distance, and Online Education: The New Economics of College Teaching and Learning*, 172-197. Phoenix, AZ: American Council on Education, Oryx Press.

Boettcher, J. V. (2003). Course Management Systems and Learning Principles – Getting to Know Each Other. *Syllabus*, 16, 33-36.

Boettcher, J. V., & Cartwright, P. (1997, September-October). Designing and Supporting Courses on the Web. *Change*, 10, 62-63.

Boettcher, J. V. & Kumar, V. M.S. (2000, June). The Other Infrastructure: Distance Education's Digital Plant. *Syllabus*, 13, 14-22.

Bransford, J. D., Brown, A. L., & Cocking, R. R. (1999). *How People Learn. Brain, Mind, Experience, and School.* Washington, DC: National Academy Press.

Brookfield, S. (1999). *Discussion as a Way of Teaching: Tools and Techniques for Democratic Classrooms.* San Francisco, CA: Jossey-Bass

Brown, D. G. (2000). Academic Planning and Technology. In J. V. Boettcher, M. M. Doyle, & R. W. Jensen (Eds.), *Technology-Driven Planning: Principles to Practice* (pp. 62-68). Ann Arbor, MI: Society for College and University Planning.

Bruner, J. S. (1963). *The Process of Education.* New York: Vintage Books.

Business-Higher Education Forum (2003). *Building a Nation of Learners: The Need for Changes in Teaching and Learning to Meet Global Challenges.* American Council on Education (ACE), 40.

Carnevale, D. (2003). All-In-One Entertainment: More Students Use Their Computers for Movies, TV, and Music. *Chronicle of Higher Education.* Washington DC: A28.

Collis, B. (1996). *Tele-Learning in a Digital World: The Future of Distance Learning.* London: International Thomson Computer Press.

Cohen, E. (1972). *Designing Groupwork.* New York: Teachers College Press.

Conrad, R. M., & Donaldson, J. A. (2004). *Engaging the Online Learner: Activities and Resources for Creative Instruction.* San Francisco, CA: Jossey-Bass.

Daniel, J. S. (1998). *Knowledge Media for Global Universities: Scaling Up New Technology at the Open University.* Paper presented at the meeting of Seminars on Academic Computing, Snowmass, CO.

DiBiasi, D. (2000). Is Distance Education More or Less Work? *American Journal of Distance Education, 14*(3).

Cooney, D. H. (1998). Sharing Aspects Within Aspects: Real-Time Collaboration in the High School English Classroom. In C. J. Bonk & K. S. King (Eds.), *Electronic Collaborators: Learner-Centered Technologies for Literacy, Apprenticeship, and Discourse.* Mahwah, NJ: Lawrence Erlbaum Associates.

Dewey, J. (1916). *Democracy and Education.* New York: The Macmillan Co.

Dewey, J. (1933). *How We Think* (1998 Edition). Boston: Houghton-Mifflin.

Demasio, A. (2000). *The Feeling of What Happens: Body and Emotion in the Making of Consciousness.* New York: Harcourt.

Dolence, M. G., & Norris, D. M. (1995). *Transforming Higher Education: A Vision for Learning in the 21st Century.* Ann Arbor, MI: Society for College and University Planning.

Draves, W. A. (2000). *Teaching Online.* River Falls, WI: LERN Books.

Eastmond, D. V. (1995). *Alone But Together.* Cresskill, NJ: Hampton Press.

Fauconnier, G., & Turner, M. 2003). *The Way We Think: Conceptual Blending and the Mind's Hidden Complexities.* New York: Basic Books.

Gagne, R. M. (1965). *The Conditions of Learning.* New York: Holt, Rinehart & Winston.

Goss, T. (1996). *The Last Word on Power.* New York: Doubleday.

Green, K. C. (1999). *Campus Computing 1998.* Encino, CA: The Campus Computing Project. www.campuscomputing.net.

Green, K. C. (2002). *Campus Computing, 2002.* Encino, CA: The Campus Computing Project, www.campuscomputing.net.

Hafner, K., & Lyon, M. (1998). *Where Wizards Stay Up Late: The Origins of the Internet.* New York: Touchstone.

Hanna, D. E., Glowacki-Dudka, M., Conceicao-Runlee, S. (2000). *147 Practical Tips for Teaching Online Groups: Essentials of Web-Based Education.* Madison, WI: Atwood.

Harasim, L., Starr, R., Teles, L., & Turoff, M. (1996). *Learning Networks: A Field Guide to Teaching and Learning Online.* Cambridge, MA: MIT Press.

Hiltz, S. (1994). *The Virtual Classroom: Learning Without Limits via Computer Networks.* Norwood, NJ: Ablex.

Howard, P. J. (2000). *The Owner's Manual for the Brain: Everyday Applications From Mind-Brain Research.* New York: Bard Press.

Johnson, D. W., & Johnson, R. T. (1993). Cooperative Learning and Feedback in Technology-Based Instruction. In Dempsey & Sales (Eds.), *Interactive Instruction and Feedback.* Englewood Cliffs, NJ: Educational Technology Publications.

Kaufman, R., &. Lick, D. (2000). Mega-Level Strategic Planning: Beyond Conventional Wisdom. In J. V. Boettcher, M. M. Doyle, & R. W. Jensen (Eds.), *Technology-Driven Planning: Principles to Practice* (pp. 13-24). Ann Arbor, MI: Society for College and University Planning.

Knowles, M. (1998). *The Adult Learner: A Neglected Species* (4th ed.). Houston: Gulf Publishing.

Knowles, M. (1980). *The Modern Practice of Adult Education: From Pedagogy to Andragogy* (2nd ed.). Wilton, CT: Association Press.

Kolb, J. E., Gabriele, G. A., & Roy, S. (2000). Cycles in Curriculum Planning. In J. V. Boettcher, M. M. Doyle, & R. W. Jensen (Eds.), *Technology-Driven Planning: Principles to Practice* (pp. 79-86). Ann Arbor, MI: Society for College and University Planning.

Kurzweil, R. (1999). *The Age of Spiritual Machines: When Computers Exceed Human Intelligence.* New York: Viking Penguin Audio.

Larocque, D. (1997). Me, Myself and . . . You? Collaborative Learning: Why Bother? http:leahi.kcc.hawaii.edu/org/tcc-conf/pres/larocque.html.

Lenhart, A., Simon, M., & Graziano, M. (2001). *The Internet and Education: Findings of The Pew Internet and American Life Project.* The Pew Internet and American Life Project.

Lessig, L. (1999). *Code and Other Laws of Cyberspace.* New York: Basic Books.

Lick, D., & Kaufman, R. (2000). Change Creation: The Rest of the Planning Story. In J. V. Boettcher, M. M. Doyle, & R. W. Jensen (Eds.), *Technology-Driven Planning: Principles to Practice* (pp. 25-38). Ann Arbor, MI: Society for College and University Planning.

Lucky, R. (1998 July-August). A Lucky Hit. *Technology Review,* 101, 72-75.

Lynch, M. M. (2002). *The Online Educator: A Guide to Creating the Virtual Classroom.* London: Routledge.

Maisie, E. (1998). Keynote speech, 14th Annual Conference on Distance Teaching and Learning. Madison, WI.

McCormack, C., & Jones, D. (1998). *Building a Web-Based Education System.* New York: Wiley Computer Publishing.

McGown, R., Driscoll, M., & Roop, P. (1996). *Educational Psychology: A Learning-Centered Approach to Classroom Practice.* Boston: Allyn & Bacon.

McKinnon, J. (1998, September 6). Online Courses Demand More of Profs. *Tallahassee Democrat.*

McLuhan, M. (1967). *The Medium is the Massage.* London: Penguin Books Press. http://www.vyne.com/mcluhan/

Moore, G. E. (1965). Cramming More Components Onto Integrated Circuits, *Electronics, 38*(8). www.intel.com/research/silicon/moorespaper.pdf

Moore, J. C. (2002). *Elements of Quality: The Sloan-C Framework.* Needham, MA: Sloan-C.

Moore, M. G., & Kearsley, G. (1996). *Distance Education: A Systems View.* New York: Wadsworth Publishing.

Muirhead, B. (1999). Attitudes Toward Interactivity in a Graduate Distance Education Program: A Qualitative Analysis. www.dissertation.com/library/1120710a.htm.

Norris, D. M., & Lefrere, P. (2003). *Transforming E-Knowledge.* Ann Arbor, MI: Society for College and University Planning.

Palloff, R., & Pratt, K. (1999). *Building Learning Communities in Cyberspace.* San Francisco: Jossey-Bass.

Pea, R. D. (1994). Seeing What We Build Together: Distributed Multimedia Learning Environments for Transformative Communications. *The Journal of the Learning Sciences, 3*(3), 285-299.

Pelikan, J. (1992). *The Idea of the University: A Reexamination.* New Haven, CT: Yale University.

Pinker, S. (1997). *How the Mind Works.* New York: W.W. Norton & Company.

Pinker, S. (2002). *The Blank Slate: The Modern Denial of Human Nature.* New York: Viking Press.

Rheingold, H. (1993). *The Virtual Community.* Reading, MA: Addison Wesley.

Riffee, W. H. (2003, February). Putting a Faculty Face on Distance Education Programs. *Syllabus,* 16, 10-14.

Rogers, E. M. (1995). *Diffusion of Innovations* (4th ed.). New York: Free Press.

Rosenbloom, R. S. (1998). Sustaining American Innovation: Where Will Technology Come From? Forum on Harnessing Science and Technology for America's Economic Future, National Academy of Sciences Building, Washington, DC, National Academy of Science. Accessed at www.nap.edu/html/harness_sci_tech/ii_4.html (4/20/2000)

Rudduck, J. (1978). *Learning Through Small Group Discussion.* Guildford, Surrey: Society for Research into Higher Education.

Rumble, G. (1997). *The Costs and Economics of Open and Distance Learning.* Stirling, VA: Kogan Page.

Salmon, G. (2002). *eTivities: The Key to Active Online Learning.* London: Kogan Page.

Sherron, G. T., &. Boettcher, J. V. (1997). Distance Learning: The Shift to Interactivity. CAUSE Professional Paper Series #17. Retrieved March 06 2003, from EDUCAUSE Publications Database.

Skinner, B. F. (1958). Teaching Machines. *Science,* 128, 91-102.

Smith, M. K. (2003) Communities of Practice. In *The Encyclopedia of Informal Education.* www.infed.org/biblio/communities_of_practice.htm. Last updated: 23 January 2004.

Swan, K. (2002). Learning Effectiveness: What the Research Tells Us. *Sloan-C. Conference,* Orlando, FL.

Tansey, (2003). Living in Parallel Worlds: Blogs and Course Management Systems. www.syllabus.com/news_issue.asp?id=155&IssueDate=11/12/2003.

Tiffin, J., & Rajasingham, L. (1995). *In Search of the Virtual Class*. New York: Routledge.

Tuomi, I. (2003). The Lives and Death of Moore's Law. *First Monday*. Accessed at www.firstmonday.dk/issues/issue7_11/tuomi/ (10-21-03).

UCLA Center for Communication Policy. (2003). *The UCLA Internet Report: Surveying the Digital Future Year Three*. UCLA Center for Communication Policy.

Visser, J. A. (2000). Faculty Work in Developing and Teaching Web-Based Distance Courses: A Case Study of Time and Effort. *American Journal of Distance Education, 14*(3).

Vygotsky, L. S. (1962). *Thought and Language*. (E. Hanfmann and G. Vakar, Trans.). Cambridge: MIT Press.

Vygotsky, L. S. (1978). *Mind in Society: The Development of Higher Psychological Processes*. Cambridge, MA: Harvard University Press.

Wagner, E. D. (1997). Interaction: From Agents to Outcomes. In T. E. Cyrs (Ed.), *Teaching and Learning at a Distance: What It Takes to Effectively Design, Deliver, and Evaluate Programs*. San Francisco: Jossey-Bass.

Young, J. R. (1997, August 1). UCLA's Requirement of a Web Page for Every Class Spurs Debate. *Chronicle of Higher Education*, p. A21.

Zakon, R. H. (1993 - 2003). Hobbes' Internet Timeline v6.1. 2003. Accessed on 9/23/03 at www.zakon.org/robert/internet/timeline

About the Authors

Judith V. Boettcher

Judith V. Boettcher is a consultant and author in the areas of designing for learning, faculty development, and the future trends of technology in teaching and learning. She is a lecturer at the University of Florida in distance, continuing, and executive education, and an independent consultant with Designing for Learning. She has consulted with an array of major universities and organizations; has been a Syllabus Scholar since 1996; serves on a number of editorial boards; and is a member of the academic advisory committees of ICUS, an e-learning company based in Singapore.

Boettcher was executive director of the Corporation for Research and Educational Networking (CREN) from 1997 to 2003, and served as program director and cohost of the first-ever series of audio webcasts, called "The CREN TechTalks," for six years. Prior to joining CREN, she was the director of the Office of Interactive Distance Learning at Florida State University and the director of Education Technology Services at Penn State University in State College, Pennsylvania. While at Penn State, she chaired the universitywide Technology Classroom program that designed and developed over 50 technology classrooms. At Control Data Corporation, she served on League for Innovation task forces on strategic planning for technology integration into the teaching and learning process and library automation. She served as project leader for the Educational Uses of Information Technology Joe Wyatt Challenge EDUCOM project from 1990 to 1992, editing the publication, *101 Success Stories of Information Technology in Higher Education: The Joe Wyatt Challenge.*

Boettcher has written features and columns for higher education magazines, including *Change* and publications from Syllabus and EDUCAUSE. She is co-editor of *Technology-Driven Planning:Principles to Practice,* published by the Society for College and University Planning, and author of a chapter, "How Much Does it Cost to Put a Course Online? It all Depends," in *Dollars, Distance, and Online Education:The New Economics of College Teaching and Learning.*

Boettcher has a Ph.D. in education and cognitive psychology from the University of Minnesota and a master's degree in English from Marquette University in Milwaukee. She can be reached at judith@designingforlearning.info, and welcomes inquiries and comments.

Rita-Marie Conrad

Rita-Marie Conrad is a faculty member, author, and the principal for RMC eDesign, where she focuses on the issues related to online course design, instruction, and evaluation. She currently teaches courses concerning learning theories and development of online instruction in the School of Education at Capella University. She has been the head of instructional development, responsible for managing the development and delivery of web-based courses, and an online faculty member with the School of Information Studies at Florida State University. She was the first online faculty member for Florida State University's graduate program in instructional systems with a major in distance learning and was instrumental in the development of the program.

Conrad has consulted on the creation and delivery of online courses, the management of technology-related projects, and the use of technology in the classroom. She presently provides training to K-12 teachers and community college and university faculty across the nation in a workshop sponsored by the Learning Resources Network (LERN). She is a frequent presenter at national forums such as the *Annual Conference on Distance Teaching and Learning* in Madison, Wisconsin.

The coauthor of *Engaging the Online Learner:Activities and Resources for Creative Instruction*, Conrad is also a co-author of *Assessing Online Distance Learners*. She has a Ph.D. in instructional systems, with a focus on distance learning, from Florida State University, and a master's degree in educational media and computers from Arizona State University. She can be reached at rconrad@attglobal.net.